Eros/Power

Love in the Spirit of Inquiry

Transforming how women and men relate

Hilary Bradbury & William Torbert

Integral Publishers
Tucson, Arizona

Integral Publishers
4845 E. 2nd St.
Tucson, Arizona

Cover Design by QT Punque
Cover graphic by Heidi Whitcomb

ISBN: 978-1-4951-5914-5

The lines from 'Stony Grey Soil' by Patrick Kavanagh are reprinted from *Collected Poems*, edited by Antoinette Quinn (Allen Lane, 2004), by kind permission of the Trustees of the Estate of the late Katherine B. Kavanagh, through the Jonathan Williams Literary Agency.

TABLE OF CONTENTS

PART THREE

Foreword One

... Love is difficult. For one human being to love another human being: that is perhaps the most difficult task that has been entrusted to us, the ultimate task, the final test and proof, the work for which all other work is merely preparation. That is why young people, who are beginners in everything, are not yet capable of love: it is something they must learn.

... The claims that the difficult work of love makes upon our development are greater than life, and we, as beginners, are not equal to them. But if we nevertheless endure and take this love upon us as burden and apprenticeship... then a small advance and a lightening will perhaps be perceptible to those who come long after us. That would be much.

Rainer Maria Rilke

In this book, my friends Hilary and Bill have opened their hearts and their minds and their histories as an invitation to us to explore "the difficult work" that love "makes upon our development." They, who have spent decades attempting to understand the brave and bewildering entwining of love and power, could have written about that entwining as the scholars they are. Instead, they offer us love and power—not to talk about it but to experience it. In the force of their grappling, in the courage of their stories, in the compelling questions they ask us, they invite us to wonder about our own histories, to trace our own developmental pathway through the forest of our most intimate relationships.

Like Hilary and Bill, I have been long captivated by these ideas, and like them, I have wondered about the missing dialogue that connects love and power and growth. Surely it is through our relationships that we find our growing edges, see our selves reflected back at us, and are able to reach a new place in ourselves. Our relationships coax out our biggest selves and spin us down into our smallest selves. We know that our attachment to our parents sets the scene for our capacity to attach to others later in life; our connection with our boss can create (or destroy) engagement at work; our relationship with a life partner shapes our health and happiness. Much is written about these kinds of connections and their developmental power. Much less is written about the often-hidden (sometimes even to ourselves) intimate friendships that don't fall into well-defined categories and yet shape our understanding of the world and our understanding of ourselves.

5

If we are really going to understand the mysterious forces of development and understand how to create contexts that enable us to bring our bigness into the world, though, we are going to have to stop shying away from conversations that seem uncomfortable or somehow too intimate. The core developmental action is when we take something that is unquestioned or unexamined inside us (to which we are subject) and move it into the light, to hold and touch it and make decisions about it (to make it an object for our reflection). Surely we cannot really understand our development and the development of others without peering into the most intimate spaces of our lives. And surely we cannot do that without pushing beyond the conventional bonds of intimate relationships and exploring new ways to love and be loved, to know and be known.

To explore beyond the obvious means we need new pathways and a new vocabulary. Bill and Hilary offer us new pathways—not hoping that we'll follow them in any way (indeed, we not only cannot, but we also see that their explorations have often circled back or dead ended). They are not showing us the right way to be in relationships; they are showing us the groping, fumbling, painful, beautiful ways they have been in relationships—including the sometimes perilous relationship with one another. They also offer us a new vocabulary for making sense of some of the relationships we may well have had—the erotic friendship—which they define as compassionate (in your mutual spiritual interest in the other's life and growth), dispassionate (in your mutual intellectual engagement of some sort), and passionate (in the spark or charge between you—which may or may not be consummated in any way).

I love many of the ideas that weave through this book, but perhaps none more than the notion of not just "falling in love" but "rising to love." Falling in love implies an experience out of our control, an event we can gain distance on only once it is over. Hilary and Bill not only call on us to imagine "rising to love" but they offer us this book as a sort of a guide. Here we see them intentionally cultivating selves big enough to fall and learn and fall and learn again, finally rising. In so doing, they call us to our biggest selves while holding and respecting the smaller and less sophisticated parts of us. If each of us reading this book could turn even one insight into the capacity to create thriving and supportive erotic friendships, indeed, "that would be much."

--Jennifer Garvey Berger, Ph.D., Cultivating Leadership and Growth Edge Network, New Zealand.

Foreword Two

The phrase "no (wo)man is an island," though much-lyricized, still sums up the central challenge and opportunity of modern-day civilizations: to understand that without relationship, connection, and communion the human species cannot survive, let alone thrive. What is at stake here is not relationship for relationship's sake, for as we all know, relationships are as likely sources of pain and disappointment as they are of pleasure and support. The shadow side of power, in its all too many horrific guises, breaks through even the most supposedly sacrosanct of human relationships. Nowhere, perhaps, is this more insidious and seemingly intractable than in relationships between women and men in patriarchal—and yes, even in would-be post-patriarchal—societies. *Eros/Power: Love in the Spirit of Inquiry*, the latest in Hilary Bradbury and Bill Torbert's important contributions to action inquiry in service of human and planetary flourishing, takes this most persistent and momentous of challenges as its starting ground.

Like the true action researchers they are, Hilary and Bill are not content to accept at face value the idealist refrain that all you need is love—tempting and catchy as it might be. Or at least not without first committing—as their deepest ongoing question, as the work of a lifetime (or two!)—to seeking out a practical understanding of what it is that love really is, and what it might mean to act lovingly in each instance, in each relationship and each encounter… even in each metaphorical grazing of elbows, and especially where subtle and not so subtle power imbalances and dynamics are at play.

With astonishing incisiveness and frankness, Hilary and Bill reflect on their own experiences of seeking and being in relationship through their own life trajectories, opening up for interrogation their own fumbling, stumbling, eventually inquiring, and ever evolving approaches to grappling with both eros and power in relationships with significant human others. In sharing such intimate, personal narratives, Hilary and Bill undertake a conscious de-robing of themselves that is as risky and uncomfortable as it is inquiring and compassionate. At times, this makes for some difficult reading. But we would be doing them, and ourselves, a huge disservice if we were to engage with this book at a purely voyeuristic level. The book is nothing if not personal and political. The overarching questions and provocations raised belong to us all, speaking to the heart(/mind/body) ache and to the relational discomforts and betrayals that are seemingly inescapable elements of the human condition. It brings home to us at the deepest of levels that our worthiest aspirations for social transformation and planetary flourishing begin with the most intimate of details: with our lived inter-subjective experiences and moment-to-moment relating with others.

Eros/Power: Love in the Spirit of Inquiry propounds a courageous and inspiring vision of inter-gendered friendships as sites for mutually supportive, ongoing exploratory quest(ioning), with the potential to heal, transcend, and transform tired patterns of relating between women and men. The book invites us, the readers, to reflect on those relationships which matter most to us: those in which mutuality and loving respect are, have been, or could be aspirations (more) explicitly shared and worked with 'in the spirit of inquiry'—including those relationships, both intimate and professional, in which structural and gendered power dynamics are salient, and all too often bruising and constraining, if generally unacknowledged. But this book does more than inspire—it also equips us. Those intrepid readers who choose to go on to inquire into how their own friendships and relationships could be awakened, (re)visited, (re)invigorated, and enlivened through Eros/Power can garner support from the action inquiry approaches that the authors have spent decades crafting, refining, and seeking to put into practice, and which they model and share in this work.

This book is a powerful manifesto, offering us a way to a radically different future. A future of infinite possibilities, enabled by a soulful, full-bodied dance with the erotic life force that pulses, all too often unbidden and unheeded, within each of us, and in the places and moments where subjectivities meet. Possibilities to craft intimate relationships nourished and uplifted by Eros/Power. To co-create meaningful work and collective endeavors empowered by Eros/Power. To speak truth to power, from an understanding of power that embraces eros. To breathe new life into our search for alternative forms of relational, social, and organizational practice more supportive of planetary flourishing. Hilary's and Bill's autobiographical writing is itself a gesture of love: a gift on their part to all out there who could/would transform in relationships, friendships, communities, and more-than-human contexts, and thus make both healing and flourishing at every systemic level possible... starting from the ground, heart, and loins up.

Patricia Gaya, Ph.D.
Centre for Action Research and Critical Inquiry in Organizations.
University of Bristol

Introduction

Eros/Power and Relational Action Inquiry

Are you breathing just a little and calling it a life…

Mary Oliver

Our intention is to cultivate love and power in a spirit of inquiry. By this we mean to practice inquiry in relationship where eros and power intersect, that very place where hurts and disappointments are most keenly felt. Too often a screaming silence holds us captive at this very intersection where instead creativity, love, curiosity and openness could thrive.

We hope that more of us may practice relational action inquiry, limited versions of which the two of us are illustrating in this book. Relational action inquiry is about cultivating eros as we develop through relationships, as though relationships themselves were containers of transformation. Eros, the creative, sensual, psychic life-force wants to be lived and liberated through and among us. Such relational inquiry, however, cannot take place primarily in the safety of reading a book, but rather in the midst of the risks and vulnerabilities of everyday life. In the following chapters, we tell you our stories and related inquiries. In the Invitations at the end of chapters and in the Interludes at the end of Parts I and Part II, we go beyond our stories to invite you to engage in your own inquiries.

Our offering here is part of the social evolution toward more deeply collaborative ways of living in support of collective flourishing – the emergent, global Third Age of Humankind which welcomes and requires new kinds of communities – friendship-based communities-of-inquiry that support us in finding our paths of continuing evolution. We urge you to join in this inquiry in your own relationships – this inquiry aiming toward mutual developmental transformation in all different kinds of relationships and circumstances.

A developmental theory about how we humans can transform during a lifetime has aided our inquiry. This developmental theory holds that we humans can develop through eight "action-logics," that is eight developmental stages or patterns of interpreting and acting in the world. We describe these in some detail in our interludes. As a foretaste we may say, however, that as we develop through the eight action-logics, we move from ways of interpreting and enacting power, love, and inquiry as if they are radically opposed to one another. We can move from wielding power coercively, without love; from loving blindly, without inquiry; and from inquiring in a detached manner, without power to later developmental stages of interpreting power, love, and inquiry as mutual and as directly entailing one another.

We define eros as the soul surging forth to know the other, to learn from and grow with and through that other, a surging that brings with it love. We like Jean Houston's definition of eros as the principle concerned with the interrelationship of psyche and nature (soul and body), with symbiosis and the connection between all things. And so we wonder what will happen when inquiry transforms the connection between eros and power among humankind, allowing our democracies to grow toward real partnership, at least enough to save us from our current unsustainable path. We suggest that Eros/Power is the kind of revitalizing experience of intersubjective flow that occurs when love and power conjoin through inquiry in the midst of relating between persons.

In contrast to this perhaps lofty sketch of human possibilities, we also recognize how warped the conversation on eros has been. The term eros too often is Orwellian-speak for carnal sexuality. The life affirming connection between sexuality and eros can indeed can become malignant. Sexuality that remains insistently ignorant of its spiritual capacity suppresses both self and other. Sexuality, however, that knows itself simultaneously as carnal and spiritually inquiring energy is truly erotic.

We believe that a taste of Eros/Power is the hallmark of a life force fully breathed, a taste of our deepest aspirations in which collaboration, mutuality, learning and creativity arise in relationship. As is made explicit in Interlude I, we count different types of power, exercised with different levels of inquiry, and see the potential for mutual power, exercised with relatively intense ongoing inquiry within a relationship. Taken together, our mutual powers, which so few people today intentionally exercise, manifest what we call Eros/Power.

In this book we suggest that relationships between women and men (or more precisely between the feminine and the masculine that embodies us in different measure) can lead an evolutionary leap. But are we up to it? As men under patriarchy are the most profoundly privileged class with the least self-interest in critiquing and transforming the source of their power and love… can women initially be called upon as primary in the leadership of widespread mutuality among the genders, the races, etc.? We believe that cultures can move from condoning relational abuse and violence to celebrating nurture and mutuality, and this is the fundamental evolutionary shift we are interested in advancing in some small way through this book. Eros, in its broader meaning of acting in coherence with communal and relational power and inquiry, is a key resource for this transformation.

Truth be told relational action inquiry is neither simple nor easy. It seems we must first confront the impulse that runs through our species, the impulse to prey upon the weak, including what appears to us as the weakness in ourselves. How it is so much easier not to hold ourselves accountable. Is this impulse the obscene secret to our ways of relating, so secret we keep it most of all from ourselves? Are women and men designed to create abusive, dominance/submission relationships? Are even good men designed to overlook the privilege they enjoy? Are too many women designed to exercise, or to enable, manipulative dominance? Is mutual erotic power and inquiry a fantasy? What sludge in the human heart must we confront in me, in you, in us, if there is to be an evolutionary, developmental transformation in how women and men relate, whereby power is subordinated to love and love to inquiry?

Our starting point is that we, the authors, are in this inquiry together. You are of course welcome to read about our slow, mostly-separate lifelong 'erotic autobiographies' in a critical vein, but we hope you will also join us by using our stumbling efforts as a chance to begin reviewing your own very different, but-probably-also-stumbling efforts to learn how to interact lovingly, inquiringly, committedly, vulnerably. At some point in your reading, we hope you want to begin keeping notes – a bit of a journal or personal blog – about your own stories so that you can return later to look for patterns. A still bigger commitment to this direction of inquiry would be for you to invite one or two or three other friends to join in your inquiry, a process for which we offer suggestions in Interlude II on relational action inquiry.

Big Fish Eat Little Fish

That things between women and men are getting better is certainly the case. We hardly miss the burnings at the stake, the ubiquitous rape of African American women during slavery, the more recent Mad Men years of organizational sexism. But it is sobering to grasp how culture shapes and scolds us. The Modern era was shaped by the prior Medieval era which targeted the feminine and women especially with clerical terrorizing masquerading as divine will. A classic evocation of the deranged misogyny that fueled this era is the Malleus Maleficarum (The Hammer of Witches), a bestseller published by Catholic inquisition authorities in 1485-86. "All wickedness," write the authors, "is but little to the wickedness of a woman... What else is woman but a foe to friendship, an unescapable punishment, a necessary evil, a natural temptation, a desirable calamity, domestic danger, a delectable detriment, an evil nature, painted with fair colours... Women are by nature instruments of Satan – they are by nature carnal, a structural defect rooted in the original creation." It's worth mentioning that this was hardly a marginal document. Enabled by the newly invented printing presses, it was one of the most available and important of church documents. An

11

issue we take up throughout our own reflections is that as misogyny danced its dance with patriarchy it was not that men did not suffer. Nor were men the sole perpetrators. The stigmatizing, victimizing, and murdering of some 200,000 "witches" is most accurately seen as a collaborative enterprise between men and women at the local level. In the roots we may find the seeds of our culture's dance of cruelty and pleasure. But enough of long ago.

Cultures change. People change. This is why we no longer burn people alive in the town square though atrocities still hover on the margins of civilization the world over, from Boko Haram and ISIS to white lone wolves creating mayhem in America. Yet the relational dynamics of women and men are, we assert, especially difficult to fully appreciate, all the harder to improve. They are neither simple nor primarily "bad." Such complexity may make it easy to overlook where we might be better off looking. Most of us want to celebrate the life giving qualities of eros between men and women, including its lunar, transgressive play. But is the sadomasochism of Fifty Shades of Gray the best we can do? Our inquiry longs for balance, beyond the extremes of a policeman or pornographic mentality, in looking amidst the interplay of eros and power in the relational dynamics of women and men. For this we must remember that power has many hues. Power is usually seen in its masculine form – hard, unilateral power with the ability to make someone do something they don't want. Feminism in particular has led us to see new forms of "soft power" which heals, provides space/time for, enhances, and grows all it touches – forms of mutual power that naturally require and encourage empowerment. So little explored are the mutual forms of power that they are widely unnamed in the popular and scholarly literature. Our effort here is to begin to illustrate these mutual forms of power so we may reimagine relational life.

Three big concepts seem to interweave as we reveal and transform ourselves to the other and to ourselves. These are themes big enough to energize a lifetime:

> Eros has a full and vacillating range from physical-sexual intimacy to metaphysical-spiritual intimacy, along with our potential to experience both ends of the erotic spectrum simultaneously;
> Mutuality informs our potential to practice mutually-vigilant, mutually-vulnerable, mutually-transforming power with one another in couples, trios, etc.;
> Our potential for exercising a daily living inquiry within a community of other adults (who may live at a distance from one another) can transform us so that we are born again and again during our adulthood.

We hold this work as being in the service of emancipation, or liberation of our human creativity in ways that cultivate personal integrity, relational mutuality, and systemic sustainability.

Hilary writes

Our book, an experiment in relational action inquiry, is intended to encourage conversations about the dynamics of power and eros in all our lives. We start with the account of Bill's and my relationship when I was his doctoral student. This relationship could stand in for many in which the woman is junior or subordinate. I too am queasy with such terms as subordinate, and describing myself as "his" student. Indeed in writing my account I realized this very aversion to acknowledging vulnerability that accrues to the one with less positional power, kept me essentially unable to properly look power in the eye. Yet such words describe the social-organizational reality to which most of us have been socialized. Therefore, this book is about power and how asymmetrical power can gradually transform toward mutual power.

If ours is a relationship with its origins in a well-known power asymmetry, what is new is that both of us reflect on the relationship together. Following that reflection, honest enough to note the centrality of sexuality and eros, despite our non-sexual professional practice, we each turn to our own erotic autobiographies. We look to our early years to understand the mostly unconscious patterns (with rational overlay) we have each developed around relating to men and women.

In meeting each other, we met precisely the one on whom projection and counter projection could yield deep insight, insight wrestled over 20 years, into how men and women do our dance together. Therefore, this book is mostly about eros and about how to transform from "unconscious love-seeking" to "mutual, awareness-enhancing love-offering."

The accounts shared, we hope, have relevance to anyone who works or plays with a someone of a different gender, or in any erotically-tinged friendship – homosexual or heterosexual – and who is willing to be thoughtful about that. We want to say that willingness to inquire probably also arises with reluctance or resistance. This resistance may manifest in you as simple irritation or repulsion at our choices in our earlier years, or it may manifest in you as the fear of being too self indulgent, confessional, and therapeutic with yourself. We know this from experience. How many times we questioned what we were doing. Deeper inquiry into that very fear has several times allowed us see how our very resistance keeps us constricted.

We find ourselves at a time of staggeringly violent backlash against women worldwide. We may wonder when waning patriarchal culture can ever make peace with women's emancipation. Dominance by men, expressed sexually, in subtle and gross ways, remains the foundation of almost all of our global societies. But women like me now have the legal protection and the benefit of humanist values that make relational happiness, with its erotic and sexual component, a possibility. A right even. In the West we no longer burn glamorous women at the stake as we once did. We never bound their feet as in China for a millennium; we never circumcised their genitalia – though it's thought that 3 million women endure the practice today in Africa – where the goal is to render women incapable of sexual pleasure. Today a woman like me may speak, supported by laws and growing civility in the intimate world of human relationships. Creativity is offered a space to take flight because eros is the heart and source of creativity with its multiple expressions.

Bill writes:

The erotic quality of friendship usually varies between the pole of remaining unnamed and unexplored, on the one hand, and the pole of being acted upon in a conventionally sexual way between two persons, on the other hand. We the authors have very, very gradually discovered through our own lives – and in the most recent years within the retreat practices of our current community of inquiry – that a qualitatively different, less-easily-envisionable-and-enactable third way of engaging the erotic quality of friendship can be discovered. This path is not new. It is as old and as rare as Tantric Yoga, the Shambhala Path, certain sufi orders, the Diamond Work, or the Gurdjieff Work, therefore a path of inquiry and contemplative intimacy, not just alone, nor just between two persons, but also in the wider container of real-life, third-person communities of inquiry. This path embraces myriad forms of expression other than the directly sexual. It is a path equally open to those practicing celibacy, monogamy, or polyamory. Yet it is rarely the path taken by any of us.

We who have adopted some version or versions of this path of inquiry in everyday life have gradually become less interested in the common phenomenon of "falling in love" and more interested in the uncommon but miraculous experience of "rising to love." In this view, true erotic friendships entail a compassionate spiritual concern for the other's development, a dispassionate mental focus around shared interests and activities, a growing sense of emotional intimacy and familiarity, as well as some degree of mutual, passionate attraction to one another – all as part of a path toward breathing more deeply and being creative with our lives together, living a life we call 'erotic' because blessed by eros – eros the integrating (if supremely tricksterish!) life-force.

We focus on friendships between women and men because such relationships, outside a commitment to marriage and exclusive partnership, are too rarely talked about or inquired into – too often imagined only as illicit infidelities, too often practiced as bruising affairs. Such friendships may be long-lasting and may constitute a serious practice of inquiry in the midst of love in its many guises, including the tricky dynamics of eros. This is a new, mutual form of inquiry or research methodology into the heights and depths of these key intersubjective realities: how eros can transform power while itself being transformed by inquiry (yielding what we call Eros/Power).

Our approach of examining our relationship and our distinct erotic autobiographies through writing and conversation with one another, and then with some of our other closest friends is an approach open to others who feel their depth of friendship merits such a commitment. Our book is therefore a re-presentation of something that is likely at hand in your life, but overlooked or misinterpreted – namely, the possibility that two or more loving adults can study and practice toward deeply meaningful change in how we understand ourselves and relate with one another.

Friendship and the Good Life

How do such friendships, under the sign of inquiry, relate to your and our most general aim of constructing a good life for ourselves with others while simultaneously engaging in the continual reconstruction of the larger global society toward greater justice in income distribution, work-opportunity, and loving-friendship-in-the-spirit-of-inquiry? We think such friendships are far more critical to co-creating a good life than most persons today make room for in their lives. We invite you to consider that you will be more likely to succeed in cooking up a good life for yourselves, with others, when you are able to generate and alchemically blend the following primary goods in the right proportions at the right times:

1) Good money (resources enough not to have to worry about them all the time);
2) Good work (bringing in the necessary resources, through work that exercises us well, makes us good friends, and calls forth our commitment, contribution, power, and sense of fulfillment),

3) Good friends (that is, people who voluntarily, mutually, and non-pos-sessively love one another enough to face our most daunting questions together [and such friends can, of course, potentially include members of our family]), and

4) Good questions (the realm of inquiry in the midst of our daily life, from our most intimate encounters to our broadest citizenly roles, whereby we may learn over decades how to make good money, do good work, cultivate good friends, and become fully-incarnated and wonder-full in each waking moment).

We have offered these four primary goods in this order because it helps read-ers to realize that our approach gives the issues of good work and good money a prominent place, even though these go almost entirely unmentioned in this book. As we imply, however, by the way we have just defined these goods, we propose that they are properly ranked in reverse order. It's our view that good questions among friends are the primary keys to the good life because they help us to determine what constitutes good work and good money for us. Resources of many types derive from good inquiry.

Each of these primary goods is difficult to attain and more difficult to sustain. Billions of humans do not have enough of any of them, and billions more may have just enough money, but neither good work, nor more than one or two good friends, nor good, life-transforming questions.

Both of us feel fortunate that our own process of inquiry put money in its proper place from early on making it possible to engage in the work, friendships, and inquiry we value most.

In a sense, you could say that each of us took the question of what love really is, and how to act lovingly in each instance, as our deepest ongoing question – whether with one's oldest friend or newest acquaintance, or when in commu-nion with life's flow in the more than human world. And, as you will see, it's probably a good thing we took this as a deep question. For, during our whole lives up to the present, we have found no once-and-for-all answer. It is the in-quiry that guides us.

Relational Action Inquiry

In this book we address the Eros/Power nexus not only as a matter of "out there," nor as work that others must do (though we applaud all that work and are grateful for it). Here we tackle it also as work "in here" that we each must do. We see ourselves, and you our readers, as implicated, as called to action. Only when we allow ourselves to see how we play the roles of victim and predator in our own lives, in our own bodies and conversations, and how little true inquiry and intimacy playing such roles permit, do we become motivated to engage in the work and play of exercising mutual Eros/Power. Bill represents the archetypal male, attempting to make an evolutionary step brave enough to look squarely, not only at his lack of experience and fear of sexuality in his youth, but also at the privilege that is his by virtue of being a male WASP (white-anglo-saxon-protestant), a privilege further emphasized as he has worked in privileged roles and institutions. And Hilary looks at how she at first archetypically condones male privilege, confused as to how to access her own, and then, based on reflection about that, develops a more sophisticated repertoire when dealing with power and privileging more generally. So ours is a tale of a journey, an inquiry, without end (a journey we find alternately energizing and daunting).

None of us knows at the outset how to engage in inter-gendered inquiry that interweaves words, touch, and feeling in ways that mutually delineate, defend, and sometimes revise boundaries in relationships of love. We certainly didn't. In spite of all our passionate experiments in love before we began writing this book, the exercise of writing it has taken on a life of it own, an inquiry that is informing all parts of our lives. We invite the same for you.

Greek Myths of Eros

The eskimo has fifty-two names for snow because it is important to them. There ought to be as many for love. – Margaret Atwood.

Eros is a Greek term. The ancient Greeks distinguished among four kinds of love. The first is storge, familial/familiar affection, sometimes taken for granted. The second is philia, friendship, a cooler, more mental love, based in a shared interest or activity, sometimes associated with a larger, implicit or explicit, community (such as a church group, a sports team, a veterans organization, or a college alumni group). A third kind of love, according to the Greeks, is agape, a spiritual, unconditional, 'charitable' love – love of a stranger that expects no return (and that can verge on the self-denying). The fourth kind of love is eros. We first experience eros as a passionate, desiring, romantic love of the beauty of one particular other, or more than one particular other. At its negative extreme, eros can lead to co-dependent addictive sex and interpersonal violence. At its positive extreme, it can lead to a mutual grace in relating that co-constructs attractive works of art – both performance-art and crafted-art.

In the Greek myths, eros, the soul's surging forth toward the other, is not solely or primarily sexual, but is, rather a complex being. Eros is perhaps most fully understood as having realities at different levels of depth; as both the fully divine and semi-childish Cupid, embodiment of the intentional and mutual wedding of opposites (spirit-matter / heaven-earth / man-woman / action-inquiry), whose sense of boundaries can be a little errant, at least by conventional standards, because still being inquired into.

In Plato's Phaedrus and Symposium we learn how eros cultivates individual development. Plato's ideas are key not least because they continue to hold Western thought in place, and the myths found in this work were of great importance to Freud and then Jung. In the Symposium, made famous for its discussion of love (all the speeches by men!), we learn of Aristophanes' theory of male and female seeking to find their "other half" to overcome the Gods' original sundering. But Socrates tells us of his teacher, the woman Diotima, and her deeper understanding of how we may rise to a higher love, eros.

Consider that erotic desire, as Diotima intimated, sets the soul off into inquiry and development. We can say that this book is inspired more by Diotima than by Aristophanes. And anyway we need to be reminded that the teacher of the most important philosopher in the West was a woman! Yes, and we need to be reminded too that the full range of inter-gendered creativity has yet to be unleashed in a world desperate for human creativity on an everyday scale.

Eros, a peer of primordial Chaos, is an ever-flowing fountain of creativity from which life emerges. Eros gives ongoing and ever changing form to the nurturing fountain of creative plenty – nowhere perhaps as delightfully and often perplexingly as in inter-gendered erotic relationships. The phrase 'eros infused or erotic friendship' connotes a relationship whose boundaries are often not entirely clear, in part because it is dedicated to the self-and-other-transforming wedding of opposites, and in part because each of us is in uncertain awareness and control of his or her erotic inclinations and projective tendencies. Erotic friendship connotes a liminal region where light, dark, and shadow intermingle and develop. Erotic friendship, one that invites inquiry while helping us breathe life a little more fully, is a difficult relationship to pursue. Yet it is crucial, if we seek ongoing developmental transformation and full mutuality as adults.

We've come to aspire to be in eros-infused friendship in which: 1) we (the parties) engage in some kind of shared interest or activity; 2) we feel a surging toward one another (which does not have to include sexual attraction); 3) we wish to become more intimate; 4) we make a commitment to develop the relationship and ourselves; 5) we passionately yearn for the other(s), but do not seek to control or possess them; 6) we experience ourselves as on a quest together, questioning as we interact what actions increase our loving mutuality; and 7) we recognize the significant role of the "third" in any love relationship – the mutual friend or community of inquiry. This third person or community provides a critique for our actions, the support to face into the critique, and the container or chrysalis or womb within which we may transform and rebirth ourselves.

This fulsome definition of erotic friendship, erotic for having redefined power to allow for nurturing collaboration and creativity, was not obvious to either of us at the outset of our eros infused adventures and misadventures. Indeed, it was not obvious to us as we initially wrote our accounts of our earliest relationship, which is the origin of this book.

Confidentiality

In this book we look primarily at ourselves as every (wo)man rather than to the large scale vectors of oppression – patriarchy, cultural socialization, economic marginalization or globalization – in our effort to reimagine more adaptive ways of relating. Insofar as doing so requires describing our friendships over time, we create pseudonyms and change background detail to protect our friends' privacy. We have also shared our stories about them with them where possible, and, in the few cases where we quote their own writing about their friendship with one of us, we do so with their permission. In the end, however, our representation of past events is of course only and always offered from our own perspectives. We hope our friends' dignity is protected most of all by your recognition that the point isn't to find out who particular stories are about, but rather to conduct your own warm-hearted, vulnerable, awakening friendship experiments.

Part 1

Chapter 1

Hilary and Bill Meet

Is Friendly Intimacy Possible Across Differences of Generational, Gender, and Institutional Power?

Bill arrived in my life on the same date that I first visited the Center for Organizational Learning whose work on transforming the workplace, like Bill's, would figure centrally in the rest of my professional life.

Working as a lowly office assistant at the time I had kept my eye out for seminars around Boston to attend as I considered how to get into PhD study. In the short term I was also desperate to escape the frighteningly dreary job of office assistant where I found myself amid frighteningly dreary office workers. My resistance to "fitting in" in this role was made pretty clear the very morning of Bill's seminar. My boss had asked, in her way that I experienced for days already as unilateral, intrusive and unwelcome: "How are you doing?" After all, I never got to pop my head in her door. Well, I didn't have a door, I lived in the office drones' cubicle-land. And I had readily replied "Go fuck yourself Marcia."

Marcia, likely appalled at how her sweet question could provoke such a rude response, summarily fired me. So I followed in the revolving door of office assistants she'd been firing for years. Humiliated on some level, of course, I was also quickly feeling happy that I could simply go to the seminar like the full human being Marcia clearly didn't appreciate me for. Harumph! In retrospect I could be a little self-indulgent with my sense of being oppressed. I was not so concerned about money just then, because of a generous severance check I'd received some weeks before when leaving the employ of my pet tycoon (the previous and far better employer than Marcia!). Better yet, my newfound location in Boston offered me proximity to the intellectual seminars that I hungered for.

So I found myself on the way to a seminar that day. I slipped into a seat beside famous organizational psychologists, just as Bill took the floor. Bill, then Director of the Organizational Transformation PhD program at his college, was advertised as speaking on the issue of developmental stages of leadership. I recall that all eyes in the room frequently went to a gentle looking man at the back. The looks seemed to check what this gentle being's feelings and thoughts were before they offered their own.

I recall how Bill was dressed. In a three-piece suit, so very different from the geeky guys (I recall few if any women) who wore jeans and T-shirts. Bill was speaking about the paucity of leaders at the later developmental levels. That long ago afternoon, rudimentary self-interest had me understand quickly that for happiness to live in the world, more people, especially those with control over the lives of others, must develop up the ladder of action-logics that Bill spoke about. I no doubt imagined that even the oppressive Marcia, who was rightfully offended by my disproportionate rudeness, might find value in inquiring, alone and with me, into her own responsibility as a manager to promote a healthy organizational environment. But what was the chance of that happening?! I certainly didn't know how to cultivate inquiry. Indeed by then, my rather elite philosophy education lent itself more easily to shutting down others' inquiry. Indeed, it is one of the active inquiries of my life even now: How to cultivate inquiry? How to move from being a knower to a learner with others?

At the time it didn't help that my only real experience of corporate worklife had been in working with my pet tycoon. What with the long boozy lunches and the Picassos on the wall, it had spoiled me. I believed a good workplace to be one that offers unbridled autonomy and playful relationships with others. Working with Marcia was but a taste of how awful the contemporary cubicle world of work actually is. No wonder regular surveys find a large majority of employees actively disengaged. This was, therefore, a compound topic – the transformation of the workplace alongside the transformation of personal capacity for inquiry with others – that Bill was addressing, in a Center devoted to the same topic. I espied my life's work.

I sought Bill out after the seminar. In introducing myself, I let him know I would apply to his PhD program. I already doubted that a degree in linguistics (which I was also seriously investigating) would get me anywhere beyond what my philosophy degrees had, i.e., a very rich description of the world but little access to meaningful action within it. In this I was experiencing the tension of moving deeply into cognitive understanding unmatched by capacity for integrating that into action that made a positive contribution to anyone. Bill, on the other hand, spoke of "action research" (an oxymoron with attitude I thought!) and offered stories of collaborating with people who affected how the world worked. I remember being impressed by his association with a local CEO of the first social-environmental stock portfolio management company. I wanted to be where the action was too! Making the world better for everyone. Besides, his doctoral program had the best scholarships and stipends in town, ideally suited to an immigrant like me, still astounded by the price of U.S. education.

I was delighted by our brief conversation and by Bill's generosity of attention. In sharing my desire to be in his program, I found he was very encouraging. I then returned to the near empty room to help the gentle guy who was clearing up the recyclables. I said to him (in my most Irish accent, which sounded even more Irish sometimes than it naturally should) "all the clever fellahs leave and don't clean up after themselves!" The quiet being laughed warmly and introduced himself as Peter. He inquired about me, saying he hadn't seen me at seminars before. Preferring honesty despite having no impressive job or internship to nod to, I came clean about my recent unemployment woes. He thought that he could likely find something for me at his Center and gave me a number and name to call. What a day! I met a mini galaxy of stars in the small universe of organizational learning in Boston, a very hot topic at the time. Soon I began to work in the Center, but more key was that I felt the attention of both of these mentor figures. I apprenticed myself for many years to come and acknowledge these generous mentors today as my most important mentors in the world of action research, an orientation to inquiry that seeks to interweave heart with mind, impersonal and personal inquiry in pursuit of a better world. I would have much to learn over the next decades.

Dressing Up, Dressing Down

Bill's Halloween Party then comes quickly to mind. It must have been just after I settled into the PhD program of which he was director. I had had enough conversation with Bill to know that he loved Halloween and the degrees of freedom it offers for self-expression. I dressed as "accessory girl" covered with all the jewelry and accessories I could find, beg or borrow, from plastic to expensive baubles.

I breezed past an anxious discussion at the door about the nominal fee charged – Bill had written postcards, with his beautiful cursive script, offering elaborate reasoning for asking for "co-investment." I dismissed the rumination and simply paid $5. This was hardly worth a discussion! Simultaneously, I was sidelining a very quiet voice inside who expressed concern about a significant but awkward issue: namely the paradox of hospitality marred by a demand for money. As I often did with vague feelings then, I simply moved on, into the unfamiliar crowd. I loved Bill's gatherings, one more eccentric than the next.

I remember the evening so well precisely because I came so close to blacking out. I recall drinking way too much of Bill's expensive Scotch, knocked back with a sense of celebration: "Yay, I will get my PhD after all!" And for reasons only the universe is privy to I started to entertain the entire room of strangers with my interpretive rendition of Melanie Klein's theory of projective identification.

Huh!? Good God, I did an interpretive dance. My subject matter was Melanie Klein's theory of group dynamics, which I was likely studying at the time. Her theory suggests we strive, unconsciously, to induce 'the other' to become the very embodiment of our own unconscious projection. Being egocentric, we tend to forget that the other is doing precisely likewise. I have been fascinated to consider that the universe plots to bring projectee and projector together. But none of that mattered in my Scotch logic, which somehow allowed me feel that an interpretive dance among strangers would be perfect. I believe it now when I hear women take off their clothes and dance on the tabletop. I understand it also when I hear young college women get obstreperously drunk at college parties. The slight difference is that I left my clothes on and danced out complex psychoanalytic ideas. It all comes back to me with a great big smile. I recall the lovely floor length silk pleated skirt I wore and how it twirled so nicely around my bejeweled arms. After some gentle applause I wandered off.

Less of a smile as I next recall sitting on Bill's white tiled bathroom floor willing myself not to throw up. I have a strong will. And then I was lying on a bed in the master suite (which I noted, as it seemed odd to me, there were a number of smaller beds arrayed around the room – Goldilocks style). I recall Bill sitting beside me and asking if there was someone he should call to inform about my whereabouts. I replied "It doesn't matter now." I do recall giving Bill a back-rub on bare skin after he removed a black T Shirt. Had I offered? Had he asked? I thought that giving back-rubs (which strikes me as a very American-hippie thing) is perfectly OK to do. Isn't it part of our Bonobo, in contrast with our chimpanzee, genetic heritage that leaves us with Bonobo preferences for sharing food (and sex) with delightful abandon? Perhaps I even offered my theory that we all live in a slightly depressed exile from our original Bonobo Eden. The pull we must feel to their fun, less stressful patterns of interaction amid our mostly uninspiring social norms. But my wisdom about Bonobos no doubt lasted longer than the grooming activity itself. I blacked out. There was no sexual contact between us then or ever.

Next day I awoke with a throbbing head to a note written in the beautiful cursive script that began with the anachronistic "Farewell." I panicked and could hardly continue. I understood the term to imply "goodbye forever" and therefore that I was out of the Ph.D. program. I had disgraced myself as a drunk with no extra credit for not throwing up! I trudged home to my husband. (Yes this wayward fool had already married.) On receiving a friendly follow up phone call in which Bill did not appear to disapprove too much of me at all, I finally relaxed. Despite my disgraceful-meets-liberated behavior the director of my PhD program seemed to maybe even like me! What a huge relief. And another big smile.

Work and Play Together

I began to work as Bill's unpaid research assistant. Early on I met and became habituated to the stuck energetics that would perplex and chaperone me for many years when dealing with Bill and indeed many men at a similar power distance. I arrived one humid summer's day wearing a favorite skirt. I recall it even now, for its lovely pale yellow and deep cut and because it was by the French couture house, Lanvin, made affordable at the then marvelous Filene's Basement in downtown Boston. I flopped on Bill's couch, talking no doubt "ninety to the dozen," as we say in my native Dublin, meaning I talked with great velocity, volubility and passion. I simply loved to meet with Bill. But quickly I became aware of how he was not listening to my words but was only noticing the way my skirt had fallen open. As the depth of the couch had taken me off balance, I recall that I joked "Hey, you need to buy more puritan furniture." But instead of feeling beautiful in a beautiful skirt, as I had started out on my day, I now felt awkward. I tried to "cover up." But what was somehow more than the apparent awkwardness was hard to adjust for. And I felt uncomfortable in Bill's distracted-from-our-conversation-gaze. I kept my hands on my covered knees as though auditioning for guidance in an Amish community. I felt I had done something wrong. I was just not sure what.

Another day, soon after, I again felt awkward. And again I said nothing – this time as Bill licked me from the V of my T Shirt along the face to the side of my forehead. A great lickedy-lick. As I disengaged a little shell shocked, I pondered what had happened. My mind was a little dazed but I decided that it was a benefit to both of us that he gave himself permission to simply be himself. I liked that in a man, someone should feel free around here! Could I say I liked that in a person? Could a woman, a female professor say, possibly express herself similarly? What would that look like anyway? But without looking too closely I felt (no, I hoped) that perhaps, at least around the edges, I also had permission to just be a more relaxed self too? Besides Bill had been smoking pot, as he often did when we spent time, so I allowed him more degrees of freedom. As someone who grew up in an alcohol-positive culture, this did not strike me as a bad thing, only a little naughty. It even felt vaguely emancipatory despite my personal aversion to mind altering drugs (well OK, except for Scotch at parties!).

Unbelievable as it is to suggest now, and as confounding as I now know it was for Bill, I never consciously entertained the idea that Bill might be attracted to me. I was, however, aware that I should be more guarded, disciplined in my self-expression. Though perhaps, I hoped, that I could at least relax intellectually…? Needless to say, given my lack of integration of feelings and intellect, I never mentioned any of this, even to myself. Perhaps I sensed the narrow, moralistic vocabulary available to me from Ireland for discussion about sexual matters would appear too judgmental. And perhaps feeling intellectually partnered with Bill meant allowing him to do as he pleased and my becoming complicit in that. At least one of us wouldn't be squelched; not feeling stymied and stifled was always a keen aspiration of mine. Yet, crucially, I was not consciously complicit.

Unfounded feelings of complicity may ultimately prove as limiting as Bill's over-stepping of physical boundaries.

Twenty years later I see my naiveté and the pattern of evoking male (sexual) interest without explicitly wanting it. Was I naïve to think I could be a little ball of eros and not have to deal with the response? Would taking responsibility for my erotic impact result in stifling myself in domains other than only sexual? eros, too precious to stifle, was kept in shadow and had remained unintegrated through adolescence in the unusually puritanical environment of Dublin. Was it simply then in my self-interest to remain consciously oblivious of my own impact on men, my attractiveness? Not that I denied my femininity. It was simply unintegrated. In truth I had too few role models, surrounded often as I was by men and frumpy intellectual women or non-intellectual Belles. But I was unwilling to "dowdy down." I would not pay that price. So I simply left it all there, unintegrated. In a way my feminism allowed me permission to express my being a woman as I saw fit. In this way, my feminism then was morphing through my own development into young adulthood (which included a punk stage replete with purple hair and a winsome "fuck patriarchy" attitude). Then as now I felt a great camaraderie with the gay community, who suffered corrosive shaming in the Ireland of my youth. I had marched in gay parades in Dublin, and I had felt courageous, if a little out of place, with the call and response "We're here, we're queer, get used to it!" But wasn't I, albeit unconsciously, seeking to establish that a beautiful woman could work and play without having her eros become suffocated? "I'm here, not so queer, get used to it!"

Rereading the term "shell-shocked," I was reminded of recent work on everyday trauma which, when triggered, leads to voicelessness. Indeed, I had become dazed and quiet in response to Bill's 'lickedy lick.' To over simplify, I have come to realize that there were two selves present. One who sought emancipation and therefore saw Bill as a role model ("someone should feel free around here"). But there was also a much younger self, one whose vulnerability was very much in shadow. Indeed my entire personality at that stage had developed to wall off all vulnerability, or at least to protect this vulnerable aspect, perhaps most of all from my conscious self. This much younger persona had developed in response to the trauma of my childhood with what psychology now calls an avoidant attachment orientation. In truth, both selves were present, but the voiceless one was not conscious. Besides I was also troubled by what my own liberated expression would be ("How could a woman possibly express herself similarly?").

A man's and a woman's erotic power are not the same. How indeed might I consciously avail of erotic capital as a 'glamorous' woman? There are few role models outside the entertainment industry for women who teach the power to "bewitch." This is the dangerous power that caused so many women to be burned at the stake! Indeed, the power of a woman's glamor remains overtly trivialized by men ("dumb blonde"). Given men's notorious inability to share attention intelligently between their brain and their genitals, it makes sense to deny women's erotic power or to blame women for men's unease.

Not that I was aware of male sexual experience for I came from a culture that obliterated any mention of sexuality. Sex was simply never mentioned. Compounding the mainstream censorship, Irish biology teachers were explicitly instructed not to teach the chapter on human reproduction. (We all studied it closely, of course!) I will admit that for an embarrassing number of years I couldn't figure out the actual mechanism of sexual intercourse – in my all girl convent school, there was hardly need to mention, much less imagine, the great male erection! This was education for life in a country suffused by erotic shame and theocratic law. (Sex education comprised an annual gory movie about the horrors of the "Godless abortion of innocent babies.")

So in a way I was unaware of any erotic charm I actually "spelled" on men, and even less about male sexual response. But at an atavistic level I did know to be self protective around men. From age nine or so on I began to experience many brushes with sexual harassment that I kept at the barest recesses of consciousness. I believe today that my naiveté was equaled only by the grace of God that allowed me to evade serious sexual violence on a number of occasions in my late teens. Could I not simply be me?! Indeed, the concept of projective identification that Melanie Klein articulates, and which had been prefigured in my debut dance at Bill's party, may even be helpful with this. What were men in our society unconsciously splitting off and projecting onto me/young women? And, so very crucial to ask, vice versa, i.e., what kept me hooked in seeking attention without consciousness of the dance?

Even harder to speak about is that women's erotic power is also often deeply resented by other women. In this way we may pretend to be a sorority of equals. Yet, we are also conditioned to enact power as a zero sum game, i.e., if you have it, I don't, so I have to get it from you or collude with you to enjoy it. Feminism – ironically often misunderstood as women seeking power over men – has promoted an entirely different conversation, namely about a new way of living and working together as partners with equal power. This conversation, so new in human history, steps outside exploitative relationship altogether. But it is hard for the previously under-powered to come to power with grace and ease. We have few role models. We are skeptical and fearful. Yet, as our species is as capable of collaboration as it is of combat, I have to trust that we'll figure it out. Women, with men, together.

Perhaps what I have been avoiding is to come clean and say that I felt no romantic attraction to Bill. I felt him to be an aristocratic yet paternal figure – not that I ever much talked of interesting things with my father as I did with Bill. With Bill we spoke of Foucault – whose work on sex and power was so compelling to me (I had written a Master's thesis with a focus on his work as I completed my graduate work in philosophy). I recall speaking of polyamory, a practice

I lauded. And I recall being taken aback by Bill's concrete questioning about the degree of openness in my own marriage relationship. Not that he shouldn't ask; I just couldn't answer. I could lecture, and perhaps did, on all the reasons a woman should not be monogamous. But only in abstract terms, at least with Bill. Yet with Bill, who understood me intellectually, or so I felt, I did not feel comfortable bringing my full self to play. But I realize now that, of course, my full self was not then available to me. It is the privilege of a lifetime to become oneself. In the meantime Bill was a partner to me in the unfolding privilege. This had always been too rare. Nothing is more precious.

Feeling the possibility of real contact with Bill, I did not, indeed could not, put into words that in addition to the intellectual delights we shared, I also felt sexually controlled and trapped by "his" patriarchal gaze. In retrospect I see also Bill's entrapment in patriarchy. It is not his fault that he carried this "stuff." Nor could I feel into how much this control threatened to leak into other areas that would threaten how we related in general. This is the domain of the subtle kinds of sexual harassment which results in so much female energy being subverted toward self protection and therefore away from creative collaboration. What a waste! Until then, I related to Bill, or at least wanted to relate to Bill, as an intellectual partner, and not a lickedy-licking one either. I appreciated him, appreciated our time, enjoying that time together. In retrospect I see how constrained I felt, yet compared to others, with Bill I felt way less constrained. That is until I took his doctoral seminar.

Our transformative undoing, only really overcome through the inquiry involved in writing this book together, started in a doctoral methods seminar. In the seminar I felt Bill overemphasized one paradigm, action research, hardly mentioning the others, which are much better known. I became annoyed and then furious to have my time wasted. His course was not well structured in any conventional sense. If I were generous, but I rapidly lost any willingness to be generous, we could say he invited a participative approach to co-create class structure. But Bill's way of working was so different from how other professors taught and we had yet to take their qualifying exams. I felt it necessary to learn in a way that would be evaluated by people not familiar with Bill's favorite paradigm. I became loudly furious. Indeed we both did. I recall how red faced we'd become in class. I believe I shouted. I left no stone unturned in my expression of disdain for this way of teaching. I advocated and agitated against him – I built stakeholder support (a key skill for action researchers!). In the hothouse politics of a PhD program people took sides. What a quiet mess I fomented. I had no idea until writing this that I likely displaced my wrath at feeling "unseen" (by which I probably mean seen in an unintegrated way that felt demeaning to me and yet was how I saw myself!) by a man I admired. In retrospect, and perhaps because the universe likes to mock us until we are ready to learn, I see now that I acted out my wrath at Bill as I had with the "oppressive" Marcia on the very day

I met him. The hurt went much deeper through as I felt Bill had doubly disappointed me by actually being capable of seeing me and then apparently choosing to reduce and constrain me. Unfortunately I was not aware of any of this. For years.

Only recently have I come to understand that men's wounding in patriarchy leaves them unable to fully own their sexual feelings. And thus men and women remain estranged even as we seek to grow close and find ourselves living and working in closer quarters.

In practical terms this meant that after the end of our seminar Bill and I did not speak. Because the dance of eros is so complex this was not a black and white matter. I really missed him! It was obvious in the departmental meetings that Bill's energy was so creative and I wanted to avail of it, learn with him. To break the ice, I finally offered an apology for all the upset I had caused. I did feel that my apology was received and, more importantly, a softening began between us. In time this allowed us to meet again as peers. In the meantime, we warmed sufficiently for me to invite him to join my dissertation committee.

Overall in Bill's presence I felt as smart and seen as perhaps ever by a teacher figure till then. I was hungry both for the affirmation and the input of a mentor I admired. I admired him, especially, for the smoothness of his ways with different types of people, for his capacity for coordinating significant action that made a difference. How ironic that I would and did simply overlook the stuckness between us. I, the great lover of truth, decided that it was not timely to tackle it. Besides, I did not yet know how to unpack that stuckness. There was no technique within my reach at that time, which in retrospect would require me to bring a great deal of vulnerability to the inquiry. That would not come for decades. Feeling warmth at least flow between us once again felt most important. Besides Bill also offered very practical help and professional advancement.

Bill opened the way to my becoming the editor of a bestselling, but more important, domain-defining Handbook of Action Research with one of his close colleagues. Bill's favorite topic, one I had fought him through the long semester of our discontent, became my life's work! And in recent years we have, finally, once again, reached toward the original potential of our friendship by becoming intimate colleagues. This time we are not bypassing the difficulties. This time we must talk about what has passed between us. Because we know we do so not just for ourselves.

I know I long to inquire more into this matter with Bill and perhaps to do so with other women and men who also care deeply about this delicate but essential topic. Warren Buffett says women are the key resource for the next economic surge, but only if those women start to see themselves without the distortion of the male gaze. In my story I sense my lifelong longing for the integration of eros with intellect in friendship that is possible with someone like Bill. And so I see us today as fated, now that twenty years have passed. Life wants us to explore this matter by looking calmly and with love at the difficulties we played out in seeking to honor eros.

Bill Meets Hilary

I met you, Hilary, in 1992. I was speaking to and with one of the organization behavior departments in town that afternoon, with luminaries in attendance. Soon you were working at the Organizational Learning Center. Nine months later you were also in my College's Organizational Transformation PhD program, taking Qualitative Research Methods with me.

I learned only twenty years later when you retold the story of our meeting to someone else at our 3-day Action Inquiry Workshop, occurring just outside Boston (at the same time as the Marathon Bombings took place) that the morning of the day I met you, you'd gotten yourself fired from your previous job that afternoon, you were therefore as much at loose ends as at any time in your life of international exploration in the six years since you'd left Ireland at 17 for Germany, Switzerland, Japan, Texas, and now Cambridge.

To me, in spite of being about twice as old as you at the time and of incalculably higher status (!), you seemed a dazzling presence of blond, blue-eyed, Nordic beauty, smiling friendliness, and self-assured intellectuality. (I think we got our mutual connections to Nietzsche and Merleau-Ponty straight at some point during our 90-second conversation after the talk, as I was leaving.) I cannot remember how often you came to see me at my home that spring and summer – certainly three or four times – in what had been the theatre of the old elementary school building before it became my condominium, with the one large bedroom where all three sons and I slept on weekends. That, unlike any of our other doctoral students, you had read European philosophy and theology, was not a small part of the attraction, nor was how you carried on conversation. Namely, you spoke as a peer – maybe sometimes a little superior! – certainly never as the inferior! Or at least so I thought.

What I remember as the first day and time we'd agreed upon (it may have been to celebrate your admission to the program), I opened the door. There you were, dressed very fetchingly like a little girl in a mini-skirt-toutou, with your hair braided on each side (a hair style I've never seen you choose again), bursting with delight at our meeting and offering me a little bouquet of spring flowers just picked. In you danced and pranced, rapid-fire philosophical conversation entertaining and entraining us both, with me experiencing more ongoingly the crush that had begun a few months before.

(I hate the word and the idea of a teenage "crush," but when I am fully honest I have to admit I've experienced an early intensity of excitement again and again in relationships with certain women since my mid-teenage years. Only recently, perhaps as testosterone relents, have I gained enough genuine distance and calm in relation to my feelings to fully experience when the 'crush' neurons start firing, as they still do on occasion.)

The College's departmental faculty had started the PhD program a few years before and I was now its Director. I had quickly learned that developing a true friendship, where both persons feel fully mutual, is an even more dicey proposition between a PhD student and any departmental faculty member (but most of all the PhD Director) than it is between say an MBA student and a professor. This is because the PhD student and professor have committed to the same profession, so the student may realistically view himself or herself as in an especially long-term state of relative dependence on the professor's good will. (And, of course, the professor's career is also at stake in a climate of heightening awareness of personal rights, political correctness, and lack of mutuality.)

Not that there was no danger of my acting on the strong attractions I felt for you. From my point of view, you acted provocatively in general – e.g., your dress and manner on that first visit to my apartment, wearing what seemed to me a provocatively-emblazoned black t-shirt to one group 'playday' I hosted that summer, your easy talk of being in a marriage that also helped secure your green card, while simultaneously feeling a strong allegiance to Ram, your French paramour (your preferred term), and a general sense of liberation with regard to such unconventional matters. So, also, did your getting drunk at my place seem, so drunk that you spent the night after everyone else had left the party.

You have reminded me that I too acted provocatively toward you during that earliest time period, once greeting you, when you arrived at my apartment, with not just a hug and a kiss, but a lick that meandered from your collarbone to just below your ear. But you seemed to easily walk around this comic gesture, and I made no further advances of this nature. For I felt very much self-guarding in your presence in general, given that you were in the process of becoming a doctoral student in our department and one whom I regarded as having great intellectual potential, as well as pragmatic savoir faire.

I was excited about the small, four-student, first-year PhD Qualitative Methods course that I was teaching that fall, primarily because I looked forward to a high level intellectually and spiritually transforming experience with you. But I was also excited because the other members of the course seemed very promising as well.

Very quickly, however, the course became the most difficult conundrum of my teaching career. Indeed, it became the only disaster from which we (the class as a whole) couldn't recover by the end of the course (indeed, the disaster is that we couldn't create a 'we' to begin with, nor a sense of responsibility to the 'whole'). The woman whom I'd counted on as an ally in examining the impact of our own actions upon others… turned out to be defensive to any direct feedback, unaware of the gaps between her espoused values and actual practice, and alternated between distracted and distracting silence and monologues largely disconnected from our topic and our conversational dynamic.

The most pragmatic of the other two very bright women – and my only quasi-ally in making subjects discussable and then offering interesting and illustrative comments, as well as emancipatory inquiries – left school altogether in the middle of the semester to go into business with her husband. I rued losing her each class thereafter.

You, to my complete shock, quickly began to speak almost pure European-postmodern-critical-philosophy, with attacks on all versions of conversational analysis and feedback about our impact and influence on one another. You called them forms of Foucauldian panoptycon-itis, along with direct attacks on me as manipulative and untrustworthy. You saw it as illegitimate for me to teach, under the title of Qualitative Research Methods, a combination of qualitative research (autobiographical writing, analysis of recorded conversations, surveys of the class), and action research (feeding the findings back to the class members and experimenting with new ways of interacting).

This line of strong attack, class after class, had (I believe, based on talking with her in the months and years afterwards) a significant influence on the last member of the course, a woman who had in fact had an experience as an undergraduate with a manipulative, group-dynamics professor. She came to join you in opposition to many of the exercises or conversation topics I proposed, until just before the end of the course, when one of our class conversations somehow made her realize she'd been projecting her former teacher on to me, and that I was actually acting differently and more constructively and trustworthily.

At the end of the course, and for several months thereafter, I felt quite deeply hurt, indeed kind of abused by you, as strange as that seems given our relative positions in the institutional hierarchy. I remember that I felt very angry and critical toward you as a cold, defensive, narcissistic, intellectualizer for a time. It took quite a while before – shining a more accepting, less presumptive light of attention in meditative moments upon the matter of the class and our relationship – the knowledge that I had not acted wrongly, but rather had come into the class with falsely optimistic expectations of how our encounter there would go – would root out much of the hurt, heal much of the wound, and make me a wee bit wiser in the future.

Although we had said a few of the right words to one another at the end of the course, thus leaving open the hypothetical possibility of further conversation in some as yet unforeseeable future, I don't think either of us actually expected anything further. We were perfectly collegial when our paths crossed (as they did more than with other students because of our joint involvement with organizational learning work), but we had no one-on-one get-togethers that spring, nor the following fall.

As I remember it, it was not until a year after the course ended that you asked for a meeting with me. Once we were walking the wooded path around Cold Spring Park, you very quickly came to the point of offering an obviously heart-felt, honest apology for how you had acted the year before, leading into a long conversation about our analyses of what had occurred. The important and immediate outcome of your apology was to heal most of the rest of my wound and to transform our relationship yet again.

What had started as a poly-annishly, polymorphously-perversely positive relationship had, first, transformed into what I experienced as an adolescently counter-dependently negative relationship during the course. Then it transformed again into an inwardly-active, but distant-from-one-another reflection by each of us during the following year. And, with your apology (and my full acceptance of it and readiness to start again), our relationship transformed to a much more nearly adult positivity.

Over the following years, we have talked deeply and easily: You becoming my research assistant and helping invent/discover the developmental model of scientific paradigms… Me helping invent bits of your award-winning dissertation action research project… You completing it successfully in what in the program remains to this day the shortest time ever… Me suggesting to Peter Reason that he co-edit the Handbook of Action Research with you rather than with me… You and he doing such an outstanding job with that first big opportunity… Quite early, I would say, you and I came to a strong foundation of shared vision and related practices of inquiry (you more yoga-ish and zen-ish; me more aikido-ish and Quaker-ish, in terms of our 1st-person forms of research).

In the years since our teacher-student relationship, you rose rapidly to various peaks within the profession (including editor-in-chief of the journal Action Research and promotion to full professor). Thus, you have become my peer in formal institutional terms. I was able to meet with you in 2012, with enough time and privacy for a further softening and emotional vulnerability to occur between us.

When we first exchanged our (different!) written stories about our relationship, we both gave "OUCH" cries by e-mail and Skype, and asked to have a face-to-face talk, including a third person we both trusted to facilitate our listening, our hearing, the clarity of our speaking, and our self-questioning of our own premises.

What I did not yet understand, in spite of our writing to one another, were two facts: first, the simple fact of your not being at all physically attracted to me in spite of your ostensibly flirtatious actions; and second, the more complicated fact that my being physically attracted to you, as a minor aspect of my overall attraction and assessment, had made you feel so awkward, unconsciously self-protective and then destructive.

I first began to allow in the thought that you were never sexually attracted to me two years ago at our Community of Inquiry Retreat. At first, this idea emerged with a strong negative feeling toward you. For perhaps a minute or so I felt angry because it seemed to me, not that you were lying, but that your mind must have been out of touch with your embodied sensation at the time. Then, in a brief flash, I felt kind of betrayed that you couldn't make your lack of physical attraction clearer to me at the time. But at that moment what I had since learned of your whole story as we moved into this joint autobiographical effort leapt back into my mind. I could see how, telescoped into the term "oral self reliant" and your reflections on your first erotic relationship, these elemental qualities of yours acted and interacted with my own preference not to differentiate too sharply among intellectual, emotional, physical, and spiritual intergendered attraction. No blame. No blame. Only sentimental regret that we did not generate this intimacy of mutual inquiry earlier on. Why couldn't your delight in dressing and ornamenting yourself not have met my nurturing delight? Why was your fear of my rapaciously "consuming" you more figural than your erotic sharing of yourself? In the projective identification dance that you began in my home, I now realize there is more than conscious and rational overtures. I am a man after all. I come prepackaged with patriarchal privilege. You seemed to me to carry your own self-generated privilege. I could not recognize it as partly a defensive invulnerability. I did not know you brought already a lot of harassment at the hands of men that was not so easily put aside.

One significant part of my joy at this point in our relationship is in experiencing you become a true peer of mine, both professionally and in terms of personal friendship (and I am now far subordinate to you in efficiency, efficacy, and work-capacity). I feel this in contrast to my very close relationship with my closest academic mentor when I was in graduate school and after. Although he and I appeared very peer-like so long as I played the student or second-fiddle role, he never seemed able to treat me as a peer once I began developing theories that, while relying on his work, also went beyond it.

Another part of my joy in our colleagueship and friendship today is in experiencing you developing additional intimacies within our wider Community of Inquiry and creating projects that involve more of our membership in the practice of the work of a similar flavor with the relational action inquiry we experiment with here. Indeed, we have both just (July 2015) played key roles in a workshop on the topic of "A Mutual Inquiry into Eros and Power." Other members offered us feedback on a previous draft of this book, and we all received extremely challenging feedback from one another about how the interplay of our distinct egos and distinct relationships are contributing to or endangering our development as a community of inquiry.

At the same time, in this writing back and forth to one another, we are both realizing anew that each of us has been hurt more deeply by the other, or, rather, by the way we ourselves have taken the other in and interacted in the past. We have each been hurt by the degree to which each of us has been more vulnerable and more unable to speak about our feelings for longer than either of us imagined. You, I think, have been shocked that my early erotic attraction to you was not only intellectual, conversational, friendly, and developmental, but also sexual; and learning that my attraction was also physical tarnished your sense of my overall regard for you. I, by contrast, have always prioritized the other aspects of our friendship and have felt positively about how restrained I have been in my behavior toward you (oh okay: except for the famous lick!). I have also believed that my passion for inquiry in conversation, my passion against using power unilaterally contrary to another's interest – and in particular for testing carefully whether we (the persons engaged) share a commitment to whatever direction of action we are about to take – all learned through thousands of hours of analyzing recordings of meetings in which I was a participant, as well as five decades of dealing with episodes of organizational and relational transformation – together supplant power asymmetry with mutual power. Now I see that while all that may be movement in the direction of mutuality, it may also not dissolve all deep feelings of power asymmetry.

As you were shocked by my attraction, I have in turn been shocked at your profession of lack of physical-sexual attraction toward me way back when… when your vivid conviviality seemed impossible to me to interpret otherwise. Gradually, though, I have digested the notion that I tend to develop a generalized crush on some women who, like my mother, I find delightful intellectual companions and conversationalists. In such cases, I presume the generalized erotic attraction between us to naturally include a sexual element, when that aspect may very well be only an aspect of my own "crush," yet whose potential for 'disappearing' the feminine voice, especially when I hold greater institutional power, had not been so apparent to me as it has now become. Or at the least it's all a much more complex experience for a young woman juggling historic powerlessness and newfound freedoms for which she has not received mentorship. Indeed, only now do I sufficiently understand that you emerged from a(n Irish Catholic) system of biologically enshrined deference to patriarchy that has offered little to women but erotic shame, ignorance and servitude. As you have also suggested, in the light of these reflections it seems all too clear how far short of fully being able to surface our feelings about one another in conversation we then felt. And I am gradually coming to see, just in the past two years or so, how rare it has previously been for me to talk this issue all the way through and accept that a woman whom I love and who also loves me in many ways may not also be attracted to me sexually. (I've just had a short series of e-mails, essays, and conversations in much this same vein with three others of the women in our Community whom I've also known for many years.)

To come to this realization only as someone aged seventy may sound both sad and comic… as it indeed is. But it is also erotically liberating in that it allows me to focus the erotic engagement I still can feel into kinds of touch, emotional intimacy, co-leadership, and intellectual exploration that we – whichever we I'm immanently engaging with – mutually desire.

Hilary responds:

Far from sad or comic I am deeply touched by this truth speaking between us. You were an older, more powerful man whom I wanted to flatter. At the same time I deeply desired to be seen by you, without realizing that it was in the eyes of teachers that I could best intuit my own capacities. I have now come to believe something that is entirely unprovable; we somehow chose one another to stop a pattern of relating that though subtle in its expression between us falls well short of our deeper aspiration, namely to love consciously and enhance mutuality. I feel that aspiration comes home in your sentence that touches me so much: "Why couldn't your delight in dressing and ornamenting yourself have met my delight?" Indeed, why couldn't eros arrive on the wings of angels as a benediction to all and not be seen as something that invited "taking"? I say that knowing that such "wings of angels" provoke an almost ridiculous contrast with what for many has become a "policeman mentality" that has so overtaken the erotic space between boss and subordinate, PhD student and advisor. We are now encouraged to think in wholly black and white terms about when sexual intimacy is allowable. In the meantime consumption of pornography grows exponentially. Eros is exiled. This exile that diminishes us all might even be bearable as a culturally transformative sacrifice if the policeman mentality had not also fallen far short of its own aims, namely to create safety from which mutuality and creativity can flower between women and men. Unfortunately, to the contrary, an erotic desert has emerged in which we all suffer, while sexual harassment, which has little to do with eros, and may well be its very opposite, continues. Predation by the powerful or resentful (we harken here back to the era of witch-hunting) on the powerless continues entirely unaddressed, merely sidestepped.

But neither you nor I see much in black and white. Our invitation here is to advance beyond that. With you, some part of me wanted from the start to break free of our evolutionary, gendered conditioning. Yet I felt vestigial self protection. As a young woman I experienced that I had to suffer men's patriarchal-sexualized gaze. And unbeknownst to both of us, certainly it must have been hard to tell when I was yelling at you, we became willing partners in unpacking this all too common dance between senior men and junior women. Until we could become peers. Would it be helpful to share a little more of "my issues," the childhood traumas at least some of which may be all too common for young women…?

Invitation

Our aim with the book is to encourage deep inquiry into the trickster domains of eros and power, with the hope that Eros/Power can flow more in all our lives.

At the end of some chapters we name what we see as an important theme and encourage your inquiry on a similar topic. Of course you may have a better intuition of what is important for you to consider, in which case go with that. For now may our questions be a guide to the trailhead.

What professional relationship comes to mind for you in which eros and power issues remain undigested? Starting with words or perhaps a picture, share a scene of a difficult interaction. Perhaps some dialogue can be added, what was said or wanted to be said, or perhaps could not be said in this scene?

Reflecting on this scene (perhaps with another person), see what additional perspectives there are. For example, what would you say now if you had the chance all over? Consider what you'd want if you could share your notes with the one with whom this matter remains undigested. What do you think this undigested relationship has still to teach you? How or where might it still be useful?

At this point you may find useful some of the additional suggestions on how to go about relational action inquiry offered in the Interludes. In particular, the Interlude offers a dialogue that begins to bring erotic issues to the surface in a work relationship.

Chapter 2

Hilary's Earliest Years

Can We Transform the Earliest Traumas?

The child is father to the man.

– Wordsworth

Developmental research suggests that over half of adults end their personal development by age 21. Of those who do transform thereafter, over half transform only once, and only a very, very small percentage transform the three further times that current research suggests is possible (see Interlude 1 for more on developmental action-logics). For those of us who sense that adult development is part of a lifelong inquiry process that leads to greater integrity and mutuality, as well as to more sustainably timely action, one practice we can cultivate is to write in a disciplined way about our early years to see, to feel more deeply into, and thus to transform the seedlings of our later troubles. In the following chapters, we alternate telling our 'erotic autobiographies,' starting with Hilary's childhood.

*****

"Was he your little lad, Ed?" asked the surgeon, an acquaintance of my father's. It seems that everyone knew everyone in the Dublin of back then. "I'm so sorry" was all the surgeon replied to my father's bewildered "yes." My father, whom I recall as tall and handsome, aged 27 or so, then fell to the floor groping for a chair so he could allow the information wash over him. He had learned officially that his only son and my big brother, Bill, age 4 had died that evening. My mother was not there. She had rushed to the other hospital to which emergencies were taken. In the chaos no one took care of each other. Years later I would find out that there had never even been a funeral. Bill was dead by the time I was two and a half. He had died falling off a milk delivery truck. That, or rather the emotional aftermath, was the defining fact of my early childhood.

My elder sister was also playing on the milk truck that day. She was six. She'd been seated in the milkman's cabin. Perhaps Bill had not wished to be left behind. Or was he feeling the need to help her? There are vague implications of pedophilia, something we now take seriously in Ireland. But the simple matter that all agreed on was that the milk truck swung around the corner and Bill had fallen off, his head had struck the curb and he had died. My older sister believed for decades that it was all her fault. To lose a four year old who'd been playing one warm autumn evening on the street outside with the other children, such things are not easily discussed or remembered, nor easily forgotten, nor spoken of later. That there was no funeral seemed almost appropriate – there had never been closure anyway.

They say I was a quiet child. I don't know if that was the case before Bill's death too. Of that I only know that he loved to pull me on our magic carpet down the stairs with me screaming in a mix of joy and horror for I usually banged my head somewhere along the path. I was aware of the deep sadness in his wake. I am sure I missed him too. I next recall being seated what seemed far away from my mother and having to watch her cry. My mother had been unable to return to our home and so had brought us all to stay with her parents in the middle of the night. In my recollection, my grandfather seems to have grown weary of her unending tears – I imagine they'd been falling for weeks. "Enough, enough," he'd said. I felt her neediness would swallow the world; I was voiceless. I was a quiet child after all, barely three. It comforts me that my mother says these were comforting days for her with her parents. Though often I wonder if she'd be able to tell the truth of how she felt. Later I would hear terms like clinical depression. But never from her directly.

Mum tells me that we went daily to Mass together and that I was very well behaved. I suppose that means I was quiet. I still like the calm of churches, the smell of incense, the candles, perhaps less so the garish statues with bleeding hearts and beatific faces. I never saw my mum as a pietà figure, holding her dying son with great sadness. She had not been with her son when he died. I realized later she also probably felt guilty. Not that it was anyone's fault. But the mind torments us. Perhaps so much so that she had become and remains a deeply devout woman. I came to learn that this was quite a transformation from her carefree youth. She had been – some even say remains – rather beautiful. Dark by Dublin's blonde standards, my mother has brown eyes and lovely hair. A little frisky she was; you can tell by the smile in the old photos. I saw a photo of her and dad on a date together well before their children were imagined, and likely just before they eloped to London. They seemed to delight in each other. My mother is in one of those great 50's skirts now popular again as "vintage clothes" in the consignment stores of major cities. She wore bright lipstick, but it is hard to tell how bright in the black and white photo.

In Ireland formal schooling starts at age 4 – thereby no doubt relieving mothers who had too many children (birth control would remain illegal beyond the 80's) of having to look after too many all at once. I was led to Miss Lorca's class a few days after I turned four. I thought teacher was lovely with her long blonde hair all done up in a bun on top of her head. My mother, wearing a green raincoat, left me at a small yellow desk. As I looked inside the desk, she must have left. All I know is that when I looked up she was gone. I didn't grasp that she was leaving me. How could that be, we were never apart. First I was startled; then, the panic set in. Then I was quiet, voiceless. I am sure the teacher was kind, but somehow this memory of my mother's desertion bleeds into my going into hospital around then for an operation. I was in for a few days because I had gone under full anesthesia. I simply refused to speak to my parents the one time they came to visit. The operation was to fix strabismus in my eye and I emerged with an ugly patch to retrain my growing brain. I would continue to wear glasses to read until I married an eye surgeon over 30 years later. I recall that I believed I had a "twist" in my eyes for those many years even after being declared "perfect" by the eye surgeon who set it straight. I rarely if ever looked someone in the eye due to my being quiet, mostly voiceless and terribly shy. It is hard to undo the marks of the early years.

School: My Salvation and Joy

I loved school. I loved to do homework when not at school. I loved to prepare for school on the weekend. I loved to have a pencil case with all my pencils and markers neatly arranged. I kept my books conscientiously, covering them with paper each summer in anticipation of the new school year. I gave myself over to homework for hours each evening as the rest of my family watched TV. I recall worrying one evening about the quality of my homework. I feared that it was so good the teacher would never believe I had done it alone! Not that anyone ever helped me. I was a bookworm they say. And this was not a good thing, certainly not for a girl in this most garrulous of cultures. I offended Auntie irremediably when we sat together in our front room, just she and I, and I had picked up a book to read. This seemed more sensible to me than making conversation that was a waste of everyone's time. I later overheard my aunt complain to my mother that I was one of the "humpy back people." I found this acceptable even if I had no idea what a humpy back person was. I assumed it meant someone who didn't fit in, someone unconventional. There was an amused tone as Auntie said it; it's not that anyone could become explicitly confrontational – not even with an odd, quiet child.

But I Am Different

My maternal grandmother was the matriarchal pole of attraction for her five daughters and one son. The extended family visited on Sundays and major holidays. The living room was always full. People smoked indoors back then. I'd remark to myself on the pictures of the pope and Padre Pio (one of innumerable Catholic saints) on the wall, while also noticing the vague outlines of ducks on the ceramic tiles. My cousins considered the Padre Pio picture somehow extraordinary, miracles were hinted at, his eyes seem to follow you no matter where you are in the room. I was nonplussed by the excitement about this matter. I had to imagine that God would surely work more interesting miracles. I recall that at age 7 or so, I offered my opinions on religion aloud to my gathered clan. The TV was on as everyone enjoyed the Christmastime Papal blessing from Pope Paul VI ("ah the miracle of TV," I heard, though I noticed that no one called it a miracle that the Queen could also offer her Christmastime good wishes on the other channel). When asked why I wasn't joining in the blessing I said simply that I thought this pope was a fool. I had proudly come to this decision pretty much as I had decided that Santa Claus was not real (something my mother first told me I was mistaken about; hearing that I insisted on sharing my logic we agreed that I not mention it at school). The loud din turned to silence in a few seconds. I can still hear the silence grow around my reddening ears as I sat on my chair in the corner. Faces became stuck in varying degrees of horror. What surprises even now is that I felt it was good to speak the truth. I found the religiosity (which so enwrapped my surroundings) oppressive, although I doubt I could have named it then. I found the familial hot house and limitless small talk equally oppressive. I had to take care of myself. I really didn't like it when I seemed to upset people by saying what I felt was true. Early on I knew it was usually better to be alone.

God knows I was not happy. God did know, because I prayed a lot and let him know. Novels no doubt helped offer hints of the possibility of things being different, happier, of liberation. The first one to really impact me was Orwell's Animal Farm. A more perfect novel for me at somewhere around 9 years old is unimaginable. I recall reading it while seated on a red velvet chair in our living room. I liked the chair because of its beauty. I also liked to drink from the very delicate Japanese porcelain cups that I would sneak from the porcelain cabinet. I thought someone ought to use them! I was captivated by the simplicity of Animal Farm and understood enough to know it was not just about animals. I felt a particularly intense sadness when reading about Boxer's betrayal. It seemed that so many around me were like Boxer the horse, plodding, oppressed and duped. Perhaps it was good that they also seemed not to know but instead accepted life as the priests and politicians insisted.

No doubt I also took the novel literally too. My father says that it was around this time that I became a vegetarian, which I remained on and off, over the decades, holding it more lightly as I transformed over the years from self-righteous, annoying vegan to more omnivorous pescetarian. My father likes to tell a story of my eating habits. "She used to love my cooking," he'd say. Dad always cooked on a Saturday night – "She'd be the first to the table to eat my rashers (Irish bacon) and sausages, fried eggs and potato cakes. Then out of the blue one Saturday she flat out refuses the sausages, no explanation. I'd thought she'd get over it, but no, she never ate them again. 'Strong willed' would be the word some might use. A 'bolschie [Bolshevik] feck' more like it." His Dubliner-isms usually elicit laughter when the story is told. I hear it as an expression of shoulder shrugging fondness and our connection over the years. He would cook and I would refuse, but he would still cook. Perhaps that was love.

Loving God, Serving Others

I recall very much wanting to become a nun when I was young. I talked with the senior nun at my school. I understood that nuns married God and some even managed to look good in their habit. My biggest hurdle seemed to be the plain shoes as I always saw clothing as an expression of the soul. I thought God would overlook my cheating a little. I was not seeking beauty for others, perhaps not even for me, but beauty for beauty's sake. In this case it would surely be beauty for God! I did love God and wanted to marry him. Sister smiled sweetly and told me to come back when I was older. I was disappointed but decided I could instead turn to cultivate "acts of charity and mercy."

My devotional self, engaged if not actually married to God, therefore suffered terribly when I felt I hurt someone, perhaps most of all of our little Yorkshire Terrier. Using the opportunity my mother provided by going to the doctor, I observed him one afternoon through my bedroom window on whose ledge I had placed him. I thought we were having great fun indeed as he yapped back through the glass. The blessing of my very short time horizon came undone when he then turned to come back to me. Of course he fell two stories, onto his little back, into the grass in the garden. I screamed as he yelped sprawling. I ran like a banshee to find my mother walking home. I delivered the scrambled narrative of what I had done, so traumatized and contrite about what I had inflicted on the most innocent one in the whole family. My mother simply looked at me and said "You'd swear something big had happened. I have been so frightened sometimes that I've thrown up." Well that did indeed shut me up. I was too young to feel compassion for what she was sharing, I felt only discounted and ashamed that I did not know that my suffering was so minuscule and my mother's so great. I knew that I should take care of her. But how?

My dad had become a teacher after my brother's death and was placed under considerable pressure to get us out of Limerick (made infamous through Frank McCourt's Angela's Ashes) where we had moved when he first became a teacher. The Irish post-colonial economy enjoyed mass unemployment at the time. But Dad had found a good position. And at the age of 12 we did manage to come back to Dublin. If Mum was happier, the transition was painfully difficult for me. Loneliness blossomed as I entered a school in which all the other girls were in impregnable cliques.

But at least I was teacher's pet. This time I loved Mrs. Healy. I was placed in a very small class with Mrs. Healy teaching all subjects while she puffed away on her unfiltered cigarettes and chattered in French. I enjoyed it especially when she shared what seemed like the madness of her own family. All Irish families are mad, but Mrs. Healy's family probably took it to a new level. In enjoying stories of her reprobate sons, I was experiencing her as open minded and I loved her for that. I gleaned through her that happiness was an important state. She also had me speak French. In retrospect I realize this little group was a "gifted girls'" class. But I had no idea my difference was positive, just that I was a "humpy back person."

Unfortunately also very present for me was my lack of friends outside of school. There was obviously something very wrong with me that I was so lonely. This was very painful to me, offset only a little by Fiachra who had a crush on me. But he was a neighbor. What use would a boy be as a friend! Boys seemed quite foreign to me. Few Irish schools are co-ed even today.

Thankfully, a school friend, Fiona, invited me to go to her house after school sometimes (I suspect at her mother's urging). And I enjoyed it immensely. Her mom would offer us freshly baked apple tart, scones and soda bread. Her father always wore a red shirt and sat in his study smoking a pipe. He seemed quiet too. He was a "professor at Trinity College," (whatever that was) and, my father told me with a huge grin, that he was "a communist." It turned out that my father had started to teach an additional class to adults in the evening at the local "Tech." He was a good and popular teacher and Fiona's mum took woodworking classes with him and used her skills to remodel her home when she wasn't baking. I can imagine the class would chatter together about their lives with my father happily telling charming stories. None of this seemed normal to my mother, (why would a woman learn cabinetry skills?) but I sensed an air of what I would now call the Bohemian about Fiona's household. I sensed also my father's openness to what was different even if he himself was stolidly by my mother's side if asked to voice an opinion. And I can now look back and see how in Ireland of the 70's a married woman who, by law, could not work outside her home was essentially forced to turn any talents into homemaking arts, whether she liked it or not. But I mustered more compassion for my friend's mother than for my own. Besides it was another indication that happiness, or at least something more pleasant, could be possible. If I look at my mother in a more compassionate way, I can see her as an unusually intelligent woman stifled by her culture. It is a bright spot that when we were grown, mum went back to school and graduated with a degree the same year that my younger brother did.

Eros Rises

The only men with whom I interacted with any frequency by age 14 were my father and my physics teacher. Perhaps both of them inspired girlish romantic feelings in me though if that was the case I was probably not that aware nor understood what it actually meant. Nonetheless I did give a rose to the physics teacher. I even declaimed a romantic poem for him in front of the physics class. Much to everyone's delight, he became red faced and flustered. By high school I had become popular with the seeming task of being playful with the teachers we liked. In the Ireland of that time where there was considerable social distance between generations and sexes, teachers and students, this playfulness required both courage and the practice of judicious timing.

Outside of school I also began to attract men's attention, which I also did not understand. Twice a week I would pop over the wall of our house to pick up fresh vegetables from the local monastery's glasshouse garden. Much as I loved crossing the fields, seeing the cows and the huge grey brick monastery itself, I wanted to run as soon as I saw Damian, the garden helper. But I'd grin and bear it as it was to Damian that I had to pay the money to receive the salads, tomatoes and greens. I found things went better when I was not alone with Damian. Once alone he would grab me and rub himself rather aggressively against me while saying rude things between his broken teeth. I found it all entirely confusing, enough even to mention it to my mother who seemed to ignore it. But Damian was merely the warm up act for interactions with our neighbor.

Mr. Kelly invited me to babysit for his and his wife's two children. If Damian struck me as puzzling and a bit pathetic, Mr. Kelly struck me as repugnant. He'd paw at me when his wife was not looking. At the tender age of 14 I was hearing things from Mr. Kelly that I was sure were not right. But I was just not that sure. So I stayed quiet. I was also a truly awful babysitter. Short of not allowing the children to set themselves on fire, I simply watched TV with them till they voluntarily climbed into bed, leaving the house in a shambles of lego pieces and crumbs. Yet I remained the favorite babysitter. Perhaps Mrs. Kelly had no choice in the matter. When they went to Brussels as part of Mr. Kelly's job, I was invited as Au Pair. My reluctance was mixed with curiosity. Brussels, after all, was not to be missed.

Perhaps the best I can say of Mr. Kelly is that I was never actually sexually assaulted. A colleague of his, also an Irish woman, when visiting the apartment one evening invited me to be an Au Pair for her and essentially took me away from the Kellys. It was all done very diplomatically, but I could see that this woman was not to be argued with. She was both funny and commanding. So I spent the rest of the summer with her, her husband and daughter in a fancy suburb. The husband, French speaking, complimented me on being "très jolie" but did so without the skin crawling effect that Mr. Kelly had. Besides he did so in front of his Irish wife and daughter who nodded. She was the first professional woman I had ever met and I liked her style. She was a professional diplomat. I recall she told me that she rarely had time to cut her nails so busy was she. She explained that she cut her toe nails when sitting on the toilet. Such sophistication! I too took up this practice.

The family laughed nicely at me when I experimented beyond my rather plain diet. Eating rabbit for dinner, why not! Escargots, but of course! I threw my vegetarian ideology to the wind in favor of new experience (but always returned). One evening Mr. Kelly called to take me out as I was getting ready to return to Dublin. The Irish diplomat agreed that I could go but insisted I return early. I recall vaguely that we went to dinner and he asked if I was shocked by his behavior. I was voiceless in response. I felt that I could not name what it was that bothered me. (O Melanie Klein I needed you then!).

In retrospect I would need to understand the whole edifice of patriarchy to understand conceptually what I was puzzling over. At a non-cognitive level I was in touch, if unconsciously, with my younger self's experience of trauma, where her needs are entirely subsumed by a powerful adult, unaware of their own neediness and the developmentally inappropriate demands they foisted on me. Into my silence, Mr. Kelly talked about what it would be like to lie on top of me – I recall exactly that he remarked upon my having such "skinny hips, that it would be sharp against him." I was glad to be walked home on time. My Irish diplomat-savior offered him a firm goodnight and never a word more was spoken of this.

When I returned to Dublin after my cosmopolitan trip I told my parents about Mr. Kelly. My revelation was met with silence. Weeks later he came to the front door in need of his favorite babysitter. My mother who'd opened the door called me. I noticed that he had not been invited in for a cup of tea, as diplomatically Irish an insult as there was, but nothing else was said. I was not asked to babysit again and my mother hushed any further conversation about him with an aggressive silence. I felt somewhat heard if not entirely embraced in all this. It strikes me as a real shame that we did not or could not speak of the matter, as I can recall too easily so many other imprecations by older men as I grew up. None led to specific sexual violence, but all were confusing to me as I could not yet name what I felt, beyond there being something wrong, something that I was causing without causing, something that was not to be held up to the light of day.

What shocks me as I look back now is how pervasive this harassment of me as a young girl was. And how lucky I was to escape physically unscathed. If anything I just ignored it, batting it away like flies. I did tolerate much too much bad behavior. At first I saw this simply as a price I was willing to pay for entrée to a world beyond. But that supposes that most girls would experience such harassment. Having asked especially my sisters over the years, I do think that I attracted more than my fair share. Why? This was not about merely attracting attention. Being pretty attracts attention, yet my sisters were at least as pretty. I realize I had become used to tolerating bad behavior in any intimate circumstance without complaint as I had learned from my suffering mother that I could not complain. She could not bear it if I did – I always simply knew that there was too much on her plate. So I had developed a kind of inner fortitude. I didn't like the attention, but I could survive it. In turn, in the vicious and virtuous cycles that nature seems to operate with, I somehow communicated an obvious eros of which I was not aware, alongside a great desire to escape a suffocating environment in which others demanded that I mend their lives. On the positive side, I could also say that I valued new experience and could bear most any, even extreme, discomfort if it offered developmental adventure. Without realizing it, I sought escape to a more urbane environment. This meant leaving the security of home, venturing into the world, ill prepared as I was.

Who owns the public space? It was not then a welcoming place for a young woman. There were constant catcalls and imprecations. This has likely been the case forever (ancient Roman graffiti is replete with pictures of phalluses!). Today, in New York City there is a counter insurgency of young women against this commonplace catcalling that young women the world over endure. The revolutionary idea is that men do not own the public space, that women too have the right to walk alone without being intruded upon. Even flirtatious comments (let alone the obscene or demanding ones) reassert a message that the public space and women are owned, and hence to be pawed and patrolled by controlling men unwilling to share what has been theirs for millennia. Women are so often called upon to be agreeable, ("Hey, smile for me, honey!"), with the consequence that women's sense of space is constrained, trained as we are not to engage, not to respond, but to be silent, pliant, getting by. One imagines the shrieks of many a rape victim over the millennia continues to be heard in our DNA. One contemplates the statistics in my bike friendly hometown where way more men than women cycle, the latter reluctant perhaps to be watched by rapacious eyes.

Coetzee's novel Disgrace describes rape at individual and national levels (he is South African). I am struck by the way he captures the "dumbness" of Melanie, who is preyed upon by her professor. Once bright and energetic, in response to his demands, she is reluctant yet remains pliant. Why, we might ask? We are answered only by her dumbness, a voicelessness I now recognize. The professor describes himself as "a servant of eros, a lover of Byron." Ignoring altogether the markings of race and class, key to the ordering of his Apartheid society, he enjoys enough oblivious privilege that he does not need to name the markers of privilege. We see how his willful miscomprehension of Melanie's dumbness (for who could bring better tools of sophisticated comprehension than the literary scholar he is) compounds her lack of choice. All of this further reinforced by her lack of words; her lack of awareness makes it a foregone conclusion that she'll become a victim of his predation. In a karmic turn-about the professor is forced to endure the rape of his own daughter by three rampaging black South Africans.

We see his more mannerly rape of Melanie is, at essence, no different from their more brutal form as both follow the imprecations of "maddened hearts." None see the women they torment as anything but an object. It is left to his daughter to transform the situation by acknowledging and accepting the men's rage for the way Blacks generally were disempowered under Apartheid. When she becomes pregnant as a result of the rape we watch with horror as she takes the offer of marriage from the father of one of the rapists so that she can enjoy a modicum of patriarchal protection in her vulnerable condition. None of this is ideal, certainly not by Western standards of justice. Yet it is how so much of the world works and continues to work.

I have been interested over the years in how post colonial traumas are exacted on women's bodies. Urvashi Butalia, a feminist writer in The Hindu, a national Indian newspaper, explains just how pervasive is rape, the most egregious patrolling of the public space. Much like the new millennium would help my own Irish compatriots see how pervasive pedophilia had been. She writes that rape occurs inside homes, in neighborhoods, in police stations, in cities, and occurs more often, as is happening in India, as society goes through change, as women's roles begin to change, as economies slow down and the slice of the pie becomes smaller.

I also read about the taboo of menstruation in India, at a level much higher than in most places, but not qualitatively different from my own experience. There is a taboo over women's bodies when men remain the standard, a standard that allows them oblivion of their privilege. With this comes a taboo over all sexuality. Perhaps because men, as their Medieval predecessors and Taliban contemporaries demonstrate, experience women's eros as a humbling of their own phallic power, so distractible is the male phallus, so erotically powerful is woman, even when brainwashed to her own compliance.

Is it part of the post-colonial mentality that encourages and even causes rape of the weaker members of society? In Ireland rape or predation has a shocking manifestation as pervasive pedophilia. Sexual predation on young adolescents, especially through the ranks of the celibate (unconsciously female-hating?) priests, has only recently been uncovered; people remain staggered and generally reluctant to address the documented extent. And we all know that what is documented is always less than what happened. I also recognize that most pedophiles experienced abuse as children themselves. And living with the shame of tormenting little children no doubt only adds to their burden. But that assumes that pedophiles are aware of what they are doing. As trite as it is to say it, my own reflection leads me to know that denial is real, apparently built in to keep the ego free of the conscious torment of shame. The urge to abuse is likely even more deeply buried.

Fault and Responsibility

No doubt some men, maybe even a punishing woman or two, and even my inner child (the one who blames herself when something is wrong between people because then at least there is the possibility of vigilance against, rather than passive acceptance of, chaos) might say I acted irresponsibly. Didn't I flaunt a precocious sexuality and bring sexual harassment on myself? I realize how important it is both to take responsibility – after all I had developed a sense of erotic safety at school where my creativity was allowed to flow and even extend to mild flirtation with the flustered physics teacher. But the cloistered environment of a convent school simply does not translate adaptively into modern life, with sexually irresponsible men, outside the high walls. Yet it's important to also steadfastly refuse attribution of fault because one was merely unaware. Feminine sexuality has been so little understood, especially by girls and women, as so much societal effort has gone to suppress, protect and render it silent/taboo, especially from ourselves.

Yet I also know and feel with compassion the confusion I did engender in men. In this regard I recall a man who must have been in his early 30's. He called regularly to the fashionable tobacco and magazines shop at which I had my first Saturday job. This handsome man invited me for a drive in his rather cool looking BMW, "… after you finish work. Just to talk, just to walk on the pier." Yea, he seemed so friendly! As evening turned to night it was clear he was not thinking of dropping me home. Somewhere at the edge of consciousness I could feel I was moving into very dangerous territory – alone, in a car, speeding away from my home. When he asked if I wanted to go to his place, I was silent. Abruptly he asked how old I was. I recall my reply even if I no longer understand it myself. I replied in terms of the new physics experiments we were doing at school – "I'm around maximum alkalinity." … His jaw dropped, an engineer, he understood that I was no more than 14. He asked me where I lived and dropped me by the end of my street. He zoomed off, angry. I knew I had done something wrong, yet I wasn't sure what. In retrospect I was lucky that he had high standards for behavior. He was a role model for others I would soon meet.

Thankfully, I did manage to draw a line at mortal endangerment. I finally learned this as I was hitch hiking into the city. Hitch hiking was then, and still is in rural Ireland, a common way of getting around. I was thrilled to be picked up in, of all things, a Rolls Royce. A 30 something man was driving and was headed in the same direction. I knew that something was wrong when he took off up the road leading to the mountains. I said nothing. He told me he lived in the US (like so many Irish who had emigrated to escape unemployment) and was home on holidays. He had a mix of charm and – by some atavistic sense, I knew – violent cruelty. As the car sped up toward the mountains and increasingly into the sparsely populated outskirts of Dublin, I quickly saw I had no other choice.

Without thinking it through, I simply opened the door of the car – barely missing a lamppost. He shouted but slowed down. Without a word – in truth I acted up rather than spoke up, I jumped out of the by then fairly slow vehicle. There were still some houses I could run into if I needed to. As I ran I sensed he would not follow me. So OK, I would splurge on bus fare after all! I carried on with my plan for the day, putting this episode far behind me. Just another obstacle to step over with a personality determined not to allow vulnerability be acknowledged.

It is not to say that I took no joy in romantic love at this coming of age time. My first crush at age 15 (I, too, no doubt could not see the real person!) was with Cormac. So deep was the crush that I remember much of what we said to each other. We had met walking to school (the Jesuit boys' school, behind its own high walls, was next door to my convent school). Cormac was so handsome and delightful that my heart simply thrilled to see him every morning where our paths crossed. He waited for me with his rugby bag slung across his shoulder and his foot resting against the wall. So cool! After endless days of flirtation on our slow walk to school, he finally asked me out. What took you so long I wanted to shout, but instead replied "Oh, yes I will!" I said, "I will." (Perhaps all Dubliners talk like Molly Bloom when romantically agitated!) We went to the movies and kissed all the way through. My heart was broken soon after when he left me for an older woman – she was 20, he was 16. He explained that it was just not fun trying to hang out with me when my parents were so strict. Naturally, I became leg stampingly furious with my parents for ruining my one chance at true love!

I remained a virgin till my 18th birthday. Having had enough of virgin status by then I asked if Matt would do me the honor. He was delighted to be of help. We can even agree he did his best. My expectations were unfortunately too high. But he was the only one of my crowd who'd asked me out. He also helped assuage the feeling that I was a little odd in never having a boyfriend. One guy had enlightened me as to why, too. "You scare the shit out of us, you're a rebel without a cause," he'd explained. This vaguely pleased me and made me feel disdain for the scaredy cat boys.

Foolishly, or was it hopefully, my entire preparation for this momentous transition to be facilitated by Matt was to imagine sexual joys of immense heights. What with the reputation sex has, all the trouble it encounters, all the rules and regulations from the besotted clergy, I could hardly wait. Even then I knew that having bad sex is a tricky problem, on one hand it's one worth complaining loudly about. On the other hand, it was completely unmentionable, though not, at least, to myself. But I could be grateful that I felt unencumbered of my virginity, that patriarchal prize. I read with interest recently that a young woman auctioned her virginity and reached $100,000. What an interesting twist on patriarchal exploitation. I wish I'd had the good sense to think of that. But we had no Internet back then.

Intellectual Horizons Come into View

I spent what would be my last summer in Dublin teaching English to Spanish teenagers. Dispirited by this work, which was no more than glorified babysitting, I volunteered in the evenings at the Dublin office of Amnesty International. A coworker advised me to read Simone De Beauvoir's Second Sex from which I took the notion of patriarchy and put it into my developing equation for understanding the lives of oppressed people. I saw myself simultaneously as oppressed and oppressor, depending on the context. I had become, if only intellectually, a feminist, which in turn sent me to volunteer at local women's groups.

I had no idea of career. My grandfather, I recall, suggested I might become an air hostess given my facility with foreign languages. I knew that didn't feel right (perhaps because I was inevitably fired from all service jobs I held and usually after being disgracefully rude to the boss or a bossy customer). But I knew I wanted to go to college. How I knew this is unclear as I was the first in my large extended family to go and career counseling in my high school was perfunctory at best. I do recall doing practice interviews for the Irish diplomatic corps (i.e., the Foreign Service), suggested as a good deployment of my talent for foreign languages. This practice took the form of role playing with parents whose actual career was in the Foreign Service. In my interview I was asked my views on the "Troubles" in Northern Ireland. I replied that I thought it simply insane that one group bombed the other for not loving Jesus in quite the right way. And for good measure I added that if I lived in Belfast I'd move to London as really "why waste one's life on one's parents' beliefs. Best to move on and create one's own life." I even thought it was a pretty good answer what with the use of the impersonal "one's own life." In the ensuing silence I sank into self-satisfaction, which was abruptly punctured by the uproarious laughter of the interviewers. The lead panelist explained, diplomatically, "Miss Bradbury I have no doubt that you will land well in life. But let me advise you to seek something different, something very far from a career in the diplomatic corps." Truth is I was puzzled by this laughter and his words for years. Only my more mature self would get to smile at my unadorned and entirely undiplomatic younger self. I was acting then like I had moved beyond the tribe's majority black and white, but without a sense of my own viewpoint as partial.

I was accepted to all of the college programs I applied to and chose what in retrospect was the least career oriented, namely a dual degree in philosophy and German at Trinity College. My parents did not support me financially, perhaps as a matter of scarcity. Not to worry, I got a great scholarship with all fees paid and a tiny stipend to boot. I was drawn to studying religion for I had always wanted to grapple with the question of God – God's existence, what my life was to be about, and to bring a little more spaciousness in my world with regard to the stranglehold of the religious verities around me. Catholicism – or really its long dull lists of moral prohibitions – had such a stranglehold over everyone, our political system included.

My voicelessness always evaporated when it came to intellectual pursuits, perhaps because I'd developed this part of my mind after my childhood trauma and in many ways as a compensation. I connected with the chair of the theology/philosophy department. At the end of the year, he took me aside and said, "You're a good and serious student, I am glad you are with us. I didn't think you'd fit in the beginning. Your pink hair threw me off at first! Now I think you may just take my own place one day." This was the first time I had heard praise for my intellect. Me, a professor! I could hardly grasp it as a possibility.

The following summer, I traveled to Germany – land of serious theologians and philosophers. I stayed for two years and I fell precipitously in love for the first time. Well perhaps it was love I felt for Horst. It was certainly an emotional disaster…

I will return to this story after we listen to the very different early erotic experiences of Bill.

Bill writes:

> But before inviting our readers into the next chapter and the beginning of my own erotic autobiography, I want to make some comments about your first chapter, Hilary, just as you offer comments at several points in the midst of my next chapters.
>
> What strikes me most about your beautifully retold story so far is how it begins with your brother's early death and how its undiscussability renders all explicit discussion of relationships inconceivable. This taboo on discussing one's live feelings about what is going on in the present is at the core of the early action-logics, which is often the reigning action-logic in family households. (The first Interlude describes the earlier and later developmental action-logics we refer to in this book.).
>
> Different children express their own early action-logic in very different ways. It is striking that you begin with the intellectual iconoclasm about the Pope being an old fool and are already developing a hide thick enough to withstand the immediate, oppressive, family opprobrium and shunning. Your mother follows up by making you feel guilty and ashamed for feeling guilty and ashamed about injuring your dog. Next thing we hear, you've transformed your attention toward the heavenly and want to become a nun married to Jesus! Soon after that you are enduring boys and men who rub themselves against you in order to be able to rub up against all that life offered.

You seem fast on the road toward independence, invulnerability, and the uncertainty about what true love is that haunts so much of most people's erotic adventuring – certainly yours and mine, as these stories unfold …

Hilary writes:

How hard it is to see my mother faulted by anyone – most of all by myself. How loyal we wish to stay to those we know loved us, even if the burdens they carried made them unable to love in a way a child, or at least this child, needed. If we are not aware enough, the apparent tradeoff between loyalty (a core element of the early developmental stage, called "diplomat action logic" and explained more in the Interlude) and inquiry (a key, if not the key, catalyst for developmental growth through adulthood) can stop us in our tracks. Loyalty, I have come to understand, is best replaced by compassion – or simply walking in the other's shoes and understanding why people act as they do. And there has to be compassion for the younger self who was quite sensitive.

As I look back with horror (and some amusement) at these early years I hear family voices that in different ways suggest that I "not speak of that; it's private." But I have come to believe that too much is kept in shadow with the excuse that it is private. So much is simply impersonal. Happens all the time. Indeed I am hardly the first Irish person to have struggled with the early years! As a culture we are blessed with the gift for poetry and Patrick Kavanagh's poem "Stony Grey Soil" comes to mind. His 'laugh' and the 'love' had to exist to be thieved. Mine would return.

> O stony grey soil of Monaghan
> The laugh from my love you thieved;
> You took the gay child of my passion
> And gave me your clod-conceived.

Invitation

Our aim with the book is to encourage deep inquiry into the trickster domains of eros and power with the hope that Eros/Power can flow more in all our lives.

At its core this chapter is about early personality formation, which as psychology tells us, happens in large part as a reaction to difficulty in childhood. We are reminded by the term personality (from Greek 'mask') that our personality is not our "true" self. It is therefore intriguing to develop degrees of freedom within our personality structure. If you do not yet know your personality type you may find it instructive to take some of the assessments now available, often for free on the Internet. The Myers Briggs is a perennial favorite. One Hilary also favors is the Enneagram. Some people also find the description of their astrological sign surprisingly informative. The point of becoming clear about personality structure is to see how it so "automatically" shapes our response to the world and our use of power, and ultimately how Eros/Power can arise in our unique patterns.

While we will always have our personality, we can learn many degrees of freedom within it through the progressive development of our character. The developmental action-logics introduced in Interlude 1 offer increasing degrees of freedom in relation to both our personality-structure and our societal role. We invite you to estimate your own developmental mindset as outlined in Interlude 1.

Beyond that it is worth reflecting on your early childhood and what difficulties may have given rise to your unique personality patterns. Write a few notes about your relationship with your mom and dad. Now consider if there is any pattern in what you wrote about in response to the last chapter.

Chapter 3

Bill's Early Years

Can We See Past Our Cultural Conditioning?

There was eros in my romances with girls all the way back to first grade, in Vienna, Austria, as I remember. In 1950 my father was serving as a U.S. Foreign Service Officer there, and we, his family, accompanied him (having lived in Madrid, Spain, the three years before that). One day I walked down the steep hill from our home and up the next, toward the home of a girl I was inarticulately attracted to. There she was, as if awaiting me. I went up and held her hand a few minutes, walking about with her, a marvelous sense of calm warmth radiating from her hand through mine and into my entire body. I cannot remember approaching her ever before or after. Nor can I recall, until recently in my late sixties, ever walking up to another woman I was so attracted to so unself-consciously, nor so simply receiving such unequivocal reciprocation and mutual satisfaction.

Still in Vienna two years later, I was smitten by a petite and precious French girl at the Lycee Français. Somehow, I persuaded my mother to invite her to our home. I took her through the hole in the fence to the home being built next door. The mountain of dirt excavated for the basement had provided an excellent run, jump, and slide experience two weeks previously, so now I showed off for her by making the same run and slide. But the dirt had become baked dry in the meantime, as I discovered upon its first contact with my lederhosen (leather pants) and my rear end, making it hard to suppress my tears at the end of the slide, as I limped back toward her trying to express my enthusiasm.

In the sixth grade at the U.S. Army school in Salzburg, I imagined tying the girl down the street onto a rock slab and touching her gently and thoroughly with my hands (but not being so intimate as to kiss her, which, even in fantasy, didn't seem fair). And in a quickening of the erotic pace, with the help of our teacher Mrs. Martegna, I also stage-managed a surprise wedding between the girl I had a secret crush on and one of my best friends. Then, as I watched in gleeful anticipation from the back of the class, some last-second hitch demanded me forward for consultation, only to find myself being embarrassingly "married" to this very girl I couldn't otherwise directly face!

Hilary comments:

Here is this term "crush" again. You appear to me as both aware at a body level of your erotic power/and or power of eros over you – which is evoked as a desire to ravish AND simultaneously you (or more specifically your super ego) will not allow this in you and translates the urge as "bad."

Bill responds:

At that time, I would say it was definitely the power of eros over me. Also, my reflection on my not kissing the girl in my before-sleep reveries is that I already judged my exercise of unilateral, non-mutual power bad. Apparently, some corner of my ego or conscience was already cultivating a self-image of mutuality in the very midst of a fantasy of exercising unilateral power.

In seventh grade, now back in Washington DC and attending the Quaker school, Sidwell Friends, I "fell in love" with one particular girl – Ann.

But this seventh grade romance with Ann was long distance and almost entirely imaginary, because Ann was in the other seventh grade section. Late in the year came my first harrowing phone call to her, which I began with my carefully rehearsed, "Of all the girls, you're number one in my book..." only to learn, seconds later, that she already had an escort to the upcoming class dance. I ended the call abruptly and rushed to my mother's lap in tears. (I wonder now whether the resistance I felt to initiating phone calls, when I later first needed to do so in work situations, came from this emotional blow...?).

Hilary comments:

Isn't your mother's birth name Ann? I am more than ever persuaded that what can seem penny-psychoanalysis with regard to superficial things like names may be really rather telling. So the idea that the mother is the Ur-Partner, the one in whose body we first feel love and to whom we retreat to cry, means the need to spend a little time on love for mom. And remember no one ever can win the Oedipal battle. Well not if they want to be psychologically healthy. Not that I am so clever. It had to be pointed out to me that your name, Bill, is the name of my brother whose death so marked my early life and perhaps shaped my expression of rage in your seminar so long ago now.

Bill's response:

> Actually, various therapists have suggested to me that I, in some ways, won the Oedipal contest with my father for my mother's primary approbation, and that that Pyrrhic victory led me to expect to win women's love effortlessly, suffering helplessly if it was not forthcoming. It is also true that I have been attracted to more Anns than one might expect by chance…

It was not until my third agonizing occasion in the movie theatre with Ann that, after an hour and-a-half of increasingly intense inner dialogue, I had dared to put my arm around the back of her seat. But by the late fall of our eighth grade year, our relationship had long since matured. That Christmas vacation I was ecstatic when she invited me to her home for lunch. I had no idea what we might talk about – my devotion to her having been limited to glances in the halls, to slow dances at class parties (I did not regard myself as capable of dancing 'fast'), and to the three increasingly intimate movies at the Avalon, the theatre a block from her home, near Chevy Chase Circle. But now, with the invitation to lunch, I had finally received an unequivocal gesture from her reciprocating my love.

Her invitation was especially welcome because it helped to put less importance on an event that had occurred only a few weeks before. At a dance party at Bunny's, Ann had told me that we should dance only one in three dances together because a lot of other boys weren't getting a chance to dance with her. Although initially hurt by this proposal, I had to admit its fairness, so I religiously kept count and approached her only every third dance. Nevertheless, this new practice remained a small cloud in the otherwise blue sky of my happiness (blue was her color), until the gentle breeze of her invitation to lunch dispersed even that concern.

When I arrived at her home promptly at noon on Tuesday, having taken the bus, I was shocked to find another couple there too. This had not been my vision of the occasion at all; but I had to admit, upon retrospection, that she had actually said nothing whatsoever to suggest that lunch was to be just the two of us.

Before I knew quite how to relate to this initial disillusionment, Ann sent my spirits soaring once again by asking if I would like to take a walk around the block with her alone before lunch. Here was the perfect opportunity, if only I had the courage, to hold her hand in a casual, possessive way and, finally, to kiss her.

As we moved out of sight of her home in a painful silence, during which my awareness was totally concentrated on the proximity of my hand to hers, she began to speak. At first I barely heard her voice, so attuned was I to the relative posturing of our hands. Then, I could feel myself resisting the import of her words, felt them threatening the bubble of my world and fought to maintain its integrity. But of course, I was already hearing what she was saying. I experienced the implosion of conclusive dis-illusionment.

Staying a step or so behind her, I fought to quell my tears as we completed the walk. Then, in abject subordination to the original scenario, I sat through lunch with the other couple, unable to trust myself to speak. Finally I left, keening throughout the bus ride home, the walk up the hill, and the whole evening.

I continued for months to yearn for her from a distance and with redoubled passion, until one day she turned on me in the school hall where a group of us were gathered, telling me to quit hanging around her like a basset hound. This fresh and public humiliation helped me gain a little distance from her, though it still would have seemed a betrayal to show affection for anyone else.

After one vacation, Ann appeared at school with a different nose, pleasantly sloped rather than haughtily hooked. She was evidently delighted by this change, but I was somehow morally offended in a way I could neither explain nor eradicate. (Consistent with this position, I refused to have my slightly gapped teeth 'fixed' for cosmetic reasons.) For the first time, I felt okay about the distance between us.

Then, as the end of the ninth grade year approached with a round of parties that were, for me, my farewell from Sidwell Friends, Ann apparently glimpsed the prestige of being associated with the departing class president (yours truly), who was headed to a distant and therefore awesome boarding school in Massachusetts as his parents and brother headed for Rome. Suddenly, in the bathhouse by Jay's swimming pool, she was pursuing me. From that moment I was unambiguously, liberatingly, and gratefully repulsed by her.

Andover – the at-that-time all-boys boarding school in Massachusetts – was no place to meet girls. But my summers in Rome with my family were an entirely different matter.

Rome

Where and when else, but in Rome, first in the summer of 1959 and then in Rome's Olympic summer of 1960, could eros have been at fuller tide?

The city, the weather, and the people seemed marvelously erotic to this northerner from the start. I would walk across the street from where we lived at Via Pinciana Vent-Uno, through the Borghese Gardens, where couples could be seen lying entangled throughout the tall grasses. What freedom and ease! I was headed toward the American movies at the American Embassy on the famous Via Veneto. La dolce vita!

A strikingly tan, svelte, sharp bosomed blonde in blue eyes and other light colors drew my shy glances in line and during the films at the Embassy, though I could not draw near, let alone speak to her, or risk our eyes meeting.

On the other hand, there was Maia and her sisters who were at once bright, serious, and fun-loving, and Maia was willing to melt into my arms. I began to ride my bike across town rather frequently to visit her family.

Hilary comments:

> Why seek to involve the whole family? I ask because I am becoming aware that the love impulse is also to overcome loneliness more generally and therefore is also a drive to create community—this seems especially to be the case with you!

Bill responds:

> Yes. I definitely fall in love with families, as well as with teams, work groups, and communities of inquiry, not just individuals. This occurred in part, I believe, because I sought out foster families for winter and spring vacations each year, when my parents were abroad during my high school and college years. (The Foreign Service supported one trip per year to one's parents' post, and that was saved for the longer summer vacations.)

Maia was not the only girl I was seeing. Diana, who lived just downstairs was my daily partner in tennis, bridge, and conversation (and she would remain a heartfelt but not often seen friend for decades). A year older than me, she could drive us at night to the parties that were becoming more and more frequent. When we returned from the parties, we talked and talked in the front seat of her father's car, about everything except, of course, our own feelings… until we started touching and kissing and talked about nothing at all.

But who was there when I went to bed on these warm nights, full of undigested and unspent passions?

Sonia

Only a thin wall separated Sonia's bed from mine. Sonia was very short, a scar disfigured her forehead, and she was 10 years older than I, but these facts in no way kept me from being magnetized by her Sophia Loren figure, by the beauty just behind the scar, and by her bouncy good cheer.

I remember being shocked when I first arrived 'home' in Rome, and this pert young maid said to Mom, "Mi dispiace, Signora, ma la tavola non ce pronto per dieci minuti." Because I did not understand Italian idiom, I thought "Mi dispiace" meant "It displeases me" which seemed a very brave way for the maid to be addressing a "Signora." Moments later, when we were alone, Mom laughed and told me "Mi dispiace" means "I'm sorry."

Sonia was certainly the reason I learned Italian in three weeks during my first summer in Rome. Our cook Margaretta and Sonia and I would watch Moduño singing "Volare!" on TV, and I would ply Sonia endlessly with translation questions, though my old Spanish and my new Latin helped some. Of course, what I really wanted to ask her was what "Ti voglio bene" meant (trans. "I want you a lot"), but I couldn't dare that, or whatever would have come next.

For, as Sonia was our maid, it was unthinkable for me to approach her. She might feel trapped, not free to respond honestly to me, or else in danger of compromising her position. Equally daunting, Sonia was ten years older than me – utterly inaccessible for inarticulable reasons. On the other hand, I could uncover no evidence that she had a boyfriend. And only that thin wall separated her bed from mine. So, in these ways she seemed excruciatingly accessible.

Via Pinciana 21, where we lived, with the other three top officers of the embassy (other than the ambassador, who had his own residence with gardens) was a large palazzo with four floors, one for each family. As one entered our flat from the elevator, the terrace and the other spacious, public rooms spread out before. The kitchen and laundry, as well as Margaretta's and Sonia's bedrooms ran back around behind the elevator on one side. The guest room, my brother's bedroom, my parents', and, finally, mine opened from a long hall on the other side of the elevator. At the back, a door, usually closed (and creaky when opening or closing), connected the servants' quarters and the family quarters.

Every night, I could not help imagining Sonia in bed just on the other side of that wall. Masturbating required no effort and was a relief, though also a bit of an inarticulate ethical question. I didn't think it was a sin, but there did seem to be something ethically wrong with – and this is what I couldn't yet articulate – objectifying a woman in one's mind like that. But, neither masturbating, nor not-masturbating did anything to quench the yearning I felt during those endless minutes when I could not sleep. Sometimes I would get up quietly and, barefoot in the dark, feel my way out front, and read in the overstuffed chairs.

Then, at some point during the second summer, I gathered my coward's courage and, moving out front in the dark, tested the door to the kitchen with infinite care and a paranoid parody of spiritual listening. It slowly swung open in silence. I slipped through and, totally alert, approached my Scylla and Charybdis – Margaretta's room and Margaretta's breathing. Twice or thrice, Margaretta, a light, restless sleeper, would awaken momentarily and call out "Qui et?" This situation gave me more practice in breathing slowly, continuously, and soundlessly. I would become immobile for twenty minutes or half an hour, then continue on. Of course, I had no idea what I would do when I reached Sonia's room.

I have often said to myself and occasionally to very good friends that the actions in my life I am most ashamed of occurred that summer in Rome. I had not yet learned, and I would not for many more years to come, how to face into the risk of moment-to-moment life with invulnerable vulnerability. I did not know that loving relationships are constructed in time, action by action, from inquiry into real material situations, into real feelings and aims, and by the real efforts at mutual awareness by the partners. To me, it still seemed a matter in each case of "She loves me," or "She loves me not" – with the probabilities heavily favoring the latter. To discover "She loves me not" seemed like crucifying myself. Hence, better to remain silent, and to keep these very thoughts subvocal to myself. The self-evident fact that this not-fully-explicit strategy resulted in a far more prolonged act of self-crucifixion was too big and too omnipresent for me to see or appreciate.

In the event, I slipped silently into Sonia's room, where the entire nighttime atmosphere seemed scented and liquefied by her presence. Approaching her bed, at first I simply gazed at her, beautiful in her skimpy, pink summer nightie – frightened that the touch of my eyes alone might waken her. Yet I was simultaneously wishing she would awake and take me into her arms before I panicked.

After several nights of simply gazing at her, and several other nights of catching up on sleep and exercising my moral fiber, I dared to go further... touching her arm... with infinite care.

She was proving to be a deep and peaceful sleeper. Soon, I was venturing further still... in the slowest and lightest of motions touching her silky nightdress over her breast, thrilling at the erotic communication, shamed by its unilateral quality.

And then I was fondling the breast itself. At moments, I found it inconceivable that she could sleep through this. Twice she awoke. Once she called "Qui et?" as I lay in complete silence on the floor by her bed, until she returned to sleep. Then I slunk away silently and stayed away for several nights. The second time she roused herself more, and I scurried out of her room as she called my name. But during the days she never gave any evidence of remembering these episodes.

There is no climax to this story. Perhaps that is why it has remained so alive as a question for me. What I have been most alive to as I've retold it here is not the weakness and exploitativeness that it points to in me and that I have been most aware and ashamed of over the years. What I am now seeing more clearly is the degree of my conscience-strickenness at my unilateral actions. I was in fact acting unilaterally and exploitatively. But I was simultaneously being inwardly repelled by the self who did so. I can now see that I was somewhere near the verge of being attracted toward becoming a new kind of self who can and does seek true mutuality in matters of power, of love, and of inquiry. (When I began to write autobiographically in my late thirties, I stopped for years just before the episode with Sonia, not quite realizing that it was because I couldn't face and explicitly reflect on these events. Once I did so, I experienced a much deeper acceptance of my own struggle.)

The next summer, my family moved from Bella Roma to a new post, this time behind the Iron Curtain, in unrelievedly-gray Budapest, Hungary. Here, amidst the general boredom I got the chance to try to be truly mutual with a 'bad' girl. She was the daughter of Foreign Service friends whom I had known since I was seven years old. She had years before taken the initiative to get us into a bathtub together and to wear one another's clothes afterwards (for about five minutes, until Mom saw us and facilitated an immediate change back). In itself, this was but kids' play. Now, a decade later, during a week's vacation by both families in Garmisch Partenkirchen in southern Germany, Mindy commandeered a chauffeur-driven diplomatic car to drive the two of us to Salzburg for an opera one day, instructing me to feed her grapes while she lay on the back seat with her head in my lap. Later that evening she snuck us into bed together and would have been happy had we made wild love (or at least so it seemed to me since she showed no restraint in inviting me further) in spite of having no form of contraception. I was definitely lustful, but found a surprising array of feelings that kept me from entering her in spite of the nearly irresistible temptation to do so. One feeling was fear of the consequences. Another fear was that, being a virgin, I would not succeed and make a fool of myself. I was also aware that, while I desired her, I did not love her. I was wary of her combination of neediness, imperiousness, and temper. The whole combination did not taste right to me. But I continued tasting for a long time, our hours together a peculiar mixture of excitement, tension, and agony. Later, I was very relieved by my restraint. By her mid-twenties, she had become a grasping and desperately unhappy alcoholic, whose earlier imperiousness had gradually alienated all those closest to her.

As I moved from Andover to Yale, also a boys-only school at that time and alma mater for many US leaders of state and business, the summers continued to be my best bet for relations with girls. In my first summer, as a legislative assistant to Rhode Island's Senator Pell in Washington, three girls attracted me strongly, and I went out to movies and for walks with each, but with little physical contact. I spent the second summer at my parents' latest post – Mogadicio, Somalia – working for an oil exploration company out in the bush, once again with no women in the proximity. In Mogadicio itself, however, I met an African-American woman from the US who was a Crossroads Africa volunteer. I found her intellectually engaging and attractive, but was once again very scared of making the wrong move. The very fact that we could speak about our sense of conversion to Christianity (my conversion influenced the previous winter by Bill Coffin, the Yale Chaplain who was deeply engaged in the Civil Rights Movement) seemed to make physical contact even more risky. So, we talked about how Jesus felt like a kind of brother to us, a brother who loved his three Marys and his disciples, a love non-possessive and non-patriarchal. And we chastely consummated our brief relationship through midnight walks and talks on the beach, with me internally torn apart by attraction, distance, and respect – not aware yet that one can speak about such inner, unresolved feelings in an inquiring way and weave a relationship through mutual truth-telling, if one is willing to exercise the power of vulnerability.

We discussed the upcoming March on Washington for Civil Rights, knowing it would be big, and both wishing we could be there, but of course not knowing how unforgettably timely and inspiring Martin Luther King's "I Have a Dream…" speech would be. I would miss the march by a day when I flew back to DC because I was stopping for my first visit to London on the way, to see my Godfather, Lewis Jones, who was the senior Foreign Service Officer there. Later that fall, I would write the lead editorial that attracted some sixty Yale students to go down to Mississippi and work for the Aaron Henry for Governor campaign – a mock campaign (because 'Negroes' didn't yet have the vote). Henry received more votes than the elected governor did in the 'real' election the following week, and this activism culminated in the Voting Rights and Civil Rights Acts passed in the following two years.

Casual Sex? Ain't No Such Thing

I had had a variety of girlfriends for short periods during college and the year following, when I worked as Associate Director for a multi-racial program for students from backgrounds of poverty. From time to time, I would return to Jan, "the girl next door" in Washington DC, though she seemed to find me too intense for the most part.

I was still very much a virgin sexually and a neophyte relationally. Remember: I went to an all-male prep school and college in the early Sixties, before "the pill." Sex before marriage, though no doubt frequently practiced, rarely with any form of protection, was still disapproved of. And the notion of wearing a condom seemed cheap, mechanical, and embarrassing to me. I continued shy and tongue-tied with girls and desperately serious about how to live life well.

In breaking up, a wonderfully bright and creative girlfriend memorably withered me with the whip-like quip, "You can't practice for life, Bill." The assertion overtly referred to my new involvement with the spiritual path called the Gurdjieff Work, where I spent many evenings and many Sunday 'workdays,' working with practices aimed at personal development, often focused on learning to move attention between our outer and inner landscape. Insofar as the Work was concerned, the snappy and equally withering response might have been, "The effort, dear, is to practice in life – now – not for life." But she was obviously referring primarily to me whom she knew a bit, more than to the Gurdjieff Work which she did not. She evidently experienced me as more stilted and over-earnest than certainly I wished to be. At that point, though, I wasn't much in the mood to take in and work with her sagacious advice.

In my first year of full-time work, I secretly fell in love with Linda, a woman some eight years older than myself and already married. While I endured the torment of my unexpressed attraction for her, she and her husband and I became close friends. Over the following summer, her husband took on a teaching assignment in another city.

At a festive staff party on a beautiful lawn one evening, another friend, laughing spiritedly, dragged Linda over to our group to share the dream she had just told him. He had immediately recognized the dream's implications, but she was still blushing with confusion as he helped her retell it.

Her dream evolved to a scene in which she was chasing me through a field of huge asparagus stalks. As everyone in our circle roared with laughter, her eyes and mine, unmasked by the slightest bit of alcoholic truth serum, met. And a boundary that we had evidently mutually maintained dissolved.

Now we experienced a new kind of torment. For, although we now began to kiss and touch ecstatically when we could steal some secret moments, neither of us wished to betray her husband (!) nor to engage in illicit or casual sex (!). He was coming home for a weekend, and I was insistent that we talk with him honestly, expressing both our love for him and for one another. But, before her husband arrived, Linda reported that during a long phone conversation he had spoken of feeling suicidal. She felt in turn that it would be unloving and potentially catastrophic to speak of our feelings for one another at this time. So, although the three of us spent some of the weekend together, Linda and I did not speak with him about our new sense of relationship.

After the weekend, Linda told me – the relational innocent – about layers of their relationship I had not imagined. They no longer had a sexual relationship, she said, because she had become completely frigid with him in response, first, to his insistence on and pace during intercourse, and later to his increasing violence in seeking her compliance. Shocked, I now felt it legitimate to say to her that I wanted nothing more than to marry her and hoped she would divorce him. She agreed.

We were both on vacation the week before he was to return. She was to speak with him about her decision on the evening of his return and then join me at nine PM at my office, where I would be waiting. We were afraid to have Linda spend even one night with him, given his prior violence with her. I'd also learned that he had badly beaten two teenagers he'd found messing with his car the previous winter.

One of the days before his return, Linda and I drove into the countryside of northwest Connecticut and gloriously enjoyed climbing in the hills and swimming in an unpeopled lake. I had never before experienced such an ease and attunement with a woman. That night she came home with me for the first time. Our loving efforts throughout the night to make love had us thoroughly glistening with sweat, laughing and weeping, but were essentially to no avail. The alchemy of cross-cutting anxieties and tensions rendered me impotent.

Ah well, so much for the mythical first time. The near future would surely be different!

And different it indeed was. I waited at the office the night of her husband's return. She did not arrive at nine. I waited with increasing dread. One hour... two hours... three hours... Finally, long past midnight she arrived to tell me briefly and in an anguished manner, "I guess you'll want to kick me in the stomach or something, but I can't resist his strength." She had chosen, somehow against her will, it seemed, to stay with him and to let me go.

I was devastated, certainly for months, arguably for years. For a long time, no other human relationship was a source of deep connection or solace, and I was anguished by the destruction I'd been part of. Magnifying my sense of isolation was my belief that I was obligated to say nothing to anyone about what had occurred in order to protect their relationship. When, after several months, I broke down and told my friend Greg, he listened and commented with true compassion and thereby became my first 'lifetime' friend.

Years later, after I'd been married the first time and divorced, and after Linda had had a child with her husband, yet also divorced, she and I befriended one another again and slept together like brother and sister, again without love-making. It was then that I learned from her that the night she had told me he was too strong for her, he had threatened to kill me with a broken bottle if she ever saw me again.

My feelings twisted once again. Seen from this new frame, I again felt more legitimate than he. His obsession with keeping her and me apart was, however, scarily powerful, even after their divorce: the two times in two years that I came to New York to visit her, he called her on the very day I was to arrive to ask if she was seeing me, angrily conveying that even though they were divorced, she should feel obligated not to see me. Linda and I wondered at the synchronicity of his calls. Could he have had her phone tapped?

Another year later, while descending a staircase at a restaurant I was astounded to see Linda's former husband. He briefly extended his hand and we shook as he said, simply "It's over, Bill." He then continued on his own way. After two years of occasional phone calls and visits, Linda traveled to the West Coast with a lesbian partner, and I have not heard from her since.

Hilary writes:

Bill, you tell of searching for mutuality in the midst of relational scenarios that make mutuality so hard. And that may simply be because it really is that hard. Mutuality is clearly not (yet!) the default human mode. Yet I also wonder why it's so hard. I notice that the maid and Linda, your great loves, share a quality of disempowerment. The maid because of social-economic realities. Linda because she is an abused wife who perhaps unconsciously colludes in her own abuse. Both evoke your tormented love. On the other end we have Ann, at first attractive then repulsive to you. There may be a power dimension here that lies at the heart of our inquiry. A core conundrum for you throughout eros' unfurling, and that shows up with Sonia, is the battle between inner desire and self-constraint. Between eros and mutuality. We are naïve if we believe that eros is always "good" or that we can rationally direct it. Yet we must try. Eros pushes up the wildflowers in the gentle sunlight, but also the tornado that rips them and us asunder. To open to eros is to open to chaos. No wonder people batten down the hatches.

A part of me wants to collude here that indeed you are a young lad in the presence of The Feminine (Sophia Loren like figure!). That it is a classic masculine/ feminine dance in which you are caught here and so you are caught in a classic power exchange that reaches no fruition – nor indeed is it even understood. However, having heard my own, I also now hear more keenly Sonia's voicelessness. And I see that part of me that wants to be complicit with you is my rational personality that seeks the emancipation you already have. Why do you have the emancipation I seek? In part it comes with the birth suit. You have the full ordination of societal power on offer for you are male, son of an ambassador, WASP, educated. Your laudable but entirely rational desire for mutuality unconsciously overlooks its shadow here, namely the trauma that you cause, unconsciously, in the less empowered one who has less social confidence and fewer degrees of freedom.

And it's difficult for me to say this to you because I know that consciously causing others trauma is not what you want either. And I know that consciously for me to say this is to risk relationship with you because what I am offering is so contrary to your rational self-image. This is why so often women turn a blind eye to the small and large harassments we experience. This is why we collude in having a man feel like we're attracted. We know that men often mean well. We know that their privilege affords their oblivion.

The effort of this, our, relational action inquiry requires that we risk. It requires that we realize that we are dealing with shadow aspects of the self. These are the inheritances of our DNA. They are not really to be treated as personal. If we won't look at them we cannot fully grasp the depth of the obstacles we must overcome on our way to loving mutuality. Such is the complex problem that a woman with a Sophia Loren figure stirs (or even without the figure), especially when it is a woman of low power.

And in case I sound like political correctness gone wild, I want to acknowledge that we are indelibly marked by those experiences in which sex and power meet early in our life. I think now of the movie Butch Cassidy and the Sundance Kid, which I saw when I was 13. I watched it again recently and yes I had not imagined a very sexy scene that plays with the power of eros. The woman lead character is told to undress at gun point. Only a few minutes into this scene do we learn that she knows and loves this Robert Redford "ravisher" character. And we realize he loves and respects her. As voyeurs we are both turned on and relieved simultaneously. We realize that this is simply how they reintroduce themselves to each other after time apart. But it is transgressive by conventional standards! Additionally, in the next scene we see the woman (a beautiful school teacher) awoken by the Paul Newman character and they ride on a bicycle together with the song "raindrops keep falling on my head." I realized she is in love with both men and they with her. She is up for ravishment AND for choosing whom and how many to love. She became my role model where eros meets power in seeking liberation from convention. But if a man already has this emancipation by default and the woman does not, watch out. Trauma will ensue. And the woman often cannot find her voice in it. Thus are sown the seeds of dominance-submission. And she may rage at him (in his seminars!) in ways that don't seem related and he will wonder what's with this hysterical woman.

Bill responds:

I love your whole reference to the Butch Cassidy trio (or quartet, including you). Other than that, I found myself sort of quietly riled up after reading your earlier bits about Sonia's and Linda's subordinacy to me and my preference for low-power women. It is true that both Sonia and Linda might see themselves as 'subordinate' in a contractual work-sense to me (though I was not either one's boss), and indeed I have described how aware of that I was in Sonia's case, but you seem not to realize, perhaps because I haven't written it directly enough, that I felt, without sham, truly subordinate to them, first in overall-experience terms and second in terms of specifically sexual experience. More generally, it doesn't seem to me that men are emancipated from convention by default, even if they have a legacy of advantage. In some ways, this legacy of privilege can reinforce men's commitment to current convention.

I do more clearly see a grand conundrum arising from our exploration of our relationship and these early chapters about early erotic experiences: namely, how does one succeed in interacting mutually when both parties have experienced emotional traumas to which they themselves cannot yet give voice?

Invitation

Our aim with the book is to encourage deep inquiry into the trickster domains of eros and power – love – with the hope that Eros/Power can flow more in all our lives.

We can see this chapter and our dialogue as containing the seeds of the ageless battle of the sexes where men (women might say) seek to take and women to evade. Can you locate for yourself a basic stance toward those who erotically draw you? Are you drawn to "get something" from them? What is it you seek? Are you drawn to give something to them? What is it you seek? Consider your earliest erotic relationships. Consider writing some notes about at least two. Are there patterns? Are there patterns that connect with reflections from previous chapters?

INTERLUDE ONE

Introduction to Personal Development
and the Developmental Action-Logics

In the body of this book, we mention only lightly the developmental aspect of our own lives and of our most intimate relationships. Nevertheless, we regard this developmental aspect as critical to our way of making sense of the interwoven stories we are telling, as well as to a more general sense of how 'Eros/ Power in the spirit of inquiry' can emerge in human relationships. We therefore imagine you may find the theory of developmental action-logics useful, both for tracing some of the patterns in your own past life and relationships and for developing new patterns in the future.

There are different versions of developmental theory, and there are strong critiques of developmental theory as a whole. The version of the theory that Bill has articulated (Torbert 1976, 1987, 1991, 2004, 2013 – see the short bibliography at the end of the book) derives not only from many, diverse field experiments and other methods of empirical testing, but also from Bill's attempts to apply the theory in his own professional practice of leadership, organizational consulting, and board of directors' work.

The basic proposition of developmental theory (as also elaborated by such scholars as Cook-Greuter, Kegan, Loevinger, Piaget, and Wilber) is that there is an invariant sequence through which humans experience the different developmental stages or "action-logics" as primary. Each next action-logic is gradually discovered (if at all) through a process of seeing through and thus invalidating the taken-for-granted assumptions of the previous stage or action-logic. Thus, each later action-logic includes, but is not limited to, the entire domain of the previous action-logics. The transformational process between action-logics does not occur by logic or conversation alone, but rather as each person faces conundrums in everyday life that his or her current approach doesn't resolve… and as that person receives some kind of inspiration and support to try new ways they never before imagined of interweaving thought, feeling, and action.

Put differently, the human development process involves gradually coming to recognize how one participates in the play among "four territories of experience." These four 'territories' of experience include: 1) the outside world, 2) one's own experience of one's own behavior, 3) one's thinking, and 4) post-cognitive, embodied awareness of the interplay among all four territories in the present.

Most children concentrate, during the first ten years of their life on gaining some control in relation to the physical, outside world – learning to walk, to bicycle, etc. During their teenage years, most youths concentrate on learning how to control their own behavior in ways that emotionally align with and/or break the invisible norms of behavior of their family, school class, and peer group(s). In their late teenage years and early twenties, many young people (especially those who leave home to go to college) concentrate on learning how to discipline their thoughts in order to become relatively expert in some craft or profession. By their late twenties and thirties, a relatively large proportion of the population have stopped developing; but a third or more learn by their late forties and fifties how to be more practically successful by bringing their partial and relative control over the outside world, their own behavior, and their own thought into alignment with one another, so that they can reliably turn plans into congruent actions that yield the intended results in the outside world. Only 10% or less of the adult population currently ventures to yet more comprehensive action-logics which increasingly engage a post-cognitive, embodied awareness… to be illustrated in Chapter 5 and beyond.

Our development from childhood efforts to master the outside world toward potential adulthood awareness of all four territories of experience is a story that can also be told in terms of how we can transform among the early action-logics that we call Opportunist, Diplomat, Expert, and Achiever; and then potentially on to later, adult action-logics we call Redefining, Transforming, Alchemical, and Ironic. None of the early four action-logics understand themselves to be a perspective on oneself-in-the-world. All of them view their model of the world as simply the way reality is. Here we offer an overview of the action-logics and types of power, along with short descriptions of the first three action-logics, illustrated by our earlier stories about ourselves. As we gradually grow up further in later chapters, we will introduce the later action-logics and types of power in a little more detail. In the shortest possible summary, these progressively discovered developmental action-logics and the predominant types of power exercised at each stage are represented in the chart below.

From early in life, we experience eros at work within ourselves directing our attention obsessively this way or that. Eros tends to control us, more than we it. However, if we transform to the Redefining action-logic and beyond, we increasingly appreciate that our own and others' visions, actions, and relationships can become self- and mutually-defined. Passionate, compassionate, and dispassionate love lies in this direction of mutuality.

Correspondingly, the types of power we experience during the early, childhood action-logics compel us and others, rather than liberating us. Then, in the later four adult action-logics, the qualities of power we use become increasingly mutual in nature, associated with the capacity of the later action-logics to inquire beyond their ego-limits and thus to be able to exercise power on behalf of values beyond their own self-interest.

New Types of Power Discovered
Each Later Action Logic

Unilateral, Win-Lose Power
Opportunist – coercive power
Diplomat – charming power
Expert – logistical power
Achiever – productive power

Mutual, Inquiring Eros/Power
Redefining – visioning power
Transforming –praxis power
Alchemical – mutually-transforming power
Ironic – the power of liberating disciplines

If one studies power closely in one's actual practice with others, gradually one begins to realize that mutual power is far more powerful than unilateral power. Unilateral power can sometimes make others conform, but only the exercise of mutual power invites both oneself and others to transform.

The Opportunist

In our Opportunist stage, and whenever we drop into it from later stages, we attempt to manipulate the outside world (e.g., with a hammer). At the Opportunist action-logic we often treat other people as part of the outside world and try to manipulate them. You may be able to see the manipulativeness of the Opportunistic action-logic at work in Bill's early fantasy of tying a girl to a stone in order to be able to touch her as he unilaterally wished. This manipulativeness is again visible when Bill tried to play a practical joke in sixth grade and get two classmates 'married.' (That was the joke that backfired on him when his teacher 'betrayed' him and got him married instead.) What did Bill learn? Probably to watch out: other people may be able to out-manipulate you.

The typical, ten-year-old Opportunist focuses on concrete things in the outer, empirical world, and has a very short time horizon of minutes or hours, sometimes days. S/he can be deceptive and tends to reject negative feedback, externalizing blame instead. Humor may be predominantly of the demeaning or practical joke variety. Emotional self-control may still be haphazard. Rules may seem like nothing but loss of freedom.

A love relationship between two Opportunistic adults would tend to be characterized by a strong sexual focus, with fiercely jealous-possessive boundaries (or else emotionally-distanced, occasional 'servicing'). It might well include lying and double-standards between the partners, strong co-dependence, and victim-victimizer dynamics. In Hilary's stories from her early teenage years, we catch whiffs of men's opportunistic orientation to her.

The Diplomat

Next, we can see the Diplomat action-logic at work, helpless in the face of erotic attraction, when Bill was thrown into such despair and self-loss by his first girlfriend who invited him to lunch at her home and broke up with him, as humanely as a 14-year-old possibly could. (She had also given him earlier 'warning' feedback ["only one of every three dances"] that he had misinterpreted.)

The typical, teenage Diplomat works to his or her peer group's standard and observes its protocol; strives (unsuccessfully) to avoid inner and outer conflict; often speaks in clichés and platitudes. In short, s/he tends to conform loyally to a referent-group (or more than one) and feels shame if s/he is caught violating a referent-group norm. Disapproval is a serious punishment. Nice, cooperative work and face-saving, especially for and with those of higher status, are keys to success.

The Diplomatic love relationship is characterized, as was Hilary's with Horst, by a clear difference in status between the partners, by the relative voicelessness of the lower status partner, by low overt conflict within the couple, and by mutually-face-saving public good cheer by both partners.

The Expert

In Hilary's childhood, as early as her statement at age seven about the pope as an old fool, she was at certain moments trying to be honest and resolve different truth claims. This inquiry of the Expert is at first in black and white terms, which reject the ostensibly irrational "popular" views of the Diplomat mainstream in favor of objective validity. There is another harbinger of Hilary's post-Diplomat action-logic in the response she elicited during her mock interview at high school for the Irish diplomatic service: "Miss Bradbury, I have no doubt that you will land well in life. But let me advise you to seek something different, something very far from a career in the diplomatic corps…" But of course, Hilary's full-fledged entry into the Expert action-logic occurred during her intellectual awakening to German Green politics, Mary Daly, and Erica Jong.

The typical Expert becomes interested in problem solving, seeking causes, based on craft logic (whether the craft be sailboating, accounting, plumbing, or law). While critical of self and others, s/he accepts feedback only from 'objective' craft masters. Principled in a dogmatic and perfectionistic way, s/he chooses efficiency over effectiveness, values decisions based on merit, and wants to stand out.

There is a definite Expert element in Bill's ill-fated love relationship with Linda. Both of them were committed to principles of honesty and mutuality in their relationships with one another and with her husband, but they were too unpracticed in how to apply these principles to succeed in the face of the intense, violent opposition that he manifested.

During the stages of these earlier action logics, both Hilary and Bill are as yet far from the exercise of Eros/Power in the domain of intergendered friendships. Later reflective notes will point to those as the stages of our lives unfold.

Part 2

Chapter 4

Hilary's Love-Catastrophe

Must We Re-enact Childhood Wounding?

We left my story at the point when I traveled to Germany to study philosophy. I had fallen precipitously in love for the first time, always a good point to examine for its early patterns around power and eros.

Horst was 22 years older than me, an academic. We'd met in the home of a mutual acquaintance and Horst arranged for me to be a visiting scholar at his University so I could stay after my summer job. I had found summer work at a Bavarian youth hostel working with other Germans, all men, who were conscientious objectors to the military training expected of them. As with most things in Germany, the youth hostels are well-financed and well run, alles in Ordnung. During the orderly work breaks, I talked about politics with my coworkers. This was a time when Germany was living into the aftermath of radical leftist politics that threatened to erupt in bombings and kidnappings in the wake of the left-extremists, anti-capitalist, Bader Meinhof gang (led by a woman and often terrorizing corporate executives).

I recall these colleagues as left wing pacifists, practicing all manner of "alternative" life styles. One had the memorable habit of standing out in the fierce Bavarian lightning storms. Having myself been struck twice (!) by lightning, it is a habit I sought to dissuade him from. He in turn suggested that I reconsider. Had I not imbibed Shamanic powers from the Universe?! This, I thought plain whacky comment, irritated my rational mind. But forced ongoing interpersonal interaction through the summer yielded an expanded capacity for entertaining erstwhile repellent ideas (and smells too for my colleague thought raw garlic consumption a cure for everything!). I stumbled into the idea that all concepts, even his, might hold some form of legitimacy. In developmental terms it was a harbinger of the cognitive preparation for crossing the Rubicon to embrace multiple perspectives and, more slowly, those who hold them. Beyond black and white thinking and the culturally pre-defined accomplishments of convention, I was opening up to multiple realities. Given the psychological leap this is from default evolutionary mind (honed to kill off what is "different") a whole new capacity began to slowly open up for me. My German friend was right after all, in his way, for this surely is a Shamanic gift.

Having been introduced to radical leftist politics by my new conscientious objector colleagues, I was prepared to proceed to dig into German philosopher-theologians and read contemporary social thought to my heart's content. Politically, I became part of the assent to power of the German Greens. A highpoint was reading the radical (eco)feminist American Mary Daly's work Gynecology: The Metaethics of Radical Feminism in German translation. I got to wallow in her amazing array of wordplays and allusions. Her radical, lesbian, separatist feminism appealed to me, intellectually. Outside my books, though, I found myself in a deeply unhappy romantic relationship with Horst. Why couldn't I have run off with a hippie pacifist? I certainly liked to talk about peace, love and understanding. But I was drawn, inexorably and inarticulately, to its opposite. How incongruous and deeply unintegrated were my intimate and public worlds. I lived in an eco-cooperative housing project where we recycled madly. On the weekends, though, I went to Horst's big house outside town. I certainly came of age intellectually. But with Horst there was mostly sex and silence. Later, when I saw Last Tango in Paris, I believed I was seeing a movie about Horst and me. The cinematic masterpiece makes the emotional disaster look bearable. It was, in fact, almost unbearable. Only at this vantage can I realize that I had "married" my mother (or to be precise and compassionate I realize it was my conditioned idea of my mother) to whom I had brought love and joy in those early bonding years and from whom I could receive only silence. With Horst too there could be no blame either. He was a child of a POW veteran (his father had been incarcerated in a Russian gulag after Germany had capitulated in World War II). The sins and privations of the parents are indeed visited on the children. And those around them.

It Gets Worse Before It Gets Better

I felt myself mostly profoundly isolated but did not or could not name this as a problem. I didn't name any problem; I just seemed to live dumbly inside it. In the language of developmental psychology very little of this was object to me, that is, I could not gain distance enough to inquire into it. Ironically, at that time I was given a prize for the best speech in the women's studies class I attended. In what seemed like a harbinger, my prize hinged on my use of close German homonyms, "force" (Zwangershaft) in place of the word "pregnancy" (Schwangershaft), when discussing women's rights. I imagined that if I'd told even some of the truth of what happened with Horst that I might have won a pity prize.

There was no integration between private and public self and a deep desire not to be seen, or to see myself, as in any way vulnerable. God forbid people would pity me. In simple terms, my subjectivity hinged on not feeling vulnerable to the need for others' caring. Of course in his way, Horst did care for me.

What was the worst moment? There are just so many to choose from. Perhaps for the Catholic Irish girl, the unintended pregnancy came as the worst. Horst, a biologist, insisted at first that it was an hysterical pregnancy. Whatever that meant. He then pleaded grief and went alone to Yugoslavia leaving me to recuperate from a termination that I didn't want to have. But even the doctor had insisted it would be best. Of course she was right. Horst was, as usual, silent on the matter. Worst of the worst was that after picking me up from the hospital from the termination, and before leaving for Yugoslavia, later that same day, he insisted on having sex one more time "because he couldn't help himself." When he did finally leave I picked up one of his biology texts on human reproduction and read that the likelihood of pregnancy is particularly high after a miscarriage or abortion. As if the body wants to recover the life snatched from it.

I could not sleep for fear of being pregnant again. School was out. I did manage to go to a girlfriend's house in the downtown area. But she was away. I conjured demons. In Germany, at least back then, terminations happened under full anesthesia even in the earliest of stages. It can also be that biochemistry also played a role in my spiraling downwards. I was left frail and frazzled. Whom could I tell of this most shameful thing? Any family members would literally freak out at the mention of abortion (it is a mortal sin by Catholic standards and therefore taboo in Ireland where it still carries a hefty legal penalty and today remains illegal in all circumstances). Any of my German feminist friends would, I felt, likely rail against my stupidity for being such a doormat with Horst. I recall the worst of it was August 8th – the feast of the immaculate conception – when I contemplated suicide. And I recall bargaining with God whose presence I felt clearly, then and always. That is to say I felt a presence of love and immense acceptance. If I live on in full health, I said, I will never again allow this kind of soul eating anxiety to close me off from life. I didn't realize that I was precisely not alone or I could not have made this promise.

Loving at that time meant not looking too closely; being loyal in a conventional way meant placing blame only on myself. It is interesting how much the world will collude in a person's low opinion of herself. Actually reaching a place from which to look with compassion at the self and others is not a foregone conclusion. Perhaps this is why in spiritual circles it is considered fortunate to have the human mind that can allow for awareness to grow. Described as the improbable chance similar to a blind turtle bobbing in an ocean and accidentally finding its head in the ring of a floating object. In other words, when that chance comes, grab it girl! It is all too rare that we get the chance to awaken from our unconscious patterns, many of them generationally perpetuated.

Leaving Horst was not easy. Yet I did return to my Irish intellectual program. An unexpected advantage of my time in Germany was that I had become a flawless German speaker. I had read all the great books in Horst's study. I ascended to my rightful position as the professor's pet! A position I always enjoyed greatly (oh how annoying I must have been to my benighted peers). My understanding of German philosophy was "systematic and rigorous, even better than the men's" – said one, German male professor. I threw myself particularly into feminist theology. My favorite self-identity at the time was "eco feminist" as I understood how nature and the feminine were trammeled by similar misplaced patriarchal impulses. I intuited that sexuality was in this mix and that it was both a spiritual path to liberation and also, especially in the absence of honest communication, a downward spiral.

I Awaken Intellectually

In my reading of all types of books, I discovered the popular and ground-breaking feminist novel Fear of Flying by Erica Jong. I loved it so much I decided I would write a major term paper on it. As was the style in my college (a sister college with the better known English Oxford and Cambridge), my tutor for this was a venerable Jesuit priest. We met alone, weekly for 90 minutes. He read everything I put in front of him and vice versa. Thus we communicated by books as he guided my reading. He declared Fear of Flying "marvelous, feminist, a fresh breeze, Rabelesian, almost Chaucerian in attitude. Gifted!" We discussed our favorite parts and laughed with delight for 88 minutes. I recall having no sense of discomfort despite the obvious erotic nature of the reading. I explain that now as an artifact of my experiencing Irish priests and nuns, who surrounded me, as entirely non-sexual. I could also state this in the negative, that they were sometimes aggressively anti-sexual. My Jesuit tutor was more the former; he was sophisticated and by professional necessity, unusually well read. He insisted however that I would not be standing up to deliver a paper on Erica Jong at the end of term. 'That just wouldn't do at all, Miss Bradbury.' In the final minute I offered a Heinrich Böll novel as a substitute. Böll is a German writer of some renown and was found immediately acceptable, for, like my scholastic tutor, he happily combined being a male feminist with little mention of sex. Thus Böll was approved as far more suitable to my senior faculty members, all of whom were men. Having run out of time to argue, I gathered my books. "Good day to you. Miss Bradbury." Aware that decorum was now called for over my pressing desire to vent righteous anger, I replied "Thank you, Professor."

I understood that I was being discouraged from commenting on what could be seen by some as a frivolous, sluttish book by a female author. Jong joined many women writers with her preference for what she might call zaftig juicy life, its sexual qualities integrated with its intellect and wit. Such a choice set it in contrast with the conventional arid scholarship of (eunuchs or merely monkish?) intellectuals, which calls us to leave our embodied life on the sidelines. In being told to ignore this type of work, I understood the implied insult to all women, and full human beings in general, and sexuality in particular. In retrospect I also know I did not have the inner fortitude, intellectual or emotional, to fend off the type of withering and demeaning criticism that a mainstream (i.e., non-feminist) philosopher would throw at me. That fortitude has taken many years to develop and perhaps must remain an ongoing intention as fortitude is not quite the right word, suggesting as it does a kind of insistence.

The feminist vision of human partnership and participation is a radical vision with implications for all philosophical thought and how we live life. It pits itself, albeit gently, against the notion of the separate individual and brings relationality to the forefront of all human endeavor. For my immediate purposes I had stumbled onto something of critical importance to me, namely, the possibility of re-imagining an entirely different way of constructing the world such that dominator hierarchy could be replaced by a more feminine-loving, partnership orientation (a formulation articulated by Riane Eisler which I so admire). Such a world would be juicier and lighter too. Wouldn't we all be happier, move alive, and not just from the neck up, in such a world? I have since spent my life trying to unpack this theme for myself in ways that translate the intellectual liberation without leaving a partnership tinged eros behind.

Not that I had experienced much of actual partnership by the time my mind had become set on its path. To ensure that I would be away from Horst who had asked, sometimes begged me to return to Germany, I decided to avail myself of a student work program for Irish students in the USA for the summer of 1985. To my great shame I even wanted to return to Germany and I cried as I left for the USA. I arrived with very little money and a few phone numbers. Again I was alone because, although I knew of some Irish friends in Boston, I wanted to avoid them. All men, they drank too much. And I would rather be with extraordinary men (a category that necessarily excluded adolescent Irish men?) or else alone.

I recall participating in a cultural training program offered by the US government to all student visa carriers on my first day there. I was entirely unable to fathom what they explained is the depth of American racism (but only the skin is different, what's the big deal I wondered). Finally, though, I got to speak with a real American! I needed help to get from the Tufts campus to the subway. My new American friend and I fell into chatter together. I learned that he was a "Vietnam Vet," and there was an air of liberation gained through fire that I immediately felt from him. I would like the baby boomer generation most of all. Perhaps I too had escaped a stupid war in Ireland. Not the one between Catholics and Protestants in Belfast, though yes I thought that was stupid. But the war from which I was a conscientious objector. Ireland was essentially an erotic "concentration camp," a theocracy whose all powerful Cardinal had line edited the founding Irish constitution. Back then, teachings on sexual morality kept the Irish hobbled with guilt in an atmosphere of powerful oppression in spiritual, moral, legal and educational arenas. At the time of my escape there was no deep understanding of the priestly predation on children, much less the more subtle strangleholds on the Irish psyche. Certainly no one thought I was right to express my displeasure. But I felt my truth in my bones reinforced by the unquestioning sycophancy towards priests that made me a little crazy. Was I the only one who saw the Emperor-Bishops as having no clothes? Hardly. But I did not know any likeminded people. My friends seemed open minded enough, but mostly just to claim their own egocentric freedoms. Funnily enough it was in Boston that I first saw a demonstration against Catholic priests' abuse of children, outside the Cardinal's house across from the university in which Mary Daly taught. The same university in which Bill Torbert was reimagining power relationships and organizations.

The connection between Catholicism and organizational structure is not tenuous. The original and deeply patriarchal Roman Army and Catholic Church is the de facto organizational model that remains dominant because its hierarchical structure has been so "successful" or at least has lasted a long time. As such it has been the only model from the Middle Ages (honed with witch hunting) into the present. The reformulation of organizations along other lines, variously known as learning organization, etc. is very much a work in progress and a radical departure from patriarchal authority. It was this topic of organizational change and at that very university that I would later get my PhD.

But on that first day I was pleased just to find the subway "T" to the affordable part of town. I heard of the campus of the University of Massachusetts and planned to look for roommate ads. Without actually knowing, I just knew there would be fliers fluttering on campus boards offering all the services and resources I needed. In any country I feel immediately most comfortable on a university campus, finding that it always provides a familiar yet cosmopolitan territory, with a funky coffee shop to boot. I pulled some fliers and called at the first address. I passed the interview with the two girls who lived there. They were surprised that I had so few belongings and no car. For my part I was surprised by how well off, decadent even, they seemed. I addressed the question on "pets" in finishing up the rental agreement by referring, deadpan, to my pet snake and baby alligator. At least I thought it was funny! I calmed the roommates down, and explained that yes I would follow the rental agreement on exotic pets. Promise! I learned quickly not to joke so easily with Americans.

I loved my room. My first old oak floored house. I kept it bare and thought it beautiful to hang my colorful clothes around the walls. My needs were simple. Nonetheless it took me three badly paying part time jobs to make ends meet in this expensive city – as a waitress, a clothing store attendant and a market researcher who accosted people to ask their opinions on all things irrelevant. Thankfully, Bostonians like Irish people and despite being quiet I had my family's and indeed Ireland's "touch of the Blarney." I could flirt and small talk with any stranger, if I had to. In return I was soon crazy about America, especially the experience of American grocery shopping. Excessive choice available even at 2 AM. For some reason I just loved walking grocery store aisles in the middle of the night, finding it the height of liberation over stuffy European customs.

Apart from lacking a sense of humor, my roommates seemed very nice, indeed. I learned that they were both vegetarians, like me. And they were practitioners of "Zen," studying with serious intent with a Zen Master in Boston. I honor them for bringing me the great gift of the dharma. Though it took quite a while for me to recognize it as a gift. They often invited me to visit their Zen Center and advised me not always to work so hard. I promised to come with them to meditate while being struck at their oblivion. "I have to work, I can't just sit on my arse, my parents don't pay my rent (harumph)." I did however look at and tried to read a book they gave me on the development of Zen awareness. It was almost literally gibberish to me, but with tantalizing moments of contact. I understood, perhaps, that paying attention without use of conceptual frames was at the core of this otherwise esoteric path. (This was before Hollywood had discovered the eternal wisdom traditions and before every hairdresser had a strategically placed Buddha in their shop window). My intrigue was piqued because as a philosophy student I was pretty sure there was no such thing that could be directly experienced; everything has to be interpreted by the neurological apparatus called mind. Immanuel Kant had been very clear about this. Surely Kant was no fool! But did I really understand mind?

More Gentle Love

Gradually I also connected better with my American restaurant colleagues. I found what was called then 'a singles bar' a fun place to work with good tips (thanks again to the Irish blarney). I went with my fellow waiters for beers after work and then I'd catch the last T home to Dorchester. I never mentioned that I was not yet 21 or that I used a fake ID (an entirely ethical protest in response to the State's crushing oppression of the under-aged, or so I reasoned). My colleagues frequently mentioned how dangerous Dorchester was – all those "blacks." But I felt safe. Besides, I had struck up a friendship with Sophine who worked in the kitchen. Being from Cape Verde, Sophine had dark skin and a foreign accent. I explained how much we had in common – what with both of us from an island in the Atlantic! Sophine helped me to send my meals out quicker than the rest of the wait staff, so I invited her for drinks, too. To the confusion of all. I realized there was an unwritten rule even in this most democratic of organizations that "back of the house" staff didn't mix with "front of the house" staff. But when she touched my face the first time and said "You the whitest white girl I ever did know," I, in turn found her skin delightfully, surprisingly soft. And we also understood each others' jokes. So yes of course I would move in with her! Categories of lesbian, straight etc. didn't seem that relevant to me then, or now. But I soon discovered that we were quite different in taste and temperament. There was no grand drama per se with Sophine – it seemed simply logical to move out after she'd invited another young woman to move in, someone with whom she regularly smoked cocaine, which I had no interest in doing. Comical to admit, but it was not the cocaine habit with another lover, but the way she wasted electricity that killed our romance – the defrosting of the fridge one hot evening by simply leaving its door open, to allow all the ice to melt on the floor. I was flabbergasted. Didn't she know that refrigerators use half the electricity of a household?! Didn't she feel bad about this waste of Earth's resources?! Sophine announced me too uptight. She also helpfully warned me against getting electrocuted while trying to save energy that the landlord paid for anyway.

But eros would not be undone. Toward the end of my stay I met an Irish American, with whom I chatted with great affinity. I was soon smitten as he listened to all I had to say. He even asked follow up questions! I told him all about myself and he listened without apparent judgment. In turn I listened to his story with many questions about American culture. Irish and American cultures seem both so very near that the distance is frequently mistaken. As our conversational intimacy grew, he told me he moved back and forth between feeling intimidated by my cool and seemingly louche lifestyle and bemusement at my apparent naiveté (OMG smoking cocaine is better known as using crack!). We began to spend more time together and gradually began to kiss passionately. I was terrified of becoming pregnant and he seemed to understand, which endeared him to me all the more. We were sad as we said goodbye at the end of the summer but stayed in touch, arranging to meet the following summer to travel across the USA together. And we did exactly that.

Our cross-country trip became a cross-continental romance as I invited him to join me in Zurich where I had taken a position as a teaching assistant at the university. It was probably ill advised that I commenced a delightful fling with one of my students not too long after his arrival. I recall this mostly because at the time I couldn't believe the upset it caused, for the Dean and for my American boyfriend.

Brought before a hastily assembled committee, I calmly explained to the Dean that the student was only two years younger than me. No doubt I rambled with self serving justifications that essentially amounted to "What's the big deal, Herr Professor Dean?!" Naturally I carefully omitted mention that the student was, after all, fabulously good-looking and had been showering me with gifts for months. I specifically did not say, 'So what's a girl with a disaffecting American boyfriend to do!' The Dean declared whatever justifications I offered "Salat" (lit. "salad," i.e., a hodgepodge of excuses), to which I replied "Well, I am a vegetarian!" The all male committee's inadvertent but uncontrollable laughter seemed to render my case dismissed. The Swiss student and I have remained in sporadic contact over the decades. Naturally, I am relieved to see he was not scarred too much by our possibly inappropriate relationship. I am even pleased that he went on to become a Jungian analyst (with, he says, fond memories of an erstwhile teacher!).

I Go a Little Overboard. Perhaps.

Next, I was delighted to win a scholarship to study philosophy with professors I considered to be some of the most exciting philosophers of our era. It only added to the appeal that the statistics for my new campus reported ten men for every one woman. Ten smart men all for me I calculated for what I envisaged as a veritable relational candy store. What fun!

What I mostly recall of the famous philosopher Paul Ricoeur was that he spoke so often of "muddles of God." Yea I could relate! So I was disappointed to learn that I had misunderstood his French accent; he really meant "models"! And Juergen Habermas was almost literally incomprehensible. The most lauded of philosophers of our era on the subject of communicative action had a speech impediment. Along with very convoluted Germanic sentences, I was left with a sinking and too often inwardly screaming sense that there had to be something more than this. But what? These were literally the greatest minds in my field. I had been lucky to get the fiercely competitive scholarship I had won. But my heart knew that I was in the wrong place.

During this time I met visiting Professor Ram Lavash, who listened to my existential woes with a keenness that I had never previously encountered. Getting to know him came to be the most indelible experience of this marvelous time. We would remain in what the French call an *amitié amoureuse* for over twenty years. His advice at the time came with a gift copy of Nietzsche's Gay Science. His counsel was to "*amor fati*," to love my fate, by which he implied I must first create it.

I wrote a thesis clarifying the difference and overlap between the categories of critical reality and myth. In using feminist and Foucauldian thought, along with reference to Irish writers like Joyce and Wilde, I illustrated that there is very little difference between these categories. I received high accolades for the thesis. Then seemingly out of the blue, while preparing to defend my dissertation proposal, whose acceptance would have locked me into at least four more years of impecunious study, I decided to go to Japan to study Zen. Just like that. Beware the effects of reading Nietzsche's scorn for conventional scholarly pursuits.

That I hardly even knew what Zen was seemed exactly right. All I knew was that Zen was not an intellectual path. No need for knowing. How I even knew that I didn't know. Perhaps it came to me by osmosis while I absently browsed the book covers over the shoulder of my alternately taciturn and droning tutor. Our boredom was no doubt mutual. He was a famed scholar of Chinese Classic Buddhist literature, a topic in which I would show no interest whatsoever till decades later. I sensed I needed to be saved from overly heady ways. Or perhaps I simply sought a zestier life. As much as I wanted to leave, I sensed my scholarly career was by no means over. In my ambivalence I wrote a letter seeking an extended leave of absence. My tutor gladly accepted...

Bill comments:

It is hard in youth to see what there is to learn from our intimate relationships. Each seems altogether unique, if we bother to reflect on them at all. You seem to me to be singing this hymn in this chapter, when you write that it's hard – as in lifetime hard – to develop compassion for oneself and others. Did your Horst experience suggest or repeat a pattern of brazen-ing your way into relationships, then suffering through them? Who knows? Especially, close to the time.

You also speak of awakening intellectually – a wonderful awakening that a larger proportion of human kind should be positioned to experience. But this awakening should not be confused with a much later awakening to awareness itself in action, which may yield in turn to the reality hidden just behind that. But now I'm talking about those developmental action-logics we've mentioned a couple of times in passing, so let's pause in our stories. Instead, let us take an interlude to 'go theoretical together' and name some of the patterns we can see in our own actions so far, in the arena of our intergendered friendships...

Chapter 5

Bill Marries

Does marriage foster loving intimacy?

In the year and a half after Linda's and my relationship was forcibly discontinued, my deep personal loneliness came to seem end-able only if I married. That's what one did then. That's what several of my best friends had already done in the two and a half years since college graduation. Of course, marriage doesn't necessarily end loneliness, and some proportion of loneliness can only be ended by becoming comfortable with one's aloneness, a process that occurred within me only over decades – decades of sometimes disciplined, sometimes lackluster first-person spiritual inquiry into the source of human intentionality, relationality, and momentary validity.

My loneliness was exaggerated, no doubt, by my having entered the Individual and Organizational Behavior doctoral program at Yale. This meant that I had no structured 9-5 job, a deficit I fixed within six months by becoming Director of the new Yale Upward Bound program for New Haven students from backgrounds of poverty. (I would also study the program for my dissertation and write a book about it and about the efficacy and inefficacy of my own leadership actions.)

Several brief relational flurries proceeded during that following year and a half. First, I had begun to see a talented and beautiful Latin American woman whom I knew through Sundays in the Gurdjieff Work, along with some two hundred others. This brief relationship included two Work-related parties that we both attended, given by my teacher's daughter. They included what might be called 'higher consciousness' party games such as sending one person out of the room while the rest agreed on a spot in the room we would all attend to without any outward indication of doing so. Returning to the room, the "outsider" would try to feel the spot of common concentration. Several times the outsider came very close to the mark. How? Intense conversation followed!

The ante-climax of our relationship occurred after a delightful evening together, with a short period of luscious cuddling and kissing on her bed before I got up and stood, hands on the top of her bureau, turned away from her. Breathing deeply, I tried to assimilate what it would be like to pair over time with this passionate and self-disciplined woman. At that moment, she came up behind me, hugged me without sensual reserve, and told me she was returning home to Brazil for a time. "Let's go slow," she said, with a warm, reassuring squeeze. Later, when she did not return, I eventually learned she had married. Whether she had already been planning to marry, I never learned. Given how fledgling a relationship the two of us had, her farewell hug and words felt to me like as loving a way to disengage as I had ever before experienced, and it left me with a permanent hint about how to interweave passion, dispassion, and compassion. But it also once again left a loneliness that seemed harder to bear ever since my catastrophic relationship with Linda.

Near Christmas time after my first summer of directing the Upward Bound program, I turned once again toward Jan, my former girlfriend from next door in Washington, even though I had earlier been the one to make the decision we should split, with no objection from her. She had said before she wouldn't marry before graduating. Now she was a senior about to graduate. (At that time, the norm for college-educated women was still to marry as soon after graduating as practical.) We had both had trouble saying anything to one another, other than my haranguing her on the meaning of brotherly love hanging on a cross, or one of the philosophers I was reading… After several dates toward the end of that fall that felt more promising than our earlier dates had been, I asked her to marry me.

She agreed, and we celebrated our wedding in early June, 1968, at the National Episcopal Cathedral in Washington, with my grandmother and the Chief Justice of the US Supreme Court among the many in attendance.

> Here we see me "falling back" to the Diplomat action-logic. Note the strong Diplomat overtones in my decision to marry: at that time, guys and girls tended to marry soon after they'd finished their expected education, whether high school or college (Diplomatic imitation of a social norm of early marriage); moreover, most of my best friends had already married I was feeling social pressure even though none was being exerted directly by my parents or friends.
>
> Whom to choose? I was in distress because my true-love with Linda had gone awry [loneliness is unbearable, pleasurable aloneness unknown (except in escapist circumstances like going to the movies)]. Since no new girlfriend appeared on my immediate horizon, wouldn't it be wonderful to bring my family even closer to our neighboring family by marrying their daughter? Diplomatic inclination to make other people happy without seriously consulting one's own preferences. In other words, my marital decision-making was strongly influenced by conforming to social norms, by imitating others, by making others happy, and by avoidance of being lonely.

My new wife and I spent a short honeymoon in St. Croix in an uncomfortable windmill next to a tourist water plane dock, where the single propeller roared to life at 7AM each morning. Our honeymoon revealed us to be equally nervous, unpracticed, and uptight in the erotic-sexual domain. From our first night in the hotel, when I knew nothing about how, gradually, to arouse her, and she played a purely passive role, which didn't help my timidity at all, we never really learned how to make love with confident, caring mutuality throughout our marriage.

Because of my commitment to Upward Bound and to living the rough life, I had arranged for my wife and myself to live in one of the student dorms for the 7-week program that started two weeks after our wedding. To say the least, this was not an arrangement calculated to optimize the growth of quiet erotic and sexual intimacy between us. Sleeping on separate single cots and being awakened by false fire alarms was certainly no help. And I was often filled with the tensions of the program, while my wife alternated between boredom and fear of the increasing violence surrounding the program. Then, the following fall, my wife soon discontinued her attendance at the Gurdjieff Work to which I had invited her, but with which she found little connection.

No, the marriage was not starting well, but we were both deeply committed to talking things through and spent untold hours trying to make the marriage work. One thing we had very definitely gotten over was our inability to talk with one another. We shared a beloved dog (Hubinger, named for the street we lived on). We shared the pleasures of tennis, mountain climbing, swimming, and skiing. We shared a delight in one another's families. And, finally, we shared that earnest belief in talking things through.

With regard to earnestly talking things through, we were delighted to be included in extensive interviews, occurring around the country, on how married couples managed their relationship. We hoped we'd provide an inspiring example of a not-easy-but-committed partnership. A year later, to our great surprise (since social science studies frequently claim they will offer participants feedback, but somehow 'forget' to when the analysis is done): We were offered feedback on the results across some 30,000 couples' interviews. We learned, with uncomprehending shock, that there was a strong inverse relationship between how much couples talked to each other each week (about anything) and how long the marriage lasted. The less they talked to each other, the longer the marriage lasted!

We couldn't imagine that many of them talked in as disciplined and open a way as we did! But, honestly, actually it's not clear that we fully understood how to conduct a good conversation that reveals our deep feelings and assumptions to ourselves through one another. All our talking often led us astray, not closer to the true issues, nor into the transformational processes that feelings and assumptions can go through if attended with deep trust and acceptance. Three drawn-out episodes concerning the boundaries of our marriage illustrate our difficulties. The first episode occurred when we found ourselves at a large dinner party one evening, with Linda – yes, 'my' Linda – and her husband as another invited couple. This was the first time I had seen Linda in over two years, ever since she had told me that her abusive husband was too strong for her (but before I knew of his threat to kill me with a broken bottle). The party was seated at a long dinner table, with me placed next to Linda at one end of the table, while my wife and Linda's husband were seated at the far end.

Although constrained by the social situation, Linda and I did have an effervescent conversation with a third dinner-mate. My wife could see and feel the laughter among us. As soon as we left the party, my wife turned very cold, and when we got home she began weeping for fear I would leave her.

I acknowledged that I continued to feel love for Linda, but tried, gently and patiently, to reassure her that I loved her as well, that I had decided to marry her in spite of this other feeling, and that I had no intention of leaving her. We talked… and we fought… and we wept all night long and into the morning hours.

As the morning continued without resolution, beyond exhausted I remembered a friend once saying that if all the different things you're trying aren't working, you should try the last thing you would ever think to do in this situation (thus, theoretically, freeing yourself from the grip of your false assumptions and habitually-embodied emotions about what will and won't work). Right now, the last thing it would occur to me to do was to get angry at my wife. I was, after all, trying to win her back from doubt about my love. I could not imagine how getting angry would reassure her of my love. Nor could I imagine what I had to be angry about. Then I remembered that I had been teased about never getting angry. Maybe I am so implicitly trained in diplomacy by parents whom I never saw fight that I can never imagine why I should be angry, I reflected. But maybe I actually am angry without realizing it. Maybe I am rationalizing away an anger I'm not letting myself feel.

I realized intellectually that I might be at my assumptive limit. I was certainly exhausted – at my physical/emotional limits. So… Having tried everything else, and without even knowing what I would say, I started making an angry roaring sound, and, to my surprise, heard myself yelling at her that she didn't trust me and my love for her. That felt totally true to me. I had finally expressed my love and commitment in an emotionally-trustworthily way.

She immediately quieted down, began to weep in a different, reconciled way, as did I, and we were out of the cycle. (This may have been a moment of transforming learning for us both, as well as a moment that I began to generalize by experimenting more frequently with discovering and expressing my emotions in reaching-a-limit situations.) I began to see that even though we had been talking a lot before, we had not been talking in an emotionally open way. Put differently, I began to understand in a different way from before that speech can either be 'just words,' or it can express and move energies (but only if we are in touch with

90

our own deeper energies). After this confrontation, we experienced a new mood of softer openness to one another that lasted (only?) a couple of months.

Hilary comments:

> Here there are echoes of the artful action of the Brazilian woman who originally taught you how to express complex things without words. This may be an important art to learn especially for those (of us?!) who are too wordy. In spending a decade with an Asian man I learned to give and receive thoughtful gifts in place of well-worded explanations and apologies. This invites us more into feeling the energetics rather than always trying to articulate the space between.

Bill continues:

Given the times in which we were living (1968-69), one of the things my wife and I talked about during our first year of marriage was whether opening our marriage could strengthen it. Quite a few married couples in our age range and intellectual milieu were having such conversations and trying relational experiments. Unfortunately, the book Open Marriage did not come out until 1972. Although only two of the seventeen chapters concerned sex directly, and we were doing pretty well in terms of the other qualities of openness, I would have learned a lot from those two chapters that might have made a difference. We were certainly trying, but trying too hard. Over the next eight years, I would alternate among trying too hard, trying too casually, giving up, and sometimes having embodied mutuality descend upon us like the grace of a mystical state.

At the outset, being the heady, Aquarian-born one of two of us, I believed in multiple, strong, mutually open friendships, with marriage as a special ongoing trust and commitment, including the joint commitment to one's children. I did not believe in brief, secret, possibly commercial sexual trysts. I thought you should make love with the one you were with only if you truly loved him or her, and that you (me, one) could potentially nurture several mutually open erotic friendships simultaneously. True Christian love, it seemed to me, must be non-possessive. I thought we could find both more friends and new ways of approaching one another erotically if we allowed ourselves to discover what intimacy with others and in other groupings besides coupling meant, and what it could teach us about our own sexual-emotional-spiritual intimacy – about which, as you can see, I had untellable dimensions yet to explore.

I could not envision how long the path of exploration might be before learning the ongoing creation and transformation of communal containers that can nurture multiple open intimacies. Nor could I envision how little most people are inclined toward such a vision, because, in matters of love, we are so often caught in the emotional vortex of early action-logic jealousy and possessiveness. Nor, again, could I see how the fact that both my parents were only children and the fact that I had left the family early to go to Andover at 13 left me a little bi-polar in my craving for intimate contact alternating with a kind of claustrophobia if relational boundaries felt too tight.

In the meantime, my wife claimed she didn't need more friends, and that brief, secret sexual trysts would probably be less dangerous to the marriage than ongoing, open friendships. Nevertheless, I pressed for a measure of openness, and she agreed to my visiting two women friends in Vermont for a weekend. One of them (who would marry my wife's brother two years later), she knew much better than I.

When I returned from the weekend, I tried to share the sense of the very deep encounter I had had with the two women, along with an invitation from all three of us to my wife to join us next time. I was shocked by her initial response of fear and dismissal, but hoped that her feelings would evolve with further attention, as they had eventually after the dinner with Linda and her husband.

I had told her that the two women and I had started our time together by climbing a hill, meditating together in a clearing at the top, before beginning to speak about our experiences and aspirations. This led us to propose a foundation, which we named "Foundations Incorporated." This foundation would serve as a 'container' wherein all members would both "give" and "get" support for one another's creative endeavors. (This vision would ten years later manifest itself in my Theatre of Inquiry enterprise, and forty years later would animate the Community of Inquiry some two dozen of us have formed in recent years.)

To my surprise, one of the two women then brought out a pipe and a little bag of marijuana, and we smoked together. I had never smoked before, except for three cigar puffs that made me slightly nauseous on the bus ride back from Exeter at the end of my undefeated soccer season at Andover. So, the inhaling was a somewhat painful initiation for my throat. I coughed uncontrollably several times, then got taught how to inhale in a slower, more gradual, and more relaxed way. At first, meditating away in my most determined way, I could feel no "effects" at all. But after a little while one of the women suggested we get off our asses and onto our hands and knees, and play about like animals.

As soon as I turned around like that, all of my bodily sensations, breathing, and emotions became vividly present to me. My images and ideas seemed like distinct tear drops. Energies were distinctively running up and down my backbone, and a more powerful attention that seemingly embraced these inner "tears" – as well as all of nature around and in and under me, and both women and the many subliminal messages passing among us – flowed through me in a splendid, liquid, wondering silence… This was the beginning of a prolonged experiential moment of continual transformation that continued through the night and into the next day.

We rolled about, smelled the earth, sounded our voices in various ways, building a basic sensual trust in one another's intentions and respect. Here was an active inquiry! This state (very much like an LSD experience, as I later learned) lasted throughout dinner and for an entire night of exquisitely intimate touching and conversation about our affinities and alonenesses. As we moved, we chose carefully and explicitly what limits we would maintain and why. (We never became entirely nude with one another, nor did we have intercourse, but we definitely did make love through our talking, our listening, in interludes of rapt silence, and only the smallest, mutually-conscious movements of hugging or touching one another's faces.)

Throughout the experience, I could feel viscerally how my four years of micro-efforts-at-attention in the Gurdjieff Work had taught me something about how to detach from each particular thought, feeling, and sensation, enhancing the shared inquiry among the three of us, and thus prolonging the inner and intimate journey.

Each of the three of us, the two women and I, agreed to take on a next task after the weekend, in furtherance of our initial shared vision. One task was to establish the legal basis for our foundation. One of the women took that on and the other, having several favorable connections for doing so, was going to explore ideas about, and sources of, funding. I, as the "social scientist," was to document our vision and to supply a kind of 'Minutes' of our meeting.

I quickly performed my duty of writing up, mimeographing and sending off a summary of our time together, as well as a description of our initial conception of Foundations Incorporated, on a single-spaced page of typing. To my dismay, I received no response. Nor would my wife engage in further conversation about the matter.

Feeling stunned and wounded from all sides, I saw one of the women several months later and learned that she had called our home to talk with me and been told by my wife not to call again because she did not want me involved with them in this way. That my wife should feel this way was not so surprising by this time. That she should unilaterally cut the communication between me and them without informing me seemed completely illegitimate. Nevertheless, true to my general dislike of conflict, I did not pursue the matter. Thus, though miraculously conceived, the new foundation was in fact aborted very early in its development.

By this time, I was completing my dissertation at Yale and had been interviewing for jobs the next fall, with the great good luck of being able to consider a joint appointment in management and education at Northwestern, positions in education at Columbia's Teachers College or management at Case Western, and in business at Southern Methodist University.

In spite of her parents' feeling that it was my wife's job to follow me to my first faculty position, my wife did not like that I accepted the faculty position furthest away down south. (I accepted the offer because it seemed to me more committed to an action-oriented educational process than the other schools even though at that time its academic status was lower than the others.) Generally angry at me during this period, my wife began to say she was considering divorce.

Human Potential Movements

That summer, my wife and I went together to the National Training Laboratories at Bethel, Maine, as part of my internship in applied behavioral science. She signed up for three weeks worth of programs, one titled "On Becoming a Woman" and another, called simply the Weir Lab, promised a two-week deep encounter experience guided by an elderly couple, the Weirs, well-known in the young group dynamics world. After the first program, my wife seemed a lot more outgoing and happy, and was now prepared to experiment with an open marriage agreement, based on the assumption that although we might each be open in principle, we would have to discover how we felt as we proceeded and be prepared to redefine limits.

She did in fact "fall in love" (her words) with a man in her encounter group during the ensuing weeks, and they spent whole nights of very intimate time together, but, as in my case in Vermont the spring before, they did not make love in the coital sense.

At some point during those same weeks, the wife of a couple we knew well called me to see if she could visit. That couple too was exploring open marriage; indeed, the four of us had discussed our feelings about doing so, and the other couple had decided to do so before us. Rebecca and I spent an exquisitely slow and gentle evening together, making love with one another in a profoundly tender, harmonious, weeping way that I had never before come close to experiencing and for which I remain grateful to this day. Like my experience on the Vermont hilltop, this experience of love was no lapse into sheer animality, but rather an unmistakably spontaneous mutuality in honoring one another's embodied and inspirited humanity.

Once again, I was shocked to discover how painful the denouement between my wife and myself was. After having proudly shared her new love with me, she seemed disoriented by my pleasure on her behalf. She introduced him to me, and the three of us spent a morning together walking in a forest, with me liking him a lot. But then she seemed to lose interest in him, and I never heard about him again (of course, we were also moving to Dallas, so sheer distance may have played a key role). At the same time, she was upset that I and the other man's wife had made love together. I believed that all four members of both couples talking

94

together could possibly shift her basic feelings... and somehow persuaded her. So we stopped at their home near the beginning of our long trip from Maine down to Dallas and had a good, quiet talk. I think it became evident that, while feeling grateful for our experience together, the other wife and I had no continuing affair in mind; also, her husband was at ease and clearly felt friendly toward me. Thus, a good deal of my wife's fear and tension surrounding these events dissolved.

Invitation

Here we share some of our own practice of relational action inquiry – taken from a recording of our dialogue about Chapter 5 – to give a concrete sense of what relational action inquiry actually looked like for us one recent sunny afternoon. We met by video conference. Perhaps you can try something similar after sharing one another's autobiographical writing with a friend of yours. (We will follow this dialogue with a continuation of the developmental analysis we began in the Interlude after Chapter 4.)

HB: Bill, I read your chapter and I just enjoyed it in many ways. I want to dig in with you a little here. So let me pose a question to get us in the ballpark of what I think might be a good conversation. I am curious how does eros relate to power and power to eros and any and all combination of those with regard to a few things I read about, namely your propensity to avoid expression of anger and generally to use thoughtful communication. And then I also want to know more about the erotic in your first marriage. I am nosy!

Bill: Laughter. Big questions. Let's see where we get.

HB: And I want to suggest a practice for us and see if it helps. Let's take some moments to listen into the dark together here. And I invite you to feel into these themes. Then you could report from that?

Hilary sets her phone alarm for 3 minutes, and we listen away into the dark...

Bill: There is something deeper than language. Language can be used either to express or to block both eros and power. I mean it can be used to block recognition of what is powerful and recognition of what is erotic in oneself or in a relationship. Talking about a situation to myself just doesn't help at all sometimes! I think I was way too identified with my own thinking and language throughout my first marriage. There is this post-cognitive reality. I refer to it as the "4th territory of experience." It's an intentional attention that is deeper than thought and can simultaneously include awareness of one's own thinking (3rd territory), one's own performing (2nd territory), and the outside world (1st territory). But it's hard to know how to find my way there. It's an issue for all of us – how to get down to deeper more trustworthy feelings, those closer to one's own core identity, core commitments.

HB: Let this wash over us some more – this 4th territory – is there an image? what's there?

SILENCE… (to invite the feelings associated here…)

Bill: Language became central to my identity as 'competent' when I left my parents and went first to Andover and then to Yale. I chose a language-based profession. Apt use of language is important in the social sciences and consulting. And because it's associated with work there was a work ethic associated with it. There was working hard, figuring it out, relying on mental process. This reliance itself became a significant part of my identity (especially during the years when my Expert and Achiever action-logics were pre-eminent). But when applied to issues of power and eros, well I can feel language is not that useful! Because of my sheltered teenage years at boarding school, I was divorcing myself both from wild eros and from raw power that in their earlier expression might have been more rough and tumble, at least to begin with. There were missing experiences for me when I was younger and I sought to make up for them.

HB: The feelings coming up are what now …?

Bill: Loneliness. The positive side is becoming more individuated, but the feeling is becoming out of touch with my real inner power and erotic experience in relationship. It was easy to feel isolated, lonely.

HB: D'you think this touched on the Eros/Power in your first marriage? The vignette that stands out for me is where your wife tells your woman friend, "Don't call!" Were you married to someone who really didn't get you?

SILENCE (to invite the feelings associated here…)

96

Bill: I feel/remember the lack of erotic connection I felt with my wife compared with what I'd felt for Linda. Erotic feelings were being denied and I didn't realize how important they were. My own marriage was evidently meant to take care of my loneliness and I found the first available person. How wonderful to marry her family to my family, or so I thought! Then we discovered how jagged our discontinuities were – how difficult it was for the erotic to express itself between us. And at the same time I felt attracted to others, but didn't do much about it except for those times I share in the chapter, on the mountain and with my friend's wife. Those experiences were erotic and had a lot of dignity and mutual power. They felt like all of us operating at our proper human potential. Although I certainly did not have the term 'Eros/Power' at the time – nor the entire concepts of mutual power, mutual love, and mutual inquiry as the triad necessary to generate true intimacy, spaciousness, and inter-personal development – I do think those moments in Vermont and later in Maine were moments of practicing Eros/Power in the spirit of inquiry. So: yes, I was married to someone who didn't get me, but I also didn't get myself. As we'll see in the coming chapters, I began to 'get myself' more when I considered seeking a divorce.

A Continuing Interlude

We have already noted at the outset of the chapter that, in making his choice about whom and when to wed, Bill appears to have been guided primarily by the Diplomat action-logic. Once married, the young couple enacted a rather Expert-like version of marriage, seeking to succeed by dint of hard-work conversations with one another, based largely on guidelines for good dialogue being developed within the applied behavioral science community to which Bill was apprenticing himself.

At the same time, in his ability to do both War on Poverty work and graduate work under a single vision of integrating action with inquiry, Bill was enacting some combination of the Expert, Achiever, and Redefining action-logics in his professional life.

The Achiever

As life grows in complexity, the Expert often finds himself or herself having to expand the mindset further toward the Achiever action-logic. Internal efficiency and perfectionism of a product gradually yields as the primary value of good work, to be replaced by external effectiveness. This latter is attained by a skillful juggling of sometimes mutually reinforcing and sometimes mutually competing values of different stakeholders (e.g. one's boss, one's subordinates, the materials at hand, the market).

For the typical Achiever the future and long-term, one-to-three-year goals are vivid and inspiring. Becoming effectiveness and results-oriented, s/he feels like an initiator, not a pawn, and welcomes behavioral feedback that helps achieve the goal. Although s/he still takes hierarchical organizational power for granted, s/he seeks to generate mutual team spirit with colleagues.

In a marriage and family setting, Expert partners will tend to believe there is a proper way to raise the children (the two partners may agree or disagree on what that is). In contrast, an Achiever couple will tend to engage in more discovery about what actually works to keep family members engaged, productive, and happy.

The Redefining Action-Logic

Bill and his first wife seemed to oscillate between Expert and Redefining versions of marriage without much experience of the Achiever action-logic.

In Chapter 5, you have probably been able to see the stumbling Redefining steps that Bill was beginning to take. The first one occurred in his all-night conversation with his wife when he desperately tried to reframe his own ineffective way of speaking and began a more emotional roaring. This can probably be described as a brief breakthrough into the fourth territory of awareness and as an exercise in the mutually-transforming power of language rather than its unilateral power.

Bill also sought to re-vision the kind of long-term intimate commitments he wished to make in his marriage and his other simultaneous inter-gendered friendships, such as with the two women friends he visited in Vermont. There on the hilltop he first experienced marijuana, and a new quality of non-possessive intimacy possible among trios and quartets as well as couples, an intimacy perhaps capable of integrating the spiritual with the sexual… (One might even argue that there was a still-later action-logic quality to this experience – an Alchemical quality. But, clearly, Bill did not know how to act regularly at this action-logic.)

The typical person at the Redefining action-logic takes a relativistic perspective, recognizing that different people have different perspectives or ways of framing their experiences and that none can 'prove' that it is right. S/he seeks to create shared visions for the future and feels the eros of vision-guided groups, causes, and callings. S/he tends to be aware of conflicting emotions and is attracted by difference and change more than by similarity and stability. S/he is less inclined to judge or evaluate than earlier action-logics, and influences by listening and finding patterns more than by advocacy.

Although Bill was quite competent at working with different perspectives in his working relationships, he was also obviously not very good at appreciating his wife's different perspective, nor at recognizing how relatively quickly that perspective was transforming. We will see the later stages of adult development in Hilary's next chapter, which offers more illustrations of the Redefining action-logic.

Chapter 6

Hilary Decamps to Japan, Returns to Boston, Marries

How as adults do we get our feet under us?

I pick up my story having left graduate school. Intellectually I believed I had exhausted the Western canon of purpose-finding for life. I was determined to plough a non-intellectual path, even as I only knew that intellectually. Being a cradle Catholic I did not overlook the importance of serving others or serving causes bigger than my own restlessness. I fed the homeless, I tutored minority kids, I played with abandoned puppies, I planted trees. My restlessness pushed me forward, though toward what I didn't know. Reading the one and only Zen book I had gotten from my Boston roommates – Only Don't Know – may have made the difference. It validated that I didn't have to know what was next for me. I just had to follow my nose (the nose being closer to where we think the mind is; it never dawned on me to tune into the whisperings of my heart). My nose took me to a one week Zen meditation retreat that lasted all of one evening.

My first Zen retreat confronted me with traditional koan practice in a private interview with the Zen Master. I had gone entirely unprepared, having no idea what was expected of me. After some ritualized bowing, the bald Master called out "Does a dog have Buddha nature?" "Of course!" I replied without hesitation. I guess I considered this the warm up, a rhetorical question. I waited for the real one. I suppose if I unpacked my response, which whirled at a speed more quickly than I could unpack it, I would have said more slowly: if Buddhism is known for anything – it's that all of life is interdependent. So they'd hardly single out dogs for special treatment. Therefore yes, woof woof, dogs have Buddha nature. But the teacher's equanimity made me question if this was the kind of answer he wanted. I began to feel, ever so vaguely, that I had blundered. Around the edges of consciousness I felt that the entire paradigm I was answering from (my brainy self!) was somehow inadequate, inappropriate to the situation. But I didn't know where my error started and ended. I was surprised when pushed – "Are you so sure?" he asked. I couldn't grope toward anything further than "Well, um, yes, maybe, no?" That the Zen master started to talk of "moo" completely perplexed me. Only don't know mind, indeed! I wondered if it was a dog or a cow I'd been asked about. This teacher had an accent even worse than Habermas. I knew that many people thought this was a great, enlightened teacher and I should feel honored, but I was sensing that this wizened, bald emperor had no clothes. Or was I so out of touch or just more stupid than I realized. But I was just not that stupid. Following an endless set of prostrations, along with complex rules for how to tie the ugly black robes, and worse still, sharing a bathroom with too many people (including men!), I began to feel faint. I just had to leave (isn't that why it's called retreat?). I longed to be with people who would at least smile. I packed to leave the next day, looked upon with disdain by my fellow retreatants. That moo would resound.

When I reflect I can locate no reason for, and every reason against, taking up Zen as a serious path. I had decided that I wouldn't think about it too much. Clearly my booking a flight to Japan with my remaining dollars could also be seen as a running away from, more than a running toward. So if I search for a reason at all, I feel that on some deep level I knew that, despite or even because of all my studies, I had no real answers to life's most important questions. Perhaps we could say that it was a spiritual gift that came having reached the end of a certain rope. Zen is for people who feel there are no other options. Why else come to a standstill, or actually a sit-still, in front of a wall to meditate till legs tingle.

What we learn, experientially, after all our reading and studying, is that experience has no (definable) essence (referred to as "mu"). And in Zen only experience (not talking about experience!) qualifies as worthy of attention. Looking closely, you get that experience is made up of all different qualities, physical and mental. The mental includes our mental conditioning and linguistic skill. So there are very many barriers to simple experience. The point of meditating is then, in Buddhist jargon, to experience that experience itself is "empty." Ironically this means it is full of interdependence with everything. The dog's Buddha nature too is empty (and so is my nature, no separation from the woofer!). Experience just is. Ironically, many worn out intellectuals like me show up in Zendos in the Western world. And we spend years looking at a blank wall. Decades. And we find there was nothing to find. And yet I say without a doubt that Zen practice is the greatest gift of my life.

Japanese Mu!

So on official leave from my PhD program, and with a quick stopover in Ireland, I landed in Osaka, Japan just as the Berlin Wall opened and as Nelson Mandela moved beyond his imprisonment. I had found a job teaching English with which I could support my study of Zen for the first year. Any 'thereafter' was entirely unclear. In yet another fit of madness and or great naiveté, it never dawned on me that I would need papers of introduction to a Zen teacher. I related to Zen as I would to Catholicism. I imagined I'd go to the local temple, which would be as accessible as our local church, and I would talk with the priest, who would be as accessible as our priests, I would tell of my great heartfelt urge to be baptized, or whatever the Zen equivalent, and all would, somehow, be well. I didn't know enough to even ask about how to start my search for a teacher! After all, or so the famous saying in Zen circles goes, when the student is ready the teacher appears. Hey, I was ready! In fact I thought financial support would be my only obstacle. That and the terror I felt at going alone to an alien country. I spent the first week howling in sadness on my new futon, distracted only by the loveliness of my new tatami floor. The loneliness, and my madness for putting myself in this situation of extreme isolation, daunted me.

I had not yet trusted that I could jump and land safely. Worse perhaps was that I'd had no practice with chopsticks! I remembered my promise to God when I promised that I would give up soul eating anxiety. I could be brave and adventuresome. I could awaken out of the loneliness and alienation. Japan was truly alien. The first monk I saw frightened me because the traditional Medieval robes worn in Japan seemed scary. I taught myself basic traveler Japanese and I could engage in rudimentary conversation. People were friendly, if seemingly made nervous by this blonde capable of talking a little (foreigners are generally thought too stupid to understand Japanese). Naturally what had begun as alien began to delight me. I felt physically safe there because there is so little crime. I was, however, too frequently sexually harassed in the evening hours. Inebriated men, so common on the way home from work, seemed to feel quite free about masturbating in public, after dark, if I was walking by. (Someone explained to me that all porn, which is ubiquitous in Japan, tends to have blonde women and hence I engendered confusion!). But for some reason this didn't frighten me too much. Perhaps because I felt sure they would not touch me, I felt as if I were nothing but a spectacle rather than a real person. Of course it's not ideal to feel so uncomfortable walking alone at night, but then I was used to far worse. I simply batted it away. I walked on.

I was well into the mind numbing and occasionally hilarious life of an English teacher when I admitted to myself that no meaningful contact had manifested with a Zen priest. I had to realize that Zen is not quite at the forefront of everyone's mind in Japan. The temples seemed to be for making money. Nonetheless, I prepared to visit temples while always thinking, this is the day, lucky me. Today I will meet an enlightened priest! I wasn't sure what that would look like. I would just know. Too many saw only blonde hair and blue eyes. Where I was expecting cosmos sized expansive mind, I was meeting priests more provincial than my parish priest in Dublin. Yet steadfast, committed, undeterred by my cognitive fixation that Zen is perfect for me, I decided 'that one must be an exception!' And so on with the next one. And the one after that. So many exceptions!

102

Well, it must be the small town I am in. They (I imagined a Zen papacy of some sort) must send the unenlightened ones to the little towns! In retrospect I am beguiled by my own unquestioning devotion. But there was no one to speak with this about. Everyone in my milieu thought Zen was an eccentric pursuit at best. In time it became enough simply to visit and sit in temples.

I had a meditation bench in my room and loved to sit on the tatami, "Japanese seiza style," which ironically was not that common in Japan. There was Kinkaku-ji's eight stories of delicate gold leaf and stone garden to visit in nearby Kyoto. Tea ceremony and calligraphy lessons in Kobe (even if the teacher wouldn't allow me to progress beyond writing the same single stroke for six months. "I am practicing f*&^ing patience," I'd say with my best smile). It was all aesthetically beautiful and I was looking on. Everywhere I was considered and referred to as a "Gaijin" or outsider. My neighbors bowed in greeting me "Good morning Miss Outsider." My landlord gave me a break in the rent as he liked to have a blonde gaijin around. Even after a year the outsider status had not budged at all. There were no romantic flirtations. No enlightened monks crossed my path.

I never realized how terribly isolated I felt. Ram called and wrote me often, but it was hardly enough to assuage the loneliness. Also through calls and letters, I filled many an evening reigniting a dear friendship with Jack Murphy whom I had met while working in Boston. Soon the eros flew. He visited for a couple of weeks and we toured Japan together. On his return to the USA and no doubt terrifying him, I asked him to ask me to marry. It was certainly not to be solely or primarily a marriage of convenience or expedience, I explained. Yet the legal employment status it would magically produce for me was a very important thing. If we were to allow our relationship to develop I'd need to be able to work. For weeks I waited for his response as he thought it over seriously. Then one evening on the phone he did indeed ask me to marry him. And so I arranged to return to the USA.

Married in Boston

I arrived back to Boston from Osaka delighted to have a place (Jack's place) I might now call home and the beginnings of some direction in my life. Before officially marrying, I clarified that Jack and I were marrying so we could live as equals in the US, not because we wished to be married in the "hegemonic" sense as I understood patriarchal marriage. I gave a little lecture on patriarchy and how I understood marriage. Nothing would change between us except that I could get a dignified job. I was certainly a little less clear on my plans for continuing to see Ram from time to time. Jack was 20 years older than me. A clinical psychologist. Our arrangement was not what Jack's more conventional family therapist colleagues considered the ideal set up for an enduring marriage.

Jack's preconceptions of marriage were assaulted, though hardly without warning. Relational experimentation had been our explicit commitment – and yet (unilateral) warning is never enough. Jack's profession and his more mature stage in life all colluded to make experimentation difficult. And soon, perhaps as in so many marriages and in such contrast to our start, there developed an erotic vacuum. For all our conversations we never really dealt with that. I felt this vacuum, his withdrawal to silence, as a cold, frightening rejection. And I just compounded the alienating dynamic by running away with my erotic (life-force!) needs. Better that than allowing myself to feel, much less express, neediness to him, or even to myself. Jack's backing away from me landed as a form of withholding from which we could not emerge. In truth had our original eros not taken flight, I would not have sought relationships with others. But the truth was that I felt his withdrawal as a deadening and felt compelled to shake things up.

If there was a catalyst for Jack's retreat to coldness, it was never explicit. Perhaps we might say it was plain obvious, he could not tolerate my self privileging and he was a man with natural possessive tendencies. I could not tolerate his withholding. I gave him a bereavement card on our first Valentines Day after marrying. It was a spiral down. What I continued not to see was the unconscious dynamic of my seeking love/life/joy from my significant other (my mom!) and finding only rejection, scorn and the other's justifiable-by-conventional-standards hurt/blame. Of course I felt that I was blameworthy for this hurt. But I also felt a primal call to self reliance,

I would take care of myself rather than be dragged down into what I felt was a spiral of depression. What I couldn't see was how the hurt was mutually shared just differently expressed – he went into himself and I sought to feel alive with others. We just never discussed it. For all that we did discuss, which was pretty much everything else, we never discussed the erotic vacuum that was opening up. Eros, or precisely her absence, was taboo. To feel alive, I simply had to escape. The lure was that strong, as if my life depended on it. Yet I was constantly drawn back, too, as I experienced Jack as one I loved so much. The various breaks we took throughout probably prolonged our agony. But we are only ever wise in hindsight.

Pet Tycoon

Unexpressed eros erupted at first at my new job. I liked this job (available now with my green card!). I became executive assistant and office manager to a real estate tycoon. It paid handsomely and offered an office with a Picasso on the wall. It brought change in many ways from the start. In filling out the paperwork I was forced to be public about being married. And so the desire for an experimental relationship of integrity was put more and more out of reach. I knew that if the company bureaucrats could know I am married, then our families ought to know. So we told. Our families pronounced 'congratulations' forgiving the secretive nuptials. Irish family members sent traditional, generous Irish wedding gifts, Waterford crystal and silver. Ram sent his Mazeltov. Jack's family was very kind and embraced me.

One of the earliest relationship experiments I brought into being, when I could finally afford it, was to move to a separate apartment. I explained to Jack that I wanted to spend lots of our free time together, but didn't accept that marriage must mean life in the same space. The experiment seemed to produce yet more distance on his part. I suspect one reason for my wanting to live separately, apart from feeling oppressed by not having a room of my own, was my not wanting to countenance how ignored I felt when we were together. But I couldn't explain that. I assume he thought I was retreating. On the contrary I felt too dependent on his love. If after all I was agreeing to become domesticated, I felt the need to figure out how to mate beyond our captivity. I also idealized my previous happiness while in graduate school. As my work began also to provide zest, I turned to Ram to meet my increasing life energy. The angels of eros were flying at work and in transatlantic calls and letters.

My tycoon boss had a serious interest in running for governor of his state. He was also, or so I thought, a handsome and charming man. I enjoyed being taken to lunch on his Harley and driving his polished Porsche around town. I was given free access to his life and soon I was a trusted confidante. We were also occasional lovers. I recall sitting in on political advisors' meetings. They explained, after taking hefty advising fees for months, that it would be just too, um, difficult to run for Governor. I smirked as the yes man looked at me and then at the walls struggling to name the unmentionable elephant in the room. The problem, Sir, if I may speak directly is that covering up the number of, um, girlfriends would be too difficult!

I was quite captivated by my pet tycoon (as I privately referred to him). He told me in one of our less than professional moments that I was "smart as a whip" and that he was "a little too afraid" of me. I expressed my delight at this confession. After all my pet tycoon took calls regularly from the rich and famous. It took me a long time to understand my feeling of delight where I might, or others might, have felt rejected. Many years later in conversation with someone not that familiar with me, but quite familiar with Wilhelm Reich's psychoanalytic classification of character formation, I learned that I could be described as a classic "oral self-reliant." By definition – a character formed in reaction to lack of nourishment between the ages of one and two and a half years of age, resulting in a basic orientation to life as having to be self sufficient or (unconsciously) fear the infant's deepest dependence and with it the fear of death. Be independent/invulnerable or die was the basic unconscious momentum of this (my) character. Moreover, I learned, on some deep level that this character is unable to differentiate good from bad relationships, all relationships evoke vulnerability and my pull is to where I feel alive, which can also happen in deeply destructive relationships. Best to stay on guard.

But all of this was unconscious to me. I rued both the accuracy and the almost fortune cookie like simplicity of this character profile. I felt simultaneously a mere cartoonish caricature. The oral self-reliant avoids feeling, much less acknowledging, vulnerability. I felt wounded by the ease with which my vulnerability was seen. Yet the healthier part of me also twigged that this pattern of character formation could be undone – precisely because it was not "me or mine," but some generic caricature, a reaction of the ego to a set of childhood circumstances that were no one's fault. This oral self-reliant was a false self, a persona. But it would take more years before I would enter a process potent enough to dissolve this persona – the transforming power of psychoanalysis.

Jack and I went to couples counseling with one of the stellar counselors in Boston (Jack's mentor). I was very fond of this slightly eccentric man, not least because he told Jack that I was good for him. (Finally some deserved recognition!). My relationship with Ram was continuing, and I thought it non-negotiable. I had flown to Paris and he to Boston. I was honest with Jack about this (which made the eccentric counselor hum with glee!) I realize I felt Ram was a lifeline to vibrancy that was clearly lacking between Jack and me. Jack, without really saying so, simply could not tolerate Ram's presence in our life. His not saying so, however, made it impossible to address.

His mentor suggested we not make any rash decisions about our relationship but continue to be together for 6 months, appreciating what life brought us. The therapist also pushed me to get more serious with my life by declaring my job with my pet tycoon "silly," in the sense that I was not being creative for myself. I was taken aback. I had felt terribly sophisticated in my job! But I quickly got off my high horse when I heard he had some constructive alternative. The therapist suggested I read two books on organizational learning, which I picked up in the Cambridge bookstore on the way home. Jack explained this systems oriented work as a form of family systems therapy played out in business teams.

I began to look at my silly job anew, sensing the difference I might make if I better understood how organizational change happens. Thus began my private preparation for the new and well-endowed PhD in organizational systems change and transformation in Boston. My tycoon was happy enough to see me leave, encouraging me to do well for myself. He also wrote me a nice farewell check that made it possible to be rather brazen in response to Marcia the tyrannical boss who fired me the day I would meet Bill Torbert.

Bill comments:

I see immense inner change in your life over your writing here. Earlier we'd had the almost horror-film-like weekend prison to which you subjected yourself, somehow mutely, Diplomat-ically dependent on Horst, the silent German professor… while you learned the language of oppression and liberation during your weekday studies and communal living – a language you could apply to every situation except the one you were in on the weekends. Rebelling at your inability to rebel, you gradually became as independent as it's possible to get, moving around the world in über-Achiever-like fashion – to Boston, Chicago, and Japan, then back to Boston – learning the language of relationships and systems, all the while on a mission to redefine yourself. But you were still unable to apply your new 'languages' to your marriage with Jack. That would involve vulnerably describing feelings and patterns newly emerging between you, a capacity your 'oral self-reliant' personality long blocked you from (and a capacity which my previous chapters show I also did not yet sufficiently possess).

So I also see how similar we are. So much talk, mostly missing the point! I see your own humor at your unilateralness, and at how ideological you were. Although your personal development had brought you to the early Redefining action-logic that permitted you to envision going to Japan, you were driving your relationships with a more Achiever-like unilateral power, not the fully mutual power that we are calling Eros/Power. There's a cartoon quality as I see you on a motorbike with your pet tycoon.

Hilary responds:

I felt completely alive on that motorbike! I was in touch with my own eros, my own confidence. I was an immigrant to the world of achievers, to male power and I wanted some for myself. The intervention by our couple's therapist about finding more creative work fostered further development for me. But your word cartoon resonates. I feel I was a caricature, a type enacting a certain formula, rather than being in and living out my own life. Maybe that is just how it is till we cross the threshold into later action logics where we get to see, to articulate, and to dis-identify with our conditioning. That seeing is needed if we are to begin to act from a different, more internally perceived, voice that includes true compassion for ourselves and others.

Bill answers:

> Yes you were an immigrant into the Achiever world. I get the joy and confidence you felt. There is an action momentum here. Eros, soul surging, is powering your initiatives, but the power is expressed more in advocacy than inquiry. I might say, eros is present but hasn't touched, in any transformational way, the unilateral exercise of your power.

Hilary replies:

> Yet, it's not to say that being a caricature, really living out that ego need, is bad. We develop within the type of personality we've developed early on. Let's face it Bill, we are both mental-intellect centered types! The growing up path for us has been to grow into the heart, to bring heart/mind into balance. The problem for me was that there wasn't much encouragement to find my heart, or at least not that I could let in back then, not that I didn't suspect was a way to control or diminish me. I had first to perceive what I was sacrificing. Frankly I think I had to meditate or I might never have seen this!

Invitation

Our aim with the book is to encourage depth of inquiry into the trickster domains of eros and power – of love under the sign of inquiry – with the hope that Eros/Power can flow more in all our lives.

And now, dear reader, it may be useful to sketch the outlines of your own developmental autobiography, bringing your relationships to the fore, examining the feelings of eros and power, presence and absence, hurts and loves. To aid you in doing so, we invite you to take another look at Interlude 1 after Chapter 4 and at our Brief Developmental Analysis after Chapter 5.

A necessary start to relational action inquiry is with yourself. Note a few vignettes from your life to date and see if you can see the stages of development as described in the Interludes. What is your best estimate of your current action-logic? What is your best estimate for the earliest action-logic you can identify? And what about your intimate partner(s)?

For those so inclined we include website resources at the back of the book which provide an expert assessment of your current action-logic. Obviously we are a bit biased about this way of looking at humanity, but based on our own development and conversations, we suggest if you feel lonely it may be that your action-logic and those around you are in a tug of war! You may be well served by developing a new friendship circle closer to your own action logic and dedicated to relational inquiry, for then your eros can flow more in life, benefitting all around you. Consider a few of the practices of relational action inquiry in the final Interlude, adapt them to your own inclinations and overall situation. Consider daring to host a new kind of conversation, or host a party devoted to building community, with the intention of personal development with and for others.

Chapter 7

Bill Divorces, Lives Communally and Enters into a Second Marriage

How *Do We* Get Our Feet Under Us as Adults?

A few things were bothering me on the drive down south to my new faculty position: the electric sciatic jolts from a summer injury, my loss of regular contact with the Gurdjieff Work, and my marriage. The most emotionally upsetting was my marriage. I was also feeling the contrast between my increasingly heavy heart and my wife's brightening optimism about it. Suddenly, I found it difficult to look at her or touch her. Once in Dallas, and experiencing the push-pull so common in life's early relationships, I now secretly hoped that she would leave.

Soon, we attended a weekend workshop, named 'Blocks to Creativity.' The exercise I chose was based on the ancient Chinese book called the I Ching, or Book of Changes, which contains sixty-four commentaries with names like 'Difficulty at the Beginning,' 'Breakthrough,' and 'The Wanderer.' How you drew the "right-for you" answer and what you took from it as helpful for resolving your dilemma seemed to me pure chance, utterly arbitrary, and superstitious.

I could not recognize my extreme skepticism about the value of this whole procedure as itself a symptom of my 'reluctance to let go' of calculative thought. But (again reluctant to let go) I was determined to be a good Boy Scout and follow through on the exercise. So I asked myself, "What's the most serious problem I have now?" The answering question sounded back loud and clear "Should I remain married, or should I separate?" I threw the coins, went through the process of finding out which hexagram they indicated, and found myself facing the word "Endurance."

"Endurance" seemed a most ambiguous answer. Since all my predilections for the past months had been to separate, "endurance" could mean that I should endure in this intention and actually do it. On the other hand, it could also clearly mean to endure in the marriage.

At the time, I did not notice that my entire interpretive set was empirical and scientific. I was attempting to locate an answer empirically, in the world outside myself, in the text. And I expected this answer to be internally consistent in

110

terms of Aristotelian logic. I had not expected to believe the answer I got, but I had at least expected a clear answer.

I asked another nearby participant in the workshop to help me. Once she heard what my question was, she replied without hesitation, "I tell you what, I will read it to you, and you see if that makes any difference." I could not see how that would help at all – I had wanted a 'more objective' opinion from her. But I lay down on a couch, closed my eyes, and listened as she read. And lo and behold, as she read and I relaxed, it became very, very clear to me that what my free association was that I ought to 'let go' of the marriage.

I also began to see that this "answer" was what I wanted, it was my answer. By responding to my question in a different language and metaphorical framework than I had been using, the text was helping me go beyond my 'objective' weighing of pros and cons, beyond my own ambivalent layers, to accept some deeper feeling or intuition which could be a truer guide – not because it was more objective, but rather because it was more truly subjective.

That evening I finally, painfully, said out loud to my wife that I wanted to have a conversation. After sharing what I felt so urgently, I agreed to one long conversation with another older married couple, both of whom had previously been divorced. I was now so sure I wanted to separate, however, that I refused to continue more such conversations as it began to seem like evasion.

A friend who was then living with us now played a small but remarkable role in this process as well. Each morning as I came into the kitchen for breakfast, he asked me the same question in the same words, "Are you going to separate, Bill?" I would answer "Yes." Without any pause, he would conclude, "Then, separate." I stayed because she was going to leave to visit her brother. But there kept being reasons why the visit was postponed. So, a week after the workshop I left our home for a small room in a boarding house. My wife stayed in Dallas for another month, then returned north for Christmas. A year later we concluded a mutually-agreeable, uncontested divorce. She went on to blossom in many ways, achieving a doctorate, becoming a professional, exploring other relationships, remarrying, having children. After some years of careful distance, we more gently re-explored our caring for one another.

What I seemed to have learned more permanently from the 'Blocks to Creativity' experience and its aftermath was what I'd experienced but not generalized from my earlier experiences of 'roaring' at my wife and discovering a whole new modality of experience with the two women on the Vermont mountaintop: namely, that there are many ways of consulting my own felt sense of deeper intent when I am a participant in contested situations. As my next adventure shows, however, I was definitely not yet able to summon and sustain this connection to deeper intent in all my relationships.

Contending with Feminine Power

After two years at my first faculty position, I took a new faculty position in Boston, and began actively seeking to befriend women of strong character, aware and in command of their powers. One striking woman, about seven years older than I, had been a teacher near Atlanta. Though herself white, Celia had become involved with the black community, and had given birth to a multiracial child whom she was bringing up as a single mother. For a time, Celia had played a political role as a public companion and administrative assistant for a Black mayoral candidate when he was campaigning in predominantly White parts of the city. Because her father had literally come after her with a gun when he learned about her interracial pregnancy, she had had to keep her home address a secret for years, neither her nor her daughter inviting anyone to visit.

What initially struck me about Celia was her commitment and bravery and political experience in difficult situations. I both respected and was attracted to her charismatic way of being able to tell a truth in a group setting and then leave the floor open for other truths. I liked that she was not, nor had been, a student of mine. Indeed, she herself felt senior to me and spoke openly of my relative immaturity as a leader – an occasional critique from which I strove to learn. True, I was put off by her smoking habit and the amount of make-up and lipstick that she used; but I turned this into a positive, arguing to myself that you can't, after the initial infatuation, like everything about someone else, good not to be wowed early on.

I suppose I gave myself over to ignoring my repulsions, on principle. Also, we both began to enjoy the sexual play between us. Soon I was inviting her and her daughter to take over the large empty room at our Cambridge commune. After all, we needed the rent, she was happy to be paying less rent, and she and her daughter promised new degrees of diversity among us.

A semi-catastrophic six months followed. Celia had very firm opinions. She was very upset at the thought of my friend Greg, who by now had realized he was gay, coming to visit me for a weekend. (Greg had become my first lifetime friend during four years at Yale together and through his listening to my agony about the end of my relationship with Linda.) From my point of view, Celia's prejudice was absolutely unacceptable. The controversy suddenly ended when Celia discovered she got along just fine with Greg.   In addition to these struggles between the two of us, Celia quickly developed a more visible, more directly (and more judgmentally) expressed dislike for the married couple in our commune than the rest of us were comfortable with… Especially coming from the newest member of the household.

Somehow, the dispassion and the compassion that Celia knew how to interweave with her passion in public was unavailable to her in her personal life with me and with the communal us. Indeed, I gradually realized that she got very upset, with seemingly chemical precision, about something every ten days, would thereupon become unremittingly hostile toward me for the following four days, and then return to amity together for the next six. Never before had I experienced such an intense emotional see-saw about what increasingly seemed to be whatever randomly happened after six days of good times. I would give up on the relationship sometime during the hostile period every time. Then, unbelievably, both to me and to my other closest friends, Celia and I would have a good conversation, or she, her daughter, and I would have a magical evening, or the two of us would make love in the shallows of a secluded New Hampshire lake… And we would turn back into one another's orbit.

Certainly, one of the reasons was her ten-year-old daughter, as sweet and bright and in-all-ways-promising a ten-year-old as I had ever known. I hope I loved her well for our 11 months near one another. I always kept a little distance between us, but not one that contradicted warmth, ease, and a nightly hug, before Mom read to her in bed. The last thing in the world I wanted to be was another disappointing, disappearing man in her life.

Given Celia's history with her own violent white father and the disappearing black father of her child, she had good reason to distrust men, and this, we gradually realized, was part of our difficulty. When an action of mine that she labeled as untrustworthy crossed her ego's bow – or when our relationship threatened to dissolve her strong emotional boundaries (which she had done so well to construct for herself during a dozen years in her twenties and early thirties) – she would react with this rabid-distrust cycle, which had somehow become entrenched.

Suffice it to say that we went through many iterations of the ten day cycle over the next six months… Including a decision by her that she would leave the commune. This move momentarily seemed to free me from her with honor… Until I ended up a few days later once again reconciling with her and deciding to leave the commune with her. When I finally limped away from our relationship, after damage to several more of my other friendships and the unhappiest Thanksgiving of my life, I ended up paying three rents for several months, before returning to the Commune and a single contribution to the mortgage. I really needed some time to lick my wounds, as much inflicted by my inability to detach from the vicious cycle of our relationship as by her. It was a time of lonely, tearful, somewhat-self-disgusted depression. At the time, my main analysis and learning from the relationship was that I was still too 'diplomatic' in my personal relationships, even if I had learned to confront strongly when necessary in professional settings. Why, oh why, hadn't I simply stayed in the commune when she decided to leave it?

Once I returned to the commune, one of my close male friends, whose wife and I gradually became attracted to one another, invited me into their bed one night. He and I each also had another lover, all open, with the five of us often at parties together. Such was my erotic ambience of those years. After a childhood with no sisters or first cousins, with two parents who were only children, whose relationship with one another and with me, though warm, was physically invisible; and after an adolescence at all-boys schools, followed by my ill-fated attraction to Linda… feeling more relaxed physically and more emotionally intimate with women was a major turning point for me.

In the summer of 1975, I took a long vacation together with my married friends, Jason and Lee. We toured England, Scotland, Austria, and Italy. Something that became noticeable only once we were on the trip was the changing power balance in Lee's and Jason's relationship. Lee was becoming more independent before our eyes, in consort with the growing women's movement, and also impelled by a change in professional status. Lee had just moved from a quiet librarian's job to a much more active consulting role in which she felt highly valued. In her new-found independence, the sharp intellect that she had previously displayed through bright quips and in her private journaling began to turn more critical. She became repeatedly annoyed and cutting with both Jason and me during the trip. Jason sometimes retreated into hurt silence, but I tended to treat her remarks with humor. Jason's hurt moved further toward withholding and retreat.

Upon our return to Boston, he moved out of their apartment, but returned again after long weekend conversations among the three of us. Still later in the fall, however, Lee decided to move into her own apartment. What I had realized during this time was that their apparently wonderful marriage had been built on a form of co-dependence. He had depended upon her emotionally (though appearing quite independent in his other relationships), and she had depended upon him practically, having him make most of the money and do all of the driving. Not only was she now making more of the money, but she also took up driving again. He was at a loss as they separated. He and I remained friends for many years thereafter.

In the meantime, however, I was feeling increasingly depressed and unproductive (in spite of being a popular teacher and publishing three books). I felt my depression lift as soon as I submitted my resignation letter. Like Hilary, I was headed into unchartered territory. I had interrupted my upward professional trajectory for something more compelling though not yet re-defined.

Spiritual Journey

I travelled to the West Coast, as I had so many summers in the past years, partly to join my teacher in the Gurdjieff Work for intensive work weeks; partly to join my brother and his partner at their goat ranch in Mendocino, where she was now pregnant; and partly to visit with friends along the way. I crossed the country in my 'new' third-hand, pine green VW camper with pop-top roof, confident that the $14,000 I'd saved over the past years would see me through the year-long 'sabbatical' that I had declared for myself.

I felt a special draw toward Lee and sought to deepen our relationship, even as I left her physically. Whether this relationship had any kind of determinate future was altogether unclear to both of us, although we were still calling and writing (ir)regularly, and I was meditating, if that's not too formal a word, on the possibility of Lee and me. Now, in spite of temporary unemployment (or was it because?), I felt ready for commitment. I had known throughout my twenties that I would want children, but not yet. Now I did feel ready.

Part of the meditation included how a possible family life could be compatible with the wider circle of my deep friendships, which with some of my other closest women friends did, on occasion, include sex. Can one be ongoingly committed to one woman in a wife-like, mother-of-one's-children, sexual, and relatively-possessive way? …While simultaneously committing to clearly non-possessive intergendered friendships that may include sex, possibly in a coitus-interruptus kind of way, at timely moments?

To be fully truthful here, I did not see how any real kind of love could be possessive in any kind of way, however committed/persevering/enduring it might be in actual terms over durational time. But to make a family commitment clearly meant to make a special commitment of continuity of co-caring for the children, which I felt increasingly prepared to make. And quite possibly with Lee.

Since Lee's and my relationship had been non-possessive from the start and had encompassed both of us openly holding other beloveds concurrently, it should be possible, it now occurred to me, to make an explicitly non-traditional, non-marital commitment to continuity as a couple and future family. So I began to try to formulate a non-possessive commitment vow during my country-crossing weeks…

> Lee,
> I wish to remain engaged to thee forever…
> in the loving educational action of this foundational friendship…
> to serve the spirit of inquiry under one another's dominion…
> in work and in play, in joy and in suffering…
> within our own family and within the still stranger, still unrecognized family humankind –

Lee, on the other hand, often felt quite fed up with my non-commitalness. What sense did it make for me to learn whether and how to be together by taking a lonely journey across the country? She had no phone number for me, nor address of course, so could do nothing but be some combination of annoyed and

115

pleased when I chose to call, just as she was sitting down to write the irrevocable letter.

Now, we experienced what I can only call a true miracle of timely interaction. I flew back to Boston and pronounced my vow of commitment amidst a long evening of delectable eating, conversing, and love making. We slept the sleep of the just, and near dawn the next morning awoke to her telling me she had her own pronouncement to make.

She said she was releasing me from all commitments of the previous evening, until I was able to digest her message. Next, she revealed that she had decided earlier that Fall that she'd like a child by me, even though I seemed unlikely to commit, and might be too much trouble anyway. So, she had not used birth control when we had last met at my parents' apartment in Washington, when I was about to head west in the aforementioned VW van.

She had learned two weeks ago that she w-a-s pregnant. In spite of protestations by several of our mutual friends with whom she shared her secret, she was planning not to tell me and to bring up the child herself.

To me it seemed like a cosmic blessing on all our decisions that I had made my commitment to her before knowing about her pregnancy. This way we both knew that she knew that I had chosen her not just out of responsibility for our child. So, with great joy, I immediately re-pronounced my commitment to living together, with child, within a wider community of inquiry.

We decided we would start over again in San Francisco and flew out before Christmas. A further aspect of the cosmic joke we were playing on ourselves revealed itself on April Fools' Day 1977, when the doctors announced that our child was in fact twins – perhaps a wee bit of a larger burden to raise single-handedly than Lee had initially been imagining!!

Needless to say, my savings for my 'sabbatical' year 'alone' began to drain away much more rapidly as we became first two and then, on May 23rd, 1977, four, six weeks prematurely. Suddenly, I was applying for jobs in the Bay area left and right, at Stanford, Berkeley, and other places; and suddenly, for the first time in my career, I wasn't getting the openings I tried for.

As spring turned to summer, we decided to return to Boston, where Lee could return to her consulting firm to give us one regular salary. I would serve as house-husband and start an entrepreneurial venture I called The Theatre of Inquiry (a story for another time and place) … until, as I hoped, I landed an academic position for the following year. Once again, however, I was not winning any of the positions I applied for, and was learning how much easier it is to leave the mainstream than to return to it.

At the last possible moment, my fortune changed once again, and I was selected as Graduate Dean at a School of Management in Boston. Promoting 'strategic prudence' to a new level of priority in my life, I remained there for the remaining 30 years of my academic career, earning what I considered to be good

116

money and doing what I considered to be good work in leadership education and research.

My relationship with Lee had been founded amidst multiple, non-possessive love relationships, and my love for her and the twins (and, later, our third son) could not have been clearer and more tangible during these years. We maintained a tradition of Saturday evening "dates" together for a number of years. I loved her cooking and her conversation, and how easily we took care of the necessities of life. We gave great parties for our friends and enjoyed visits with and from both our parents. My boss used to kid me about how in love I was with Lee, which I took as a gigantic compliment.

Nevertheless, Lee and I were stretched right to, and sometimes beyond, our limits, during our first family years with our two very demanding full-time jobs and our two very energetic twin sons. She asked that I not engage in any other intimate, sexual relationships for two years after the twins' birth, and I was glad to agree.

I loved singing all the childhood songs to the boys, including the ones in French and German, and later reading out loud all three volumes of the Lord of the Rings to the twins. (I was crushed seven years after that when my voracious-reader-of-a-third-son was too impatient for me to read them out loud all over again and devoured them much more rapidly by himself instead.) My love for my three sons has always seemed the most 'natural' and ineradicable love of my life: mountain climbing, ping pong tournaments, coaching their soccer teams, Saturday evening religious observances of Star Trek, skiing, bridge, swimming off Marblehead lighthouse point, conversation – serious or light – and one or two occasions with each boy of fierce fatherly boundary-setting. As with many of my other close friendships with men (and some of my close friendships with women as well) there is an erotic attractiveness in these relationships that is not at all sexual in flavor.

Continuing Interlude on Developmental Analysis of Events

In the previous chapters, we have seen Hilary and Bill begin to exercise Redefining action-logic and visioning power. We see the beginnings of this in Hilary's commitment to Zen in Japan – to 'Redefining' herself through the power of committing to a vision. Visioning power entails the use of one's imaginative, artistic, mutual-trust-building faculties and disciplines, alone in nature and with committed colleagues or friends in society, to create new visions of the future of this conversation, meeting, organization, nation, etc.

In Celia's and Bill's relationship, we witness a repeated cycle of stuckness between the two of them, neither of them capable of sufficiently appreciating the pattern, nor capable of offering and receiving and acting upon the kind of double-loop feedback that can reveal and break such a pattern. Their praxis power was limited.

By contrast, two years later the dance that began with Jason, Lee's, and Bill's European trip, then led to Lee separating from Jason and Bill separating from his university and later included Bill's repeated departures and revisits with Lee over six months became an exercise in mutually-transforming power that blessed us with timely commitments, long partnership, and children.

Mutually-transforming power includes the first-, second-, and third-person practices of vigilant and vulnerable presence to, and timely interaction with, one another in community that generates power via love and inquiry more than via the first four types of Unilateral Power. This kind of power becomes available at the Alchemical action-logic. It welcomes triple-loop feedback: A response that awakens us into all four territories of experience at once (the outside world, one's own enacted sensations, the structures of thought, and a bare observing attention), with a profound feeling of the inter-independence of the universe and of our own congruity or incongruity herein.

Invitation

Our aim with the book is to encourage deep inquiry into the trickster domains of eros and power with the hope that Eros/Power can flow more in all our lives.

Referring back to Bill's struggles with Celia, how do you contend with women's power? Bring a powerful woman to mind and examine your feelings in response. Is there any relation to how you related to your mother? Consider if there may be patterns here when looked at alongside responses to earlier invitations. If you are married or in a marriage-like relationship recall the early days of learning to negotiate power together. Is there a pattern you have fallen into? Is it what you want?

Chapter 8

Hilary's Inquiry into Relationships
Across Power Differences

My Ph.D. dissertation about organizational change was award winning, a form of action research, that is, research "with" rather than simply about people. And I thank Bill for his influence on that work. Upon graduating I started my career as assistant professor at one of the best Organization Behavior Departments in the world (at least according to the Financial Times that ranked such matters!).

My new department was known as an oasis of radical humanism. I loved the graduate students, many of whom were seekers on their own unusual paths. Whether out of loneliness or sheer bravado I started a romantic relationship with one within a few weeks of arriving. He simply insisted I love him back. That I was lonely, albeit still formally partnered, didn't help me resist. That he was an extraordinarily handsome student, who grabbed my hand to dance the tango in the local Coffee shop, by way of personally introducing himself, probably didn't dissuade much either. My faculty colleagues seemed amused more than outraged.

Thus began a thrilling eight weeks. Because that was not complicated enough, I experienced early and insistent sexual harassment at the hands of a senior professor. In truth we had much in common intellectually. But his sexual overtures, repeated, direct and blunt, worried me. I could not just simply slap him in the face. Stressed, I turned to Bill for advice. Bill's worldly counsel proved speedily effective. His advice essentially amounted to my calling on institutional power-holders; Bill specifically dissuaded me from seeking to reason with the senior faculty member myself (as had been my wont). Nervous and quite aware that my own illicit relationship (about which I was honest) certainly had me appear as less than an innocent angel, the institutional process worked like a charm. Sexual harassment really is about those with power using it over those with less.

The harassing professor and I even managed to make peace. "It's not the Sixties anymore," he remarked with both a hint at apology and some sadness about this contemporary sorry state of equalizing gender relations. He even threw in a

119

little advice: "If you'd just stop being such a pushy broad, don't talk quite so fast, you'll go far!" I laughed, feeling a mix of sadness for learning opportunities lost between us and relief to be freed from the unspoken demand for obsequiousness that he had enjoyed for too long. Unfortunately, neither of us could benefit from a mentorship relationship where oblivious sexism went unchecked. I could not bring myself to be appeasingly appealing. Despite or because of this start up (all this in my first semester), my career took off. I brought my professional focus to how action research might better address itself to the complex needs of stakeholders seeking a more sustainable world and published in the all important A level journals. I also did well teaching executive and part time students. This first few years I enjoyed myself professionally. I also enjoyed mutual support with other women faculty members.

The personal side of life was less successful. Perhaps in the void I felt when things had ended with Jack in Boston (he had never moved with me to my new college town and we had formally parted on one of my monthly trips to Boston), I carelessly fell back into what became a three-year relationship with a graduate student. The overall effect was to make me feel old. My half-hearted attempts at ending things were brushed aside. He moved himself into my new house. I sought peace elsewhere and contemplated that suddenly I had become 35. My biological clock began to sound like Big Ben. A friend set me up on a date with a lovely man and within minutes of meeting, we seemed to see in the other a potentially excellent partner! But yes, the awkward fact that a lingering (and handsome!) love object was living at my house was hardly an unambiguous statement of my availability. Yes, of course he was right to request that we not date till the handsome one had moved on. But he would not move on! Short of calling the police – an idea I never entertained seriously – I simply didn't know how to get him to let me live my life. To put it simply I wanted a child.

Forced to vulnerability as the specter of remaining childless my entire life truly frightened me, I was even agreeable when the graduate student agreed to co-parent once he had completed his studies. What was I thinking?! In truth I wasn't really thinking at all about the bigger picture. My professional work seemed to absorb so much of me, plus it seemed that every article written on age-related infertility now found its way onto my desk. Quiet panic was running the show. I did, however, give birth to a stellar resume (which like a Tibetan mandala would be burned some years later). There was to be no child between us. The graduate student started his career as assistant professor elsewhere, leaving (without telling me when!) a few days before my 36th birthday. I understood he must move on. My gift to him was a perfect editing of his excellent dissertation. I was also deeply hurt bordering on fully enraged that I'd been forced to waste "my childbearing years."

This reminds me of other situations I've seen you struggle in; I wonder what's the kryptonite in these situations that so paralyzes/disempowers you?

Hilary responds:

At the risk of being repetitive, (I am amazed at the simplicity), my insight is simply that I was seeking the emotionally familiar, seeking Mom! Or to be more careful, I was continuing to seek my early experience of Mom. There had been an early conditioning to meet the needs of an intimate other without complaint. Intimacy implied fulfilling the others demands even when they conflict with my own. But it was so unconscious for me. Finally, now do I begin to see it more clearly.

The Urge to Have a Child

I saw myself in a New Yorker cartoon around this time in which a group of Thirty Something career women sit around. One, looking at her watch, shrieks: OMG I forgot to have a baby!" I turned to Ram.

In order to convey a little more about what it meant for me to turn to Ram, I first look more closely at the love shared with Ram and its transformation over the 23 years we were eros infused friends. Since first meeting while I was in graduate school, we'd seen each other, albeit infrequently, usually for just a few days at a time in Paris. One of my inquiries is simply to understand the nature of our love. We have too few terms in English. Perhaps the contemporary, if crass term, "friend with benefits" is appropriate; the French use the term "amitié amoureuse" – loving friendship. When I listen to Leonard Cohen's song "I'm Your Man" it describes – sentence by sentence – our togetherness over the 23 years of our amitié. Ram also looks like Leonard Cohen. The interweaving of conventional and self-authoring relationship forms is so clear between us. Let me reflect more on the Eros/Power that played in different guises between us. I look backward from the latter part of the relationship, for it did end, though not for many years after our attempt to have a child together.

BFF (best friends forever): the near enemy of the beloved?

I texted Ram after a brief voice contact on the fly, literally because I was be-tween terminals at the Chicago airport: "How appropriate that we just spoke– I forgot to mention that I am in Chicago." "Appropriate indeed" was his immedi-ate reply. "It was in February, my darling, 22 years ago that we met, more than the double of your romance with your current love." I wondered about the words "romance" and "current." But Ram is not a native speaker of English so I let it go. We arranged to talk soon, after I'd had a chance to rest, for I was returning from Ireland, city of birth, home of my family and extended family where I had gone to celebrate my parent's 50th wedding anniversary on Valentine's day.

Ram and I rarely spent extended periods of time together, but we talked on long Skype calls. The intimacy, the sense of authentic and deep contact would simply emerge again and again between us. Yet again we were planning to get together Perhaps it was a mistake to try to understand this relationship? I could see from observing my parents that one could just muddle through. Longevity is its own excuse. But with Ram there was only choice – there was no cultural structure for our relationship, no real support for it. It's hard even to define it – half lovers, half friends, perhaps soul mates, at least on the good days. But I had also begun to doubt us – begun to doubt that the friendship was one of virtue, which for many years I had believed it was.

Ram's presence in my life over the years was both a thorn in the side and a benediction. I would not – perhaps could not – give him up. My relationship with Ram carried on through my own marriage-like relationships. I learned over the years not to talk about it too much. Here my silence was different from my early years. Now it was that the issue is almost unresolvable. I had come to feel and believe that there are specific channels that open between lovers that, if kept with integrity, promise to keep alive a passion that is unmarred by any other relationship happening around it. In simple terms there is always more room for love. And this love does not have to diminish any other love. I held an essentially polyamorous stance about relationships.

I see Ram as the one who allowed me to stay in relationships that were not quite perfect (e.g., so what if my new beloved doesn't have a dazzling mind, I could talk to Ram and have the need for brilliant conversation met). Our friend-ship seemed to be based on a need for conversation at a level of intensity that is usually unmet, i.e., for being intensely listened to and understood by one so in-telligent and quick, was the friendship. Not that sex was absent. To the contrary. The sex was terrific – but honestly – if I had to choose, and thankfully I never had to, it was secondary. As with most great loves there was simply being met where I was.

Our most intense time together came when I was looking for a father for my child. Using an ovulation predictor kit to decide when to fly, I was happy that

Ram and I had easily agreed to become parents. We failed miserably. It was as if the universe intervened and declared "No way!" We were literally mugged with teargas when our train to Paris stopped in the infamous banlieux (suburbs where immigrants of North African origin live) on the very day I arrived. Our plan, that is my plan, became almost physically unexecutable. The aftermath, which left me with literally nothing – no money, no passport, no clothing – had left Ram with a broken arm. Though that was not quite enough to confront the craziness of the baby plan. But if anyone knows the cavernous yearning that a ticking biological clock leaves, you may fill in the blanks. It is evolution at work. Fourteen billion years of unstoppable momentum. Acceptance of failure would not come easily, especially not to one grown used to being a "winner." At first I grew angry and impatient at Ram's need to convalesce, ("it's just a broken arm for God's sake!"). Comical scenes played by two wounded egocentric intellectuals making mutually exclusive demands. Then Ram's mother went into hospital and called him back to Jerusalem to hold her hand as she passed away. And because that was not enough (I could join you I offered!) the second intifada erupted in Palestine and buses began to explode on a regular basis. He apologized, heart broken over the demise of his beloved mother and perhaps also for our plan. He packed.

Our only contract had been to always be there when needed. I felt forsaken. The contract of our friendship was finally broken. I surrendered.

In retrospect this friendship may have been part true love. But in part it was likely also love's near enemy by which I mean so close as to allow me to fool myself. In the intervening years we had even discussed this – no stone would remain unturned between us in our long and life probing conversations beginning many months later.

I pondered more privately my rather bizarre and unusual (in hindsight) indifference to getting married. Why had I not equated parenting with marriage? Could it be my own childhood? I hadn't looked for the longest time! My own skirting of the issue was perhaps a way to avoid recognizing my deep neediness and the vulnerability it produced. I chose to try to become a mother through a psychological contract with a father, a contract I could shape and define. I could not, so straightforwardly, become a wife. To become a wife I would have to be chosen. I preferred to choose. In this way, Ram and I were like porcupines – truly intimate, truly committed, but stopping short of nuzzling up together. Porcupines do not nuzzle. Ram's father, an army officer, was hardly warm and fuzzy. Ram's upbringing in a kibbutz, in the era when kids were not directly cared for by their own mothers, had traumatized him. We were, I recognize in retrospect, extraordinary friends-in-trauma.

Did I relate too selfishly to Ram? Because we talked and listened so well, the underbelly of who we were to each other was that much harder to see. Listening was the form that love most took between us. Ram was what family therapists call the "third" – the one who brings sustainability to other marriages but usually with a cost. That third can be a mistress or it can be a job, or alcohol, or a child. Knowing this I reasoned that it's unreasonable to ask everything of any one relationship anyway. Having Ram "on the side" made my life complete for the years our friendship endured. His too. Right?! For his part Ram's main love, as he liked to explain, was for his only child. Though in fact there was usually an adoring female companion close by also.

Perhaps it became a habit, to talk and then occasionally plan to fly to meet Ram. Despite the particular hiatus after the Parisian assault, as ever we'd managed to make up, over time, over email and over phone. But all things pass away and indeed there came a final meeting. With Ram I never felt the vulnerabilities of clingy love, but I finally allowed myself to see that I was not actually fed by our relationship. I was met, seen, understood. But I was not fed. In simple terms our eros was not easily in touch with mutuality. When should relationships end I wondered?

On what would turn out to be our last day together, as like so many times before, we walked for hours in the city of Paris whose history Ram knows, street by street, and narrates between mini lectures he is preparing for his graduate students. Having originally met me as a graduate student, perhaps he continued to relate to me as such. But now it irked. There was also the semblance of peer-like status, moreover replicating a tried and true interdependency that was a source of sustainable erotic energy between us. And perhaps I was flattered to feel young still. In practical terms, however, by our last meeting I had become Ram's professional equal. Not that we ever mentioned that, indeed we rarely mentioned my work. And in conventional academic terms (citations, academic title), I had become more successful. But to mention that would be taboo given the erotic energy that originally propelled us. Women must be appealing, perhaps even more so when they outrank their male peers. Eros and power were not transforming together easily.

Just as leaves wither and fall when they should, so perhaps too with relationships. I found myself talking to Ram about my spiritual life, my spiritual teacher. As usual I loved that Ram understood the complexity of what I shared. In his self appointed position as Nietzschean therapist, with me as colluding patient and Ubermensch wannabe, he also diagnosed my lazy spiritual concerns as an escape hatch from my successful bourgeois life. Was I not perhaps overly influenced, living in California, by Madonna's infatuation with Kabbalah? Ouch! But any truth he might be speaking seemed almost beside the point. I felt him speak to me as if from on high, while I knew him to be firmly on the ground with feet of clay beside me. Realizing that I was in a relationship where there was too little mutuality, and that it didn't seem likely to transform itself, left me to face the incongruity between my vision for my life and the reality of this relationship.

Without any forethought or perhaps even recognition of how deeply uneasy I had grown with this lack of mutuality, I simply stopped walking alongside him.

Then I turned and walked away. Perhaps my years of meditation and increasingly serious practice had made a mark that led in a different direction. Perhaps the shell around my heart had softened to the point where I could voice my more tender emotions. By our last meeting I had also developed the heart of a mother. Whatever was the catalyst, Ram's and our amitié came to its end while walking in the Montmartre cemetery. We'd been walking and talking that day and I realized, 'No, he is walking and talking, I am following and listening' and I said, "Enough!" I left him startled and took a path that interested me more to visit the tomb of Charcot, Freud's teacher and therapist to hysterics (talk about finding trauma in the context of eros!). Ram caught up to express his vindictive wrath at my walking away. His anger grew more murderous (and in a cemetery!). Clearly he did not like to be abandoned. But in fact I was not abandoning him. That I could even walk away came as a new idea. It was no longer a time for dialogue. In time we might again reconfigure ourselves, I thought, but this lack of mutuality is over. Now. I chose instead to snap a photo of Charcot's tomb. And so our ignoble end arrives, I thought to myself. In a cemetery. And I am walking away.

Developmental Commentary

If we return to the first page or so of Hilary's chapter, to her story about her relationship both with the graduate student and the Department Chair, we can perhaps taste mutually-transforming power, with both double – and triple-loop feedback, at work. Most obvious is how Hilary as the institutionally lower-power member via her Department Chair used institutionally-sanctioned logistical power to create power parity, not in a way that made the two of them enemies, but rather able to relate in a new way; indeed, with him still alive enough to offer her single-loop career advice ('don't talk so fast') ... As the chapter continues, we see other signs of Hilary's early Alchemical action-logic, in part in her walking away from her relationship with Ram as she increasingly recognized his unwillingness to drop his 'superior' role, an act of walking away suffused by a synchronicity of metaphors (fall, the cemetery, Charcot's tomb). We also see how labile the Alchemists' action-logic is, running back and forth along the trombone stops of the octave of development, as she endures a sense of powerlessness to define her own home space in the face of the graduate student who came to dinner and stayed.

Our Reflection Together on Redefining Our Lives

Bill comments:

I have been thinking about your 'amitié amoureuse ' with Ram. You managed to co-create a relatively permanent institution for inquiry over twenty-three years. It played a key role for you. I do feel that your primary tone now is recrimination, an effort to topple the statue, even as you acknowledge the positive. But I am also seeing in your amitié an experiment that just didn't fit too easily in the conventional frameworks we must continue to answer to at all stages of our life. You kept this amitié separate to cultivate its erotic energy enough to redefine your life. It was a private but not secret relationship. You clearly struggled with ethical questions. From the perspective of convention, there is little perhaps that can be claimed as inherently virtuous in that amitié… yet it cultivated you into your post conventional years. We might say that you were brave enough not to betray yourself, even as you betrayed others. At the end when you walk away in the cemetery I see a metaphor. I also laugh a little at your comedy. Relationship death by inattention in a cemetery! Perhaps in hindsight I wonder if you can also see that it's a triumph. There is finally an odd mutuality in walking away, something that had been so difficult for you previously. At this ending, and who knows if it is truly the end of your amitié, you permit each other to keep your own ego in the condition you each wish. You've learned how to end a transformational relationship without violence. Brava!

Hilary responds:

In turn I hear words of Blaise Pascal as I consider the development of the Redefining and later action-logics in both our previous chapters. Pascal said, "We know the truth not only by reason but by the heart." More famously he also said, "The heart has its own reasons that reason cannot fathom." Pascal comes to mind especially when I recall that compelling moment of escape from what I want to call the Temple of Reason that you, and I, were imprisoned in until we settled into a more redefined stage of living. That moment when you cast the I-Ching, which so flummoxed you, is key. For me it was my encounter with Zen. We get first significant tastes of going feral, away from the conventional path, away from the dominance of what we have internalized. Both of us had become professional academics, which is to say we were priests in the Temple of Reason. What excellent Cartesians we were. Redefining was certainly not a sure bet. Eros broke us out of the Temple! We see your fall back when you ignore your repulsions with Celia's make-up and cigarettes. If ever there is a clear message from the heart-body it is when we feel erotic repulsion. Of course repulsions also need to be discerned, they need to be felt into, as opposed to rationally examined for political correctness. Repulsions may well convey the whisperings of the heart's saying, "Not this way." But rationality doesn't listen to whispers, only loud, well-articulated insistences count as important. To talk about grace and polyamory in the same breath is conventionally shocking, but it's grace that allows us to awaken. Your developing the relationship with Lee and Jason then offers the beginnings of a deeper venture into relationship patterned by heart and hand as much as by reason. I so love Mary Oliver's lovely poem, which is really about moving confidently into the redefining period of life. It's called The Journey:

> "But little by little,
> as you left their voices behind,
> the stars began to burn
> through the sheets of clouds,
> and there was a new voice
> which you slowly
> recognized as your own,
> that kept you company."

Invitation

Our aim with this book is to encourage depth of inquiry into the trickster domains of eros and power – of love under the sign of inquiry – with the hope that Eros/Power can flow more in all our lives.

Has there been a relationship in your life that is most dear and honorable to you and yet quite unconventional and perhaps difficult for others to understand/accept? Can you claim what is honorable in it? Can you see what is dishonorable (if anything)? How much space do you grant others, really, to live what feels true for them? Do you have rigid boundaries for yourself and others? Does anything go? What feels like a healthy middle ground?

Chapter 9

Bill's Polyamory and the Frontiers of Post-Conventional Relating

Are There Limits to Human Nature's Capacity to Embrace Mutual, Non-possessive, Erotic Friendships?

I (Bill) chose to remain celibate during the first year after the sexual relationship with my second wife, Lee, ended. I wanted to learn what I could by drawing a strong intentional boundary around my sexual action. I certainly saw the tidal power of my desires again and again. I also began to recognize, in meditation when feeling that pull, how empty I was of sensual pleasure in my own embodiment. Could I take erotic pleasure in my separate embodiment, in my aloneness? What would it mean to love myself – not as a thought, but as a sensation in the body? What would it mean to take a voluptuous pleasure in my breathing and the energies traveling up and down my spinal column – indeed, from the top of my head to the bottoms of my feet? One could not very well love another, let alone humanity as a whole, without love for oneself. How did these first-, second-, and third-person gestures of love interweave with and inform one another?

After my celibate year I entered into the early stages of a trio-relationship with two women, Patricia and Liz, who were also friendly with one another. We had several actual get-togethers as a threesome and other get-togethers in one or another of the three pairs that made up the trio. The trio occasions included one long back-to-back-to-back meditation interspersed with short face-to-face-to-face and knee-to-knee-to-knee conversations. There was also another long, memorable evening of touring Cambridge music bars and restaurants, each of us having been assigned a role for the evening that was particularly difficult for us to play. For example, the least assertive of us was to take a strong lead in suggesting what we do at multiple points in the evening. (Everything quickly became very hilarious.)

Because I was by this time vaguely aware that I was setting out all over again to live out a new kind of non-possessive adult friendship, I had not only been hilarious with my two friends, but had also talked my good serious talk about

the primacy of non-possessive erotic friendship as a form of love in my world…
More specifically, I illustrated why I thought a sequence of three specific acts
would help interlace newly forming erotic friendships with more senior friendships in a way most likely to make all parties feel respected and treated mutually.

"William's Rules of Order" for non-possessive friends, when potential or actual sexual relationships are at issue, included:

1) You let the senior friend know about the new friend as soon as a strong
feeling is felt (and prior to sexual intimacy);
2) After conversation and reflection between the two senior friends, if you
wish to go forward with the new relationship, then you let the new friend
know about the senior friend if you haven't yet, as well as about the kind
of conversation the two of you have had about the new friend, and about
the idea of non-possessive love in friendship under the sign of inquiry you
wish to play out; and
3) If the new friend hasn't run away by this time (!), you invite him or her
into a trio conversation with the senior friend or with some other group-
inquiry constellation early in your new friendship (in order to enact and
experience a trio or group inquiry, not just talk about it in the abstract).

I realize these "rules" sound rather absurd presented so skeletally, but I had
good conversations with each of the women about the details. Indeed, at the
time, each woman seemed to like the sense of commitment these priorities represented for the senior friendships (each of ours with one another). A key omission, however, may have been the lack of a good conversation early on among
the three of us together about this.

After my divorce, both relationships were already beyond the sexual-coupling
period (and there had been no trio sexual engagements). But what I am actually
most proud about in regard to this experiment in explicit trio-ing from the start,
is how both friendships continued transforming after that time, one of them lasting actively into the present.

The short-term wasn't as pretty. Within two months of our conversations
about our non-possessive, inquiry-based friendships, Patricia began a sexual relationship with another man but without first discussing it with me. This man
almost immediately made it clear to her that he was seeking a monogamous marriage (why don't my fellow men ever seem interested in my non-possessive approach?).

I was deeply wounded – by Patricia's evident preference for that man and his
commitment to monogamy over our five-year, mutual, non-possessive relationship, itself only recently having become fully sexual. We had promised one another the gift of bringing such potential love relationships to one another before
becoming sexually involved with the other. This promise evidently meant noth-

ing to her! This made me feel angry as well as wounded (at least I was finally getting in contact with my anger a little earlier in such sequences).

At the same time, believe it or not (and she didn't for a long time), I was also genuinely concerned for her that the new relationship, so founded, could not last. She was sure at the time that my high-mindedness about senior friendships and my concern for her new relationship was bullshit to cover my jealousy about her good fortune.

She discontinued our occasional sexual relationship because she wanted to give monogamy with the other guy a chance. We agreed to keep our five-year friendship open, which, in practice, meant no more than a phone call every third month or so.

Later, I worked with Patricia in tandem serving a consulting client. That was more pleasurable than painful because we did have a kind of intimacy that permitted complete candor between us, and that, in turn, permitted us to work together very efficiently and effectively. Still later, she entered into an enduring marriage in a different part of the continent.

Five years later, after intermittent phone conversations between us, Patricia came to Boston, and we had a more deeply reconciling talk. She had come to apologize, she said, and to thank me. A year before her visit to me, her husband had proposed opening their marriage and beyond some moments of panic, she thought of how practical my three "rules" could be as protections for her (and him) if they were to open the marriage. During a week of initially-difficult conversations between them, he in turn accepted the three steps. They actually enacted the espoused strategy, and now they were happier than ever…

She later apologized for how unjust she had been in her interpretation of my motives before. This change of feeling brought my inner vulnerability in contact with my physical containedness, during a long and fully felt (but not sexual) hug with her. I was reminded of the feeling I had experienced when I was hugged from behind twenty-some years before by the Latin American woman in the Gurdjieff Work. It was possible for me to remain physically-sexually alone, with equanimity, even while in deep physical-emotional communion with a woman. This had been possible since my middle twenties with men, but only in my 50s began to become possible with women like Patricia.

"The Other Woman"

The other woman in our trio, Liz, extends into my present. Liz wrote about the early period of our friendship, and her writing, shared with me, became a transformational trigger for our friendship. Her artistic initiative began to more fully "mutualize" us. She chooses to tell a longer story – a story of finding more dimensions of her own voice and beginning to assert creative peer power. She definitely surprised and shocked me with a perspective on me and on our love-making that I had not known she held at the time… But over several re-readings spread across a week, I came to receive Liz's offer of her story to me as a loving educational act – a beautiful example of relational action inquiry.

Visitor

He came into my home and moved quietly through each of the high ceilinged rooms – taking in the art on the walls, examining my floor-to-ceiling collection of books, scanning the New York Times article "About Men" framed above my desk, reading the calligraphied testimonial above my bed that had been presented to me by my co-workers many jobs ago now.

As I watched him standing reverently at the foot of my bed reading the hand-lettered words of the plaque, I thought with both irony and amusement that my bedroom had a funereal quality about it. The bed, a mound of soft blankets, burying me in warmth and darkness each night; the framed plaque, a beautiful headstone; and its words, an epitaph by which anyone would like to be remembered, I guessed.

He stood tall, arms folded. His eyes and shoulders sloped in perfect parallel to each other. He drew in a deep breath, his torso heaving upward, and he closed and opened his eyes in a single, slow blink. A meditational move, I thought. "It's you," he said.

I had an annoyingly habitual smile. Annoying because it found its way to my face in moments when it was least welcome. This was one of them. Quick and broad, my open mouth and smiling teeth did nothing but destroy the meditational aura of his presence. "Yes." I said, imagining myself a grand dame standing in her parlor, dramatically gesturing about the room to display its riches. Only the effect I created was quite the contrary as I spoke in nervous syncopation, my arms waving like noodles about me. "Well, yes. Well, everything here means something to me. I mean, there's a story behind every piece of furniture, everything hanging on my walls."

"No," he said quietly, "I mean it's you – the high ceilings, the long windows, the mirror. Like you, like your form, long and tall." "Form," I repeated the word to myself chuckling. It gave away something about him. I wasn't sure if it was his age, the other side of 45, or his breeding. Someone more common to me in age and upbringing I was sure would never think to say form for figure or body. But I felt suddenly very beautiful, and to myself I added other architecturally and anatomically descriptive words. Graceful, columnar, arched.

The evening gave way to an unusual combination of silence and movement. We smoked some marijuana and I put on some music. I sat silently, moving rhythmically back and forth in my ladder-backed rocker, the habitual broad-mouthed smile glued into place on my face by the pot. I watched him as he moved into the open space of the dining room and on the rich maroon carpet that became his dance floor, moved silently with abandon and absorption to the ethereal sounds of the music. At some point no longer clear to me, the spell was broken. And he put on his leather jacket, picked up the beat-up leather bag that had become his security, his companion. It went with him wherever he went these days, in contrast to everyone and everything else in his life that seemed to be leaving him. His wife was leaving, his house was for sale, and his lover had left him for a man who promised monogamy. Around his neck he wrapped a black and orange and red and yellow crocheted scarf, so wide and so long that it hung to his knees. His wife, before she had become his wife, had made this. They'd called it The Confusion. He swaddled himself in his knitted Confusion and went off into the cold night.

I returned to my rocking chair and thought about what he'd said. "It's you." I looked up at the long tall ladies of the brass rubbings praying down at me. They wore elegant headdresses, flowing vestments, all in black. My best color. I looked at the long windows, at the breast plates, as I called them, in the upper corners. You know, those two carved wooden squares, inside a circle and at the center a nipple. My best features, my breasts, I laughed to myself. I looked at my face in the long oval mirror between the two windows, and saw the face of a Modigliani woman, painted with exaggerated length and sadness. I looked at the flowing lettering of the calligraphied testimonial, paragraphs arranged to form a collage whose final form was longer than wide.

His comment hung in the still air of my apartment for weeks after his visit. I moved through my rooms and among my possessions feeling strangely detached. No longer could I hear their stories, or feel their comfort. I became instead obsessed with their symbolism. Once precious possessions, they now had become artifacts, things to be studied, to be examined carefully for the smallest possible clues, maybe even answers. The more detached I felt from these possessions of my past, the more alive I felt in this game of symbols. It was a game of Hide and Seek. "Come out, come out, wherever you are," I whispered into the air. But the more alive I felt in my game, the

132

more I became aware of the many images of death amidst which I lived. The brass ladies lifted from their tombs in old English countryside churches, the testimonial that hung and read like an epitaph. On my nightstand the obituary and last letter from a past love. And under my rug, I remembered one evening, was the oil self portrait I'd done and buried, to keep it flat, I'd told myself. I peeled back the rug, and saw staring up at me my image, strikingly nondimensional. I remembered painting that portrait. The face seemed to come easily to me. But the hands... I'd worked on the hands for days trying to put them perfectly into position at my chest crossed over each other and crossed over me.

Months went by and my caller became a more frequent visitor. Not that there was any regularity to these visits. He'd phone sometimes on a Sunday afternoon wondering if I "might like to have a visitor." His boys, I imagined, were out playing on their own. His wife was probably at home. And without the purpose of his boys and in the presence of his estranged wife, I imagined him to be left a most uncomfortable guest in his own home. Sometimes he'd call when he happened to be in the vicinity. It was all very unpredictable and though I tried to be annoyed by it, it was hard to deny the pleasure of feeling pursued. Over time, I'd let those hands of my self-portrait drop for him. He caressed and coaxed them away from me, somehow convincing me to lay down these hands that were my shield and to dare to expose myself to the world. And so I did, and I felt sublime in my nakedness before him and before the world. The brass ladies stared down at me.

It was Fall. And as the weather grew colder, my spirit grew numb from changes that while warming for him, felt chilling to me. Liberating structures, he would probably call these changes. The divorce and his new condominium were the structures. The liberation was, I imagined, being able now to have public relationships with other women. I was a remnant of his secretive married past, and I stood shivering alone in my nakedness. The brass ladies looked down at me over their stone black cheeks.

We were sitting on my couch, pillows bunched behind us, each of us cross-legged at opposite corners of the couch. Dinner was cooking – linguine a le vongole, an unhealthful but delectable meal of clams simmering in a deep buttery, wine, and garlic sauce. The table was set, we were sipping wine and having hors d'oeuvres. The foreplay of all fine dining, I smiled to myself, imaging this possibility with him. Only ours had become a friendship, I kept reminding myself. Just a friendship. So we'd gone to bed on more than one occasion. So he'd chanted over my body. So he'd said his experience of my caressing was unprecedented. So I knew there'd been many before me, some during me, and others to follow. So?

I stared at him. Invisible, venomous darts of anger emanated aimlessly from me. But so lacking was my power to initiate that I couldn't even get them to stay their course. Him. The search and destroy mission turned suicidal and I sat there, a vulnerable and cooperative target for my own anger. But once jetting through my veins, my anger lost all its lethal power and turned from venom into sedative. My eyelids drooped. My stare turned into a gaze, and he became not a target but an object upon which I became transfixed with a knowing sadness. I knew this about him. He was capable of commitment. If nothing else, to irony. For his commitments were to breadth when it came to relationships and to depth when it came to honesty. But when you put the two together, the combination seemed always to self-destruct.

I kept listening, or at least trying, to his words becoming muffled hollow sounds. I felt myself being pulled under as if by some strangely soothing yet threatening current. My thoughts bubbled to the surface for air, searching with all their logic and reasoning for life. You had to have stamina to be with him, I thought, the stamina of a long-distance swimmer. And I didn't have it. If you could endure the others, survive the exhaustion, and reach the other side with him, there probably were some possibilities for exhilaration. If you could plunge the depths of his honesty, so unfathomable, so murky, and overcome the fear of the dark and of going that deep, there too were probably untold, never before experienced treasures to be found with him. I recalled the time we went swimming together. He could dive deep, and he could swim far, but he couldn't float. If only he could have put aside his indomitable Initiative, his drive to out pace and out distance himself and everyone else. If only he could just have learned how to float with me, I thought. I had been raised a good woman, taught to believe that initiative, commitment and honesty were the generics of a good and lasting relationship. But his was a particular, if not peculiar brand, something he called Living Inquiry to which he dedicated his life, engaged a following and in the process sacrificed more than a few. The most important ones it seemed, were the most intimate ones. The wives, the lovers.

I half listened, did more wordplay. "Living Inquiry" I mused, "Living Hell," I concluded. My fingers combed slowly through my hair. It was a gesture of distraction as I felt my face, any minute, about

to crumble, thin cracks moving out from the corners of my mouth
making me look like a china doll with a fractured porcelain face...

I will readily admit again to feeling naked and flayed on first reading Liz's version of our early story (and again as I include it, with her permission, in this book). At the same time, I was impressed and delighted by how much her masochistic-comic-wisdom-of-the-first-voice made it easier to accept her perspective as genuinely hers. Her vulnerable, 'powerless' voice was having a powerful influence on me, and also left me free from a sense of having been judged or having to defend myself.

In spite of Liz's sense that our relationship was ending, our friendship, after a passive period of separation, has continued over the past quarter century – at first, understandably, almost entirely at my initiative. Later, Liz and I began a long period of co-family-ing a dog beloved by many. Still later, my friendship with Liz picked up more merriment when she re-discovered her true love from her teenage years.

Over the years I think I can say I have become much more than the distant visitor I early on seemed. But do I know what she's really thinking??? In any event, in later times I have decided, in order to give myself some credit, that it cannot have been pure chance that – shortly after she wrote the story, thus finding her voice as a peer in a man-woman relationship with me – she entered her first long-term, public relationship with a man.

Learning About Love

My two marriages had been very different from one another – the second so much longer; with children; with a partner with whom conversation felt amusing, creative, and productive; a partner with whom I felt emotionally, intellectually, spiritually, and sexually engaged during the early years; with a partner with whom I had shared in an open, polyamorous relational web before we made a special commitment to one another. If I look at all the criteria Hilary and I name as essential to true love as Eros infused friendship in the Introduction, Lee and I were in love in so many of those ways in our early years together.

For eight years or so, my sense of spontaneity emerging from discipline and her sense of control yielding creative results wove fine patterns together – our three sons, our two jobs, our wide web of close friends. But over the next period they became threatening enemies instead. Enemies who sowed mistrust, created claustrophobia, and ultimately destroyed our friendship, leaving the marriage a husk.

The formal marriage, I now believe, had been a mistake to begin with. We had long since had our unique mutual commitment ceremony, and the twins were a year and a half old, when we got married by a justice of the peace at city hall, on a day we were both so sick that our honeymoon consisted of sneaking through the back door into our bedroom for a nap, leaving the babysitter to deal with the twins out front in the living room for another two hours. We told ourselves we married to make our relationship less problematic at the Catholic college where I worked (an odd rationale given that I'd already been hired without any inquiry into our marital status). We believed marriage wouldn't make any difference to our real and already-established relationship. We were wrong. As differently as they began, and as much longer as my second marriage lasted, both my marriages came to feel first claustrophobic and later dead to me. Is it marriage itself that doesn't agree with me? Marriage is the most powerful, conventional social institution and as such co-opted my own deep conventional habits, setting them at odds with my aspirations toward post-conventional development. Again, as after my first marriage, I committed not to remarry.

Another way of reflecting back on that time is to divide the time before I reached the age of forty – still in love with Lee, in love with my children as I still am, and in love with my career of teaching, researching, and dean-ing – to the time when I was between forty and sixty. At forty, I felt that the disciplines I had learned for self-, group- and organizational-observation and for timely, trust-building leadership were standing me in good stead. In contrast, between forty and sixty, I sought out insight and intervention from different therapists and body-workers, sometimes for prolonged periods of time in efforts to better understand my relationships with women.

Still another way of thinking about my lifetime is to compare myself to my lifetime friend, Greg, who was pretty crazy from twenty-three to thirty-four, when I first knew him, but thereafter got saner and saner. Why? Because he got over his nihilistic depressions and alcoholism once he came to terms with his homosexuality – the love that still could not speak its own name until well into the 1970s. What, I wonder, is a name for my more ambiguous combination of spiritual and erotic relationships that have a communal vector as well as a personal one? I still did not know, so I still could not come to peace within.

Hilary comments:

> I live in Portland, polyamorous Portland as it's called. Perhaps experiments in sexual relationships go hand in hand with experiments in more conscious living (sustainable local food, good coffee and microbrew)? An English professor friend tells me that whenever she invites freshmen to write on a topic of their choosing, 90% write about their polyamorous relationships! A delightfully tricky topic for it forces sexuality and transparency together. We see this combination of candor and goodwill in all your relationships, too, Bill.

Opening up our relationships – whether and how – is an inquiry in which our genetic and cultural (Judeo-Christian) heritages keep us in check. We don't know how far we can stretch until we reach relational breaking point. And because children are often involved we must be very careful, indeed! My favorite book on this topic is Sex at Dawn, which discusses evidence from early hominid groups to suggest that polyamory has always been with us. I also enjoy the contemporary work of author and syndicated advice columnist Dan Savage who suggests that given the mess that cheating and divorce causes in our lives, we should all strive for "monogamish" relationships in which we are GGG (good, giving and game)! Just as the body is not designed only for vegetarianism, yet can thrive on a vegetarian diet with minor tweaks, so too sexually, we appear to be designed as, um, omnivores; yet it is a good and healthy practice to make monogamy work.

Many can. Some stay celibate. And many founder, daring hardly to even feel from the waist down. I am pretty sure that serial monogamy accompanied by expensive divorces is not the answer to our erotic malaise. I am pretty sure that ignoring our malaise is not the answer. I am pretty sure, like Reformation's Martin Luther, that healthy celibacy is for the very few. And so it is a surprise and delight to see that women's role in the polyamorous community calls men to a higher standard of relating: talking honestly! The famous foundational text is Ethical Slut. So polyamory is important in so many ways. Yet also in Portland (support-land!), I have learned the term 'manarchist," which suggests the ways in which efforts to create new social forms can sometimes cover up an untransformed predatory-masculine behavior in the guise of "liberation." Generally speaking, it seems most wise that women and men truly partner and speak honestly. Given the historical novelty with this, we are called to tread carefully.

Key in a phase of inter-independence in relationship is also maintaining a live erotic polarity within the couple, including but certainly more than sexual intimacy. Figuratively speaking, if eros exists at all as chakras (consider the erotic charge of a well turned out journal article! the erotic charge of a finely wrought dinner! the erotic charge of sexual connection), then a practice through life is cultivating eros on all chakras. The natural desire of eros to arise – as the soul surges forth to know the other – doesn't diminish. And I have been surprised by that! But it may seek many different manifestations. Awareness of the demands it makes is key. And in truth I know sometimes the demand is simply too great and eros and love hurt one another. Let me pick up this topic as I share more of looking for love. Adrienne Rich says it well:

An honorable human relationship, that is,
one in which two people have the right to use the word love
is a process delicate, violent, often terrifying to both persons involved.
A process of deepening the truths they can tell to each other.
It is important to do this because it breaks down
human self-delusion and attachment to isolation.
It is important to do this because in doing so
we do justice to our own human complexity.
It is important to do this whenever we can because
we find so few people to go that hard way with us.

Bill responds:

I do see, Hilary, how you have woven different beliefs at different times around the exigencies of your actual relationships and your continuing inquiry into them. In the past five years alone, I have known you to practice and to preach (at least for yourself) celibacy, monogamy, polyamory, and now this more subtle inter-independent monogamy under the sign of inquiry. I too experience this stumbling comedy of erotic inquiry, but have found a qualitatively different balance, which includes both long-term, deep, and carefully limited polyamorous friendships, as well as a stable third marriage and home life for the past twenty years (from my 50th year to my 70th). My marriage is to a woman who knows my other friends, as she knows you, and to whom I have committed not to write about our relationship, other than this brief acknowledgement.

For now I have three additional reflections to offer about patterns of action in relationship that took me decades to see. One pattern began in high school when I befriended my friends' families in order to be invited back again during school vacations (although the process wasn't as conscious and selfishly goal-oriented as the words "in order to" imply). I acted especially responsibly with my friends' parents, keeping my room neat, making my bed, doing my laundry, washing dishes after every meal, being unfailingly cheerful – whereas at home (in part because we had servants when abroad) I was a lazy, passive, good-for-nothing. By the end of my first marriage, I could see I was treating my time in my married-home somewhat the way I'd spent my time in my parents' home, and treating my work-teams more like my friends' parents' homes. This pattern was less obvious in my second marriage because life with children was so demanding and enthralling that I couldn't get away with being a good-for-nothing. I will have more to say about my ongoing inter-independent friendships after your next chapter.

Invitation

Our aim with the book is to encourage depth of inquiry into the trickster domains of eros and power, of love under the sign of inquiry, with the hope that Eros/Power can flow more in all our lives.

Has polyamory appeared anywhere in your life? What is your reaction to it? How is your reaction grounded in your earlier experience? Have you experienced being "cheated on" (which is actually not a form of polyamory)? What are your commitments around fidelity at this season of your life?

INTERLUDE TWO

Practicing Relational Action Inquiry

Once you understand this you understand all. This idea that love overtakes you is nonsense. (Tis but a polite manifestation of sex.) To love one another you have to undertake some fragment of their destiny.

– Quentin Crisp.

We now invite, not just your reflective inquiry, but also your active relational inquiry into how you too can cultivate more mutual, more balanced, more loving, more supportive, more erotic, more inquiring friendships. Here are some suggestions.

I. Practice relational action inquiry at the check-out counter

This one is based on Hilary's practice, having shopped almost daily at Trader Joe's supermarket for 10 years. The basic principle is to hold open the possibility that this is an opportunity to be surprised and delighted, or at least to pass a few moments well. A few moments in which with an appropriate opening received ("Did you find everything you wanted?") or offered (I might say that you're almost done for the day; how's it been for you?). There is space for the other to arise as a person rather than solely or primarily a customer service representative. I have been surprised by how many are actively living the Good Life as artists, enjoying a flexible work schedule that permits their passions. I communicate my interest in them. Nothing is self conscious, we're simply making heart centered connection. It's simple enough – starting with listening into the space between myself and the check-out person. I listen for, are they open to relating authentically, or should we stick to interacting at the transactional "professional" level? I am not especially extraverted, but I find I enjoy these time limited interactions. Worse case scenario I get to practice being kind, and being receptive to their kindness (and great suggestions about personal food favorites). More often than I can recall the interaction has been about as delightful as a grocery store allows!

A reader might wonder: Well, isn't this "just" being nice, something the associates are paid to be. Yes and no. Eros flies through commonplace positive emotions. And sometimes, now and then, someone tells me something profound and I get to listen to the unexpected as the soul surges with interest toward the other. There has been much more goodwill, laughter, flirtation and interesting news updates than would have emerged without the effort at listening into the other. There is no downside. So if there is a bedrock principle for relational action inquiry, it is listening into what surprising or unique pattern of relating can emerge here and now between us, be it in interactions of less than five minutes or in more cultivated environments as we describe below.

IIa. Relational Action Inquiry between Partners

Choose a date and time that you consciously practice relational action inquiry. Be careful to not mix in "business as usual" by dedicating special time and taking care of business as usual either before or after.

The following describes a weekly practice of Hilary's with her partner for which they set aside 60 minutes. (It's also possible to do a shorter version. Longer may feel burdensome over time). It is possible to do most of this by videophone also. It is useful to alternate which partner facilitates/time-keeps to demonstrate care for the relationship and to feel cared for.

Begin with reminding yourselves of your heart centered purpose in using your time in this unconventionally care-full way of relating. Remind yourselves also that your partner is an ally and that cultivating Eros/Power between you is a gift to you and the world. For the aesthetically inclined you might light a candle or conjure some spiritual support. The following can be modified to work more appropriately with your inclinations:

Our purpose in talking together for the next hour is to transform our partnership's darkness into light together; to liberate through welcoming along with our joys and appreciations, those shadow parts of us so easily triggered in this relationship. We remind ourselves that without truth there can be no love and that without humor there may be no point.

- Start by listening into the unknown together, perhaps with silent eye gazing (timekeeper may set an alarm for 2 minutes).
- Invite a check in, simply asking each other, "How are you?" or "What is your experience now?"
- Listen to what the other is saying with your whole body, noticing your sensations as you listen.
- Speak back the essence of what you heard, especially the emotions

present. AND share some of the sensations you had (tingling around the heart; constriction in the throat, etc)

• Pick 1-2 items or topics from what has been spoken. Check if you both are willing to pursue a topic together. Once agreed flesh out a little more why this topic is important. Monitor your reactivity.

• Invite and share relevant mental images or vignettes (especially from childhood) that may be associated with emotions and reactions that are arising. Go back and forth as before till each feels complete, and with each practicing listening with attention to sensation…

It's important to pause regularly and take a breath. This will allow you savor, and/or listen further into, and/or channel strong emotions constructively and/or to discern together if/how to continue.

End with a brief check out that includes appreciation for eros that may have flown between you. It's quite probable that you may also sense incompletion with a particular topic. Don't worry, that can be brought to a next conversation. Be sure to create your next relational action inquiry date to signal there needs be no scarcity of sharing generously of your time, (bring your calendar).

Where there is a physically intimate relationship consider holding hands as you speak or touch mindfully more often than you might. Note how touch, mindfully given and received, anchors you in what's real, often bringing simpler language and stopping a spinning into abstraction and distraction.

Where there is sexual intimacy consider wise use of sexual communion as a way to communicate. This is not primarily pleasure-oriented communication. The process would ideally follow all of the steps outlined above! The only suggestion is to go very slowly and remain in eye contact, emphasizing appreciation given this especially vulnerable state. As this is quite a profound practice, don't use it till you are versed in the process and then, use sparingly, keeping it as a guarded time in addition to other more free flowing or regular sexual intimacy.

As a general hint, it is best to err on the side of giving more appreciation than you might normally. There is likely no such thing as too much and it will feel good and create a virtuous cycle for you both.

It is wise to expect a mix of jaggedness and generosity especially if you have not been bringing truth to your interactions before a conscious practice of relational action inquiry. If however, after a number of dates, you find things becoming more jagged rather than more generous between you, consider inviting a third to join. This could be a trusted friend or a professional couples therapist.

Repeat this practice regularly, as much as is helpful.

IIb. Take the Global Leadership Profile

Consider doing the GLP assessment along with other personality assessments and have your partner do likewise. The GLP action-logic assessment may well be a particularly useful key ingredient for sustainable matches. We often feel lonely when the distance between partner's action-logics is too great. For example, if partners find themselves on the opposite side of the Achiever/Redefining line, then a real tug of war can occur, because everything before Redefining is about stabilizing; on the other hand, the Redefining and later action-logics are about the dynamics of peaceful, mutual, and timely transformation of self, relationships, and systems. So it is helpful to find yourself in relationship where action-logics are close, or, if in a relationship, to seek to bring them closer, between partners. See resources at the back for more information.

III. Convene 2½-Hour, After-Dinner Meetings of Three to Twelve Inter-Gendered Participants

Invite several friends (start small, say three) to your home for an evening meeting that will have an intentional structure of limits to it that you let them know about ahead of time.

Devote the first 30 minutes of this after-dinner meeting to meditation; begin and end the meditation with a ceremonial gong of some kind. Different ones of you and of your friends will lead this meditation in different ways; just be sure to spend most of the time in silence.

Open the second 45 minutes of the meeting to group conversational play, focusing primarily on how participants are experiencing and impacting one another during the conversation itself. (This is, of course, a primarily relational or second-person form of research-practice. Like the subjective, or first-person meditation exercise, this is a form of research in the present that is by and large unknown in the empirical sciences.)

The final half of the meeting can become a party with music, song, and dance for all those who wish to stay. However, the party must end promptly on the hour. Subgroups are free to engage in after-meetings if they wish, but such are not encouraged, and the meeting convener in particular ought not to leave his or her home, nor allow anyone to stay.

Sometimes these meetings develop some consistency of attendance to become every-other-monthly. Hosting them on a Full moon (as Hilary does) offers an opportunity to share what has happened in the past month and to "lean into" the new by sharing some aspirations.

IV: Lead a Conversation into an Entirely Different Realm than It Has Manifested Before

We can see a courageous conversation occurring in the following email exchange between an older female, who is the formerly-teacher member of a dyad, of which the younger male member is the former student. The pair is exploring creating an organizational consultancy together. The senior member is in the midst of reading an earlier draft of this book as the e-mail exchange begins.

On condition of anonymity, both have agreed to a wider sharing of the following parts of their e-mail transcript. The transcript suggests some of the challenges of conducting such a conversation, as well as some of the humor.

Junior Colleague (male, early 30s): What are you working on?

Senior Consultant (female, mid-30s): Reviewing some really interesting work on eros and purposeful work by Bill Torbert and another colleague... then writing my own response intended for collaborative discussion about the Greek sense of Eros, erotic love/friendship

You are linking erotic love to corporate psychology?

Well, yes, in the sense that it is a wholly ignored force/power within organizational work, professional relationships and friendships that usually ends up relegated to conventional setups, or within organizational life, sublimated to cheap affairs or passive aggression or avoidance. If harnessed or "integrated" in an intentional, mutual, structured way, it could ignite the pro-creative work that needs to be done in organizations and in the larger world...

You mean if people had actual sexual relationships with each other in the work place?

No.

That's what I understand "integrated" to mean.

Ok, well, integrated in the sense that we work to incorporate the power of the attraction in relationships for the purpose of the work at hand, rather than bury it. The argument is that in not doing so we relegate a very strong force of attraction to quick carnal satisfaction

144

– just having sex – when in fact it could be powerfully productive to use it otherwise... though everyone has to be post-conventional enough to be brave enough to do so... with great vulnerability come some very powerful working relationships.

Yes, but I don't know how you would stop two people from having physical relationships.

Ironically I think its a little bit of what you and I have going on, at least from my end... some sort of attraction that is at its root more about how we interact in relationship intellectually and psychologically (the potential for innovative thinking, effective work partnering, intellectual friendship) than a superficial sexual attraction. How we use it is up to us (if its mutual). When I've actually made this available to talk about and work with other times (only very few times so far) it has been SO COOL. I am learning...

Yeah, I agree we do have a well functioning relationship but if you were a guy and the same conversations were taking place... I don't think it is erotic.

Ok, fair enough, but if your concept of what is erotic is (to use our recent theory's lingo) "5th ordered", then it can be very much so. If your concept of erotic attraction expands and enlarges to include experiences of more than just physical, it begins to blend...

Well, our relationship started out as a teacher/student relationship with very defined boundaries and expectations, so we both sort of know what to expect from each other. (Pause) I'm saying in general, in a corporate setting, when you push people to open up with the opposite sex and take away boundary it would be inevitable for them to test the water.

I know, it pushes boundaries, tests them, and invites the setting of new boundaries. And, hence the precariousness of sharing something like that... but it's what I'm working on today and you inquired!

I (along with these colleagues) don't buy the inevitability of acting on the impulses in a sexual direction. And I would, with you, also challenge the notion that you need sex to know if you're attracted... phooey.

Figuring out attraction through the act of sex is so limited... because the attraction and the place from where it stems is so much more complex than that.

(The developmental approach) is basically an argument for making Object the experience of sexual attraction so you can examine how deep and far reaching it actually is... not just hormonal or visual. And how powerful it can be for people who want to do meaningful work... not just dealing with it by having a quick release or getting away from the object of attraction (normally what happens with unexamined attraction).

(He mentions the sexual difficulties of his divorce, essentially that sex doesn't equal happiness)... I've worked to move myself past this stage.

This is exactly what I'm/we're saying... relying on the physical aspect of sex to make or break our relationships is shallow, basic, limited, and yes, disappointing. One of the people I have talked a lot with about this is a minister colleague of mine (I end up running in ministry circles which are particularly difficult places for eros to become integrated or even acknowledged). This has become the primary way he understands his own sexual desires/attractions/impulses, as something deeper and more indicative of the people he could/should(?) be doing difficult work with. He and I experience an intense attraction and are working to open it up reflectively (not physically) and focus it on a shared sense of important work we are doing together... this would be what "moving past that stage of sex as a natural need or desire" means to me.

Well, and like most difficult or unintegrated things, we're socialized not to think about it, we're enculturated to understand sexuality as merely based in the physical act... We're rather dumbed down sexually. Reactions?

So what do you tell your minister? When I'm around you I'm super aroused, but I'm learning to express it more rationally?

Hahahaha! He's not "my" minister! But yes we sort of do that, but in a very specific purposeful context, with a very intentionally constructed understanding about how we will inquire, and with the hope of eventually having others reflecting on it with us. He's very post-conventional, and we are both still learning about how to do work like this. I like to think we are aware of the dangers of it, but we can't be fully and so at least we agree to make them available to reflect on.

No matter how complex you are, I still think that sexual release is a normal and natural thing. I mean, he must be a dumpster fire of pent up sexual anxiety…

Well yes, that's his business really and he WOULD be pent up except that he (and others including me) are practicing these disciplines in such a way that doing this kind of work does offer an experience of release that is greatly satisfying. Now, some central voices in the discussions I'm currently in would include physical satisfaction of these attractions in the exploration of a more full understanding of integrating sexuality/eros into meaningful work. But, I'm happily and actively and monogamously married. I don't do the abstinence discipline now. But I abstained from sex until I (in my late twenties) married my husband (in his early thirties) and so did he… a very intentional, interesting conversation that's linked to this one…

So I do have myriad experiences of both avoiding sexual attraction in order to not have to deal with it (in varying types of taboo relationships, professional and personal) as well as trying to use it in a different productive way in as many. The latter is FAR preferred but very complex and difficult to hold at first, as well as ongoingly… I am certainly still a learner and intend to continue as one.

(He shares about sexual partnering and inquires about the limitations of having only one partner)

Regardless, my experience has been that although I've only had one partner in sexual intercourse, I have had many sexual partners, just in other ways, expressing many aspects of my own deeper and wide felt-sense of sexuality. Some have been romantic (boyfriends) whom I definitely shared a sense of physically-boundaried, mutually-satisfying sexual expression with. But the others have been friendships that had sexuality integrated as a source of power and inquiry based in academics, ministry, co-teaching, supervision, or friendship. These are what are most interesting for those of us writing and exploring this topic…

Do you ever regret having only one person?

It is AMAZING! For us both, having no history, no hangups, no "well my last partner..." or "my next partner…" We're learning together in the context of the fullest human commitment we have, I have deep psych and emotional security... as well as our central, shared spiritual connection. Perfect storm for me, indeed. For him as well. We regularly revisit the decisions we made separately and then together with gratitude that is ecstatic!

Do you think you'll ever regret it?

How can I say now, but I can't envision it… BUT I will say (just to complicate things) my sexuality can't be fully creative solely in a physical relationship with my husband, my sexuality flows through everything I do, my work, my play, my relationships. I'm for the ongoing integration of it rather than categorization of it, sublimation or separation of it... crazy enough for you yet? You asked!

It doesn't sound that crazy. To use a golf analogy... my home course and the one I grew up on is probably my favorite course. I've played it a million times but to be a better, more complete golfer, I need to be playing other courses not only to improve myself as a golfer but also to improve how I play mine, because I learn different shots and techniques that I wouldn't otherwise learn or be exposed to. I think different "partners" can have this effect too.

That is the prevailing theory, and I won't know since I won't ever choose to test it but... there is also the angle of never really playing the same course twice: you are different, the wind is different, the day is different, your heartbeat is different, the other games are still present to you, etc. It's how deep you take your perspective of experience, how finely attuned you are to the subtle yet very present differences... What are you thinking at this point?

That: aren't there psychologists who say that having multiple partners is good or bad? What's the healthiest mean number? And how do they determine that?

I'm sure there are such numbers, but what we're thinking about is less (if at all) about how many physical sexual partners. It's not about physical expressions of sex at all but about attending to our experiences of our sexuality in relationships beyond the physical act that I'm/we're are interested in …

I've probably given you too much of my research-from-the-margins (not to mention my personal life!) for today. I'm off for lunch… if you want more on this, I'll gladly and honestly engage. But perhaps I should let you initiate…? We can talk about what you're interested in next time …

V: Convening Three-Day Alchemists' Workparties of a Dozen or So

A final, and an obviously far more advanced example of intimate, relational action inquiry, in terms of the level of commitment required, is the convening of a three-day workshop for friends or friends-of-friends, half men, half women to create a powerful, loving, inquiry-based, peer environment for one another to transform together. Each member of the group leads one 2 ½ hour session.

Each word of the title – Alchemists' Workparties – is carefully chosen and sculpted. The first word "Alchemists'" refers to the intent of conducting mutual social alchemy, within oneself and with others, to creatively marry opposites (spirit/matter, man/woman, elder/younger, theory/practice) rather than treating them as inherently alienated from one another or warring enemies. The members commit to engage in creatively marrying such opposites whenever they can imagine what that entails and can manage to do so. Also, as the apostrophe in Alchemists' makes clear, the Workparty belongs to all present. The word "Alchemist" also refers to the title of the rare leadership action-logic that Bill has found, through 50 years of leadership research, to be most adept (among the action-logics measured by the GLP) at encouraging personal and organizational transformation.

The second word of the title – "Workparty" – refers to the sense of these occasions as reconciling the particular 'opposites' of work and play, of being occasions engaged in for their own sake (leisurely play), but also part of a lifelong project of inquiry (intentional work). Politically speaking, the term "workparty" has a sort of comic 'Communist' overtone, given how non-abstract and non-ideological the good times of work and play together are. Perhaps, though, our workparties have had a Marxian quality of praxis – that is, efforts to attune our theory and our action through reflective conversation (Marxists, in contrast to action researchers, generally have been better at talking about praxis in theory than enacting it in practice). Even more apropos of our efforts, the word "workparty" can also imply a project that entails adventure and danger, such as trying to rescue people or rebuild washed-out bridges after natural or social disasters.

To give more of a taste of these occasions, here is an account of one Work-party at The Abbey in the English countryside.

On the first morning of our workparty, after convening the previous afternoon and evening, one participant shared an overnight dream. The dream included a scene where all gathered in The Abbey's shabby-comfortable living room, as we were now. In the dream, animals were looking in at the windows from outside, and three dead moles lay in the middle of the floor. It was suggested that the live animals looking in might have indicated we were meeting on behalf of all species, not just humanity. The dead moles seemed to refer to death and the underworld. But why? And why were there three moles?

Within minutes, however, Sarah and two other members, Catherine and Peter, declared themselves to be the three dead moles. Each of the three felt they had been living a kind of underground, deeply singular, solitary life, that each now felt ready to be born beyond.

The dream, and the three self-identified moles, proved to be enacting an ongoing transformational dance. Peter joined Catherine and another in monthly trio phone calls for two years afterwards. It was on these calls – that created symphonies of words, intonations, feelings, and silences filled with conscious inquiry – that the larger community first learned about the mutually-transforming power of such mutual, triadic, meditational, long-distance voice conversations.

Meanwhile, Sarah and Peter quietly rose toward love during the workparty itself, both feeling drawn to one another, until at the final evening's Masque Ball, each in their own adopted character and self-created costume, their mutual attraction reached overt verbal and non-verbal expression. Sarah, with her blue sapphire hanging at the place of the third eye, danced with Peter, who was playing the Vicar Something-or-Other.

That workparty left many a mark on most of the participants, the most marks of all on Peter and Sarah. These two erstwhile "dead moles" – she in her mid-forties and never before married, he in his mid-fifties and long divorced – married one another less than a year later.

The evening of their wedding outside London brought together representatives of distinctive spiritual traditions mingling easily with her parents' crowd, one entire large dining table reserved for Alchemists. The dancing after dinner was wild, until the even wilder rain outside flowed in over the flooring on the lawn and everyone slipped and fell in a hilarious wave of very wet folks in their best but besotted dress, giggling and hugging and fleeing for the inside-the-club-wedding-room…

Six months later, during their honeymoon in Italy and in spite of both plans and assumptions to the contrary, Sarah and Peter found themselves pregnant. And soon after that, Bill found himself dandling their newborn daughter in their new home southwest of London, during a long weekend's quartet among the four of them.

Hilary writes:

I have so appreciated the Workparties and what has come from them. I recall that I went to one of the first ones where I found a delightful tribe with whom to cultivate personal leadership and a deeper understanding of adult development. Professionally, too, this has become so important for enriching my teaching and coaching/consulting with regard to action research and leadership for sustainability. What with Peter and Sarah, myself and Nathan, and some others, it seems important to note that there may be a higher percentage of partner-matches that result from those parties than from most! But of course that is not the point. More key is this practice of active befriending which has been a great offering to many people. It is a seed I would love to see flourish for many more as we, society wide, seek to enrich our ways of community making. It sure beats watching TV. Thank you Bill. We are only beginning as a species to cultivate community with non-blood relatives. I think it may be the most important work for us this century.

We now invite readers who are interested in practicing more deliberately with likeminded people, or who seek support to practice with their own friends and communities to do so. Please contact us to learn more.

Good luck. Your relational action inquiry contributes to the evolution of us all!

Part 3

Chapter 10

Learning with Integrity

Big Love as Motherhood and a Guru

Born in a hot tub, my daughter's appearance marked it as one of the greatest moments of my life. All the preparations made were well used – even the selected soundtrack was perfect. The active labor was very long and in its way painful. And I loved every moment of it. Crazy to say perhaps, but it felt like a perfect meditation retreat. Nowhere to go and nothing to do but breathe.

I felt cared for by competent people. My husband, whom I'd met a little less than two years previously, was a surgeon at the hospital. Arriving in my life at a perfect time, like me he was also a professor and he was also single. We were ready to settle down. Well, what more could I wish for. We'd loved each others' minds from the start and had gotten engaged within six months, agreeing to become parents sooner rater than later?

I sat in the tub rather bovine-like. I used the time to marvel at my body. I had put on 60 lbs., which came as a great shock! It had become difficult to move. I had even gotten stuck in bed one morning, like a beetle. Unable to turn over, I had to wait for my husband to return from work. But my usual self-reliance took a vacation in the hormonal flood of relaxation. I declared it the most marvelous pregnancy ever, despite having no comparison. The constant nausea never actually bothered me – it's an odd kind of nausea where one feels pressed to eat just to feel better, but never actually does feel better. My sense of smell had become a superpower. I found for the first time in my life I forgot things, such as meetings with the Dean. And when I remembered I just didn't much care. I had fallen into a kind of blissful state. I felt myself as a Goddess – a sometimes rather demanding Goddess – God forbid I was made to wait in line at the grocery store or take the inside seat on a flight. Also a sometimes sweet and much softened Goddess. I started to offer more generous comments on student papers in celebration of my getting a semester off to take care of the baby. By the time I lumbered into the hot tub, our daughter was set up with clothing, a changing table and a cot by our bed. I even got all the accoutrements for breast-feeding as all upper middle class women aspire to. I would be shocked to find it so painful that I had to give up after a few days. But that was after I saw how perfect my daughter was.

When she emerged in the hot tub we locked eyes. I counted her little fingers and toes, marveled at her soft skin and knew she was perfect. After I heard her APGAR scores were fine, I allowed myself to faint. For the first time in 9 months a ravenous hunger arrived for it had been a 72-hour labor with no food.

Vision Realized

I had gone on a vision quest after my husband, my daughter's father, had asked me to marry him. I had gone to find out what was the right thing to do. Marriage made me nervous. And I felt needy which made me very careful about expressing the exuberance I felt at the excellent timing of meeting this marvelous man. On that quest, however, I had dreamed of a daughter and then settled into the idea that marrying would be the perfect thing to do. The vision quest came back to mind during the birth because like on a quest, which is a Native American coming-of age practice where one is alone for five days and nights deep in the wilderness and without food, I could not hide from the fear I felt.

Childbirth was also a time to go without food. As I had survived and thrived on my week's quest, so too again with childbirth. I had even become quite dependent on those around me. I experienced the birth as simply happening. Nothing to do. I learned that nature does not leave important things to us to decide. I learned – not in my mind but deep in my bones where it really matters – that life knows how to live. I just need to let it happen and stay as relaxed and awake as I can. It is not actually my life. Just life.

Suffice it to say, I can confidently claim that motherhood has gone well for us (famous last words!). It is one of the few places where I feel little need of advice. I usually simply know how to act. Life has moved beautifully. Clearly this teaches of love and its transformation. Perhaps the paradigm of transformational creativity in its most concrete manifestation is a child. And I have been blessed in this transformation. But if it sounds as though some equanimity had been reached, I was fooled.

Our delightful baby grew up a little and no longer needed all my attention. My husband's career had taken off and his creativity flowered. I followed his career to California. In turn I nurtured various projects having settled into an adequate academic position at a respected institution where I even enjoyed a promotion. I founded a not for profit to help reduce water use and to educate school kids about global climate change. In doing this I learned of the laws on the local books that rewarded unsustainable behavior. I joined the Green Party, remembering my coming to sustainability consciousness in Germany. I was encouraged to run for local election. I very much enjoyed beating a Republican incumbent. I took to local politics as a duck to water. The being in the know, the power plays, and most of all the ability to actually influence important things were very appealing to me. Not that I'd admit any of that except to fellow insiders. All politicians are painfully aware that most of our fellow citizens see budding politicians as little more than lost or poisoned narcissists. Certainly there are too many of those. But really, and perhaps to sound a little idealistic, why devote one's time to politics if not to make a positive difference? A liking for power is necessary. I liked power and felt fairly comfortable with it, wanting to feel more comfortable. I was intrigued by how to use it for a cause much greater than me. For sure I was also forced to deal with the smaller potatoes, the tiresome, politicized (surprise!) arguments that taught me a lot. I also saw that it was a way to assuage my growing personal restlessness.

Living in the Gap between Contentment and Reality

Something gnawed. It was not enough to simply recognize it as how life just is, evolutionarily designed as we are for dissatisfaction and restlessness that propels us forward as a species. Without fully knowing what "more" was, I felt I needed more. My "elsewhere-ism," a term coined with Ram, renewed itself. Elsewhere-ism refers to the desire to have things and be places other than being here, being now. On top of this, I felt ambivalent about admitting that I was unhappy. But with Ram gone I had lost my usual escape hatch. I felt I had exhausted all forms of earthly entertainment this life offers (home, family, career, politics, environmentalism,..). Beware the zealot. I turned with renewed zeal to Zen practice. When there is no exit, you sit down and shut up.

Now into my 40's, a common age at American Zen Centers, I had found a spiritual community at which I felt at home and in which I practiced as often as I could. A zealous Zen practitioner meditates daily, sits quarterly retreats (essentially looking at a blank wall for 12+ hours a day for a week) and meets with a teacher to discuss spiritual matters on a regular basis. She also reads about and listens to dharma talks, i.e., talks about Zen practice now available from all over the world on the iPhone (thank you Steve Jobs with himself a Zenophile).

Because the universe has a sense of humor, it so happened that my spurt in zealousness coincided with my community's taking up the issue of sexual scandals surrounding spiritual teachers. Our teacher, Daishin, a newly ordained Asian American priest, came from a lineage of teachers on the forefront of cleaning up the sexual scandals that had originally rocked the San Francisco Zen Center some twenty years previously. As our community had not had any incidents, it was perhaps more a sense of community solidarity but without any specific need that led to our lazily addressing this topic. My only intelligent contribution in our community meetings was to point out that the old style hierarchical relationship between teacher and students could, indeed, become problematic. More democratic structures were likely warranted which, as an organizational psychologist, seemed clear to me. I also heard myself say out loud that for me sex and power sum up to the lifeforce itself, that it is eros' job to mess with our boundaries. I added for the heck of it, "We'd be wise to expect things to go a little haywire if we are lucky enough to have eros come to play with us!" Silence greeted that visitation by eros and I laughed with a frisson, quite probably, of wishful thinking. Despite my explicit ambivalence on the matter of containing eros, there issued an invitation to me to join a committee to help develop new democratic structures for our sangha. Thus I met more frequently with a smaller group and, on occasion, the gentle Daishin himself.

Zen Mistress Not

Soon I found myself anticipating our committee meetings. I found myself thinking about Daishin far too much. But was that really so? Wasn't I just a zealous Zen student committed to helping my sangha? I grew skeptical of my effusive feelings. But then for maturing adults at least, isn't love to be invited to flow through and enwrap us with the energies of the life force itself? But really, wasn't my desire to attend committee meetings a tad too enthusiastic given our rather dull mission? It is hard to tell even now if the unfolding was tragedy or comedy for soon my puzzlement would end as I found myself sitting in a dejected heap – tears threatening, falling, drying up, starting over. I noticed the grin on the face of the seated Buddha on my home altar and I am sure Sidd (as I called him Sidd, for Siddharta) whispered, "What on earth were you thinking?!"

I say his name, Daishin's name. Surprised to find such tremendous love. Tears start over. There is even a touch of the benediction of the absurd.

In a perfect world, of course, I would not find myself in a dejected, deflated heap on the floor late one Saturday night after a sangha committee meeting. A Sinead O'Connor verse was breezing in my head: if he were just a little weaker, if I were just a little stronger. But in that same world I would not have just told my beloved spiritual mentor that I wanted to – well, it's what I'd implied that made me cringe. I had been unprepared for what I'd said. I doubt it was anything too cringe inducing. In all honesty though, I felt strong erotic pulls. It's just not my style to be so direct. And certainly not with Daishin. I realized that it had been so many months of yearning and longing for him and I could no longer measure out my love in coffee spoons.

Daishin had been very clear in response. He gave me a lovely hug. He'd been, as ever, kind. I mumbled apology. I was left with "ouch." Sadly this is no kiss and tell. Yearning, neediness, irregular eruptions of need to express my love, got all entangled in red hot sexual desire. Why should this be easy! I watched the moon poke through the dense clouds. Mars and Venus visible in the sky. The parents of eros, chaos and lust, the meeting of too much and too little.

It would be a minor omission if I didn't mention that it was not the first time I had expressed my desires to Daishin. I had just not been aware that I was doing so (so much for my years of mindfulness practice!). Not that these declarations were so clearly erotic in my mind – but certainly the same ballpark. I guess I'd started what I must admit were serial admissions of undying love some months previously. To my credit there had even been a decline of sorts. Very little had been expressed too indiscreetly. At least not face to face. And really, if you over-look my expressed desire to have a child with him (again, easy enough to miss), there are really only seemingly endless articulations and re-articulations of love, all of which are mere variations on the words "I love you," which are perfectly spiritual in their way. And along with this a few imprecations that we run away and live together Oh yes, those! But all in all, it was not too bad. Not really.

OK, we'd best overlook all the late night emails. How many? We could count them in the mere dozens. The Valentine cards were not as numerous, and there had been just a few small gifts. All in all though, a few months is a long time, what with holidays in between. So really, as we say in my country of origin, a blind man on a galloping horse might not have even noticed my ardor.

But my heart remembers the ocean when in touch with my feelings for Daishin. It's hard to fight an ocean. I had never known the longing for a "love su-preme" before. I love my daughter with a passion. I had loved my husband in our passionless way. But this love for Daishin was of another order of love altogether. Having come, finally, to recognize this love, it just seemed to keep bubbling over. I realized that my body seemed to know him when we first met. I was electrified. And I use the word advisedly – as I have been twice struck by lightning. Like a cat that got "furred out" when confronted by another creature in her territory. Some kind of response was called for.

When I finally got honest about the level of emotion I felt (which is not un-heard of between spiritual students and their teachers), along with its vast ele-ment of sexual desire in addition (much less is shared about that!), I explained to myself that I simply wanted to know and share the gift of life in this body. That part of this miraculous incarnation is to be loved – sometimes, impolite as it is to suggest it, that really means being fucked with love/love fucked, fuck-loved. I mention that just so there is no mistake that it was some sweet romance to fuel a mid-life crisis. Well, that may not be entirely true either. I wanted everything. I imagined, in G rated language, more about what I actually wanted. Delivered in the third person – just to add the merest hint of distance – she wrote a note to him:

She wishes then, just this once, without concern for others
feelings, to be able to nestle into his arms and listen to him speak

of himself. She might interrupt, but only occasionally to stroke his fuzzy head. And maybe kiss him lightly on the lips. And smile. And tickle his face with her eyelashes as he's talking – they are much longer than they look.

She'd make tea for them, it wouldn't be a big deal. It would be time out of regular time. Time to be together.

To touch him and feel his touch. To be wanted. Without all these words.

To inexorably reach to kiss him and be kissed and not to feel too bad if she gets a little undone – perhaps more cat than puppy. For she imagines a great well of sensuous expression and delight below the surface.

To give expression to what the heart wants. To be wanted. Like that. The way these things naturally unfurl, like desire itself. Always a surprise, a delight.

And why you ask would she want that –to be wanted – where could it lead and what would be the point?

To that she has no answer. Not now anyway. And frankly she is a little weary of feeling she has to have an answer. Feelings have no because. She wants simply to be wanted by the one she wants.

Next, she, my romantic, took the first dangerous dive in. She spoke to Daishin through Keats – written on a card for him during a duller than dull committee meeting. Somewhat apologetically:

I am forgetful of everything but seeing you again. My life seems to stop there. I see no further. You have absorbed me.

In response he was unfailingly kind – told me he loved me too, AND that nothing sexual could be/would be part of our love. Seeing me a little distraught he continued that he agreed it was a shame as the loving heart always wants to flow naturally and easily..."It's just that it can't. Not in our situation." I believe I heard hints at other lifetimes.

And perhaps because there is so little to hold onto I hold on dearly to what happened to close my first clear declaration to him offered in person. I had lingered to draw out discussion on some of the more esoteric meanings of the Heart Sutra (such a torrid scraping of the romantic barrel!). As he escorted me to the door, Daishin reached out his arms and asked me to dance with him. As he held me to him in a waltz of sorts, he stroked my hair and shared a favorite line "We are poor indeed if we are only sane." And we danced for a blissful eternity. He then helped me with my coat and saw me to the door where the brilliant afternoon sunlight of Los Angeles burned my already burning face.

The next step became immediately obvious to me. It was time to get married! Marrying things, all sorts of things, like rivers and mountains and even people occurred to me as a great idea. Inspired by performance artist Annie Sprinkle whose notion – very vague – of eco-sexuality intrigued me, I felt attracted by this term – a sexually infused eros that was more than just interpersonal, it was about saving all sentient beings. At the same time I was giving up – or giving up was happening to be more precise – that I could control too much of how this love would unfold. It seemed my job was to stand by and be embarrassed and charmed alternately by my activities. In this way Daishin was a significant erotic playmate – even as I joked I was so bored by the G rating of our play.

So soon enough I found myself arriving to Daishin and asking to be married "to the universe." Clearly the universe would include him, but I had enough delicacy not to be too pointed as to actually name him, for he seemed to have a great delicacy about him. Without missing a beat Daishin said he'd better put on his priestly robes to officiate. Using the formal text of a wedding ceremony and borrowing a rokusu (part of the formal Zen garments worn for ceremonies), I said the traditional Zen precepts and with Daishin's help married a universal self, vowing always to love life as it is. This vow I felt would best help me accept how this love between me and Daishin was to be. I wore my favorite blue Asian silk dress. Perfect. The honeymoon, however, was a real non event.

A song from what seemed like a previous life echoed. How do these old songs come back to us? I had to search for John Martyn's music in the recesses of my mind and then Google. I listened to the song Angeline far too many times. Angeline with her taste for trouble, loved without possessiveness, without fear of loss.

To love without attachment – perhaps that was the path on which this heart, mad for love of Daishin, was taking me. I wondered if perhaps all love affairs try at this – but we normally get so sidetracked by passion and its attachments. Then there are passion's lesser cousins – the shared furniture, dishware, life plans, plants and children. With Daishin I had none of the furniture and certainly no shared plans. I first decided and then began to actually feel, that love is just as it is and was somehow a gift not yet fully unpacked. And slowly I began to notice the freedoms offered by the lack of attachments – not that I wasn't deeply attached, but there was no formality to my attachment. This love could ebb and flow. Daishin asked little of me while allowing me the space to express what I felt. Holding what must have been a precarious balance, he neither encouraged nor shut me down. I felt it was OK to love him. I began to taste the freedom of a love affair in which I was entirely free to feel what was there.

Just as in my childhood desires were ignored, here I also experienced no resolution, but with a difference that made a great deal of difference. Daishin still ignored me, but kindly. Was Daishin perhaps my mother or father, or both when they were on their best behavior?! I did wonder if the gift here was an opportunity to right past emotional wrongs and to stand up as I had never done as a child (during silent meditations perhaps!), and scream my demands so as to overcome my being the ever self reliant? Thankfully, my soul stopped me in those plans and there was never anything too excruciatingly embarrassing. Certainly I missed having someone to advise me on so complex and delicate a matter. This is a rare kind of situation. If I looked a little more closely (of course by now I no longer trusted that I could even see the nose on my face!), I could see that my personality patterning was coming a little undone. Just a little? Thankfully by virtue of the personal dignity of all involved, and because the universe knows when enough is enough, my sense of scarcity of love began to move toward celebration of this rare gift whose effects began to be felt in other relationships where there was more freedom to act on feelings.

Clearly eros was also having a little fun – trifling with me. Certainly, a whole universe away from the torture of loving someone cruel! Some of that eros expressed itself as a number of little and big liaisons that even my conscious mind could see were an almost childish Daishin-sublimation-seeking effort. And such subtlety on my part – I even started up a romance with a priest of my own, a woman priest no less, though not of the Zen variety I hasten to add. But I won't digress as this is not a tale of kiss and tell! But, yes, I did occasionally also feel the need to fill the erotic void Daishin had created and Ram had finally vacated. It led me to consider that there are many types of love, of eros unbound. Though as Daishin put it, there is only "One Love" (or was that Bob Marley?). With and without guidance, our love story became a customized gateway to the magic of life, that lovely feeling of the excitement of infatuated love but somehow embodied in a lasting way as an ongoing chaperone through my life. Kind of like The Matrix, if happier, but without that really cool coat Keanu Reeves wears.

In moving to Portland I found another teacher who proved very helpful in integrating what had transpired. I could finally begin to see that my job – all our jobs – was simply to 'catch and release' – catch whatever experience is there, including a crazy love, and like a fly fisher release it. Some days I'd still feel hooked enough to be wounded, but more and more I could simply receive, feel enlivened, and let go. And in its way, this love for Daishin came to seem like an advanced course in catch and release – an advanced course with no class credits.

Developmental Discussion

In the past two chapters, we have seen some micro-examples of the power of liberating disciplines. One example occurred when Liz offered her story about her and Bill, which Bill then had the opportunity to read and reread, gradually absorbing the double- and triple-loop feedback inherent in Liz's very different patterns of interpretation of his acts and enactment of her feelings from anything he had imagined. Daishin's responses to Hilary's effusive declarations of love also have the quality of liberating disiciplines. Both his invitation to her to dance and his donning of robes to marry her to the universe are ironic responses – at once playful and serious, at once reciprocating intimacy and maintaining a distance, honoring the space between. We will see more examples of liberating disciplines in the Interlude that follows this chapter.

The main thing we see in this chapter about two kinds of supernatural natural love – Hilary's birthing of her daughter and her love with Daishin – is how much the biggest and most meaningful lessons of our lives catch us by surprise, like the earlier example of what Bill learned from the I Ching Blocks to Creativity exercise. As Hilary has repeatedly noted one of her primary personality characteristics can be named 'oral self-reliant.' As Gurdjieff said, our chief feature is precisely the one we ourselves have the most trouble seeing and liberating ourselves from. In neither of these two grand experiences of love could Hilary be fully self-reliant and control the outcome unilaterally. In one case she was wise enough to yield to Mother Nature herself. In the second case, she could do no other than yield to her Zen teacher in LA, who exercised the extraordinary wisdom of not yielding to her Siren-like entreaties to merge sexually. Thus did she begin to appreciate post-self-reliant experience, more consciously vulnerable and more mutual inter-independent ways of exercising power together.

Invitation

The first stage is to believe that there is only one kind of love. The middle stage is to believe that there are many kinds of love and that the Greeks had a different word for each of them. The last stage is to believe that there is only one kind of love. – Frederick Buechner.

Our aim with the book is to encourage depth of inquiry into the trickster domains of eros and power, of love under the sign of inquiry, with the hope that Eros/Power can flow more in all our lives.

Consider how sexuality and eros are, or are not, bound up with your spiritual life. Are these separate facets (as is the teaching of mainstream Christian religions)? Are eros and your spiritual life growing more integrated? What feels like the work that wants to be done and the play that wants to be had in this domain?

Chapter 11

Ever Tried, Ever Failed

The Interplay of Eros and Power with Bill's Beloved Work Partners

In the period after my retirement from academia in 2008, I put a lot of time into hosting 3-day Alchemists' Workparties among friends and colleagues. Even more of my time was invested in Paynesdonne Consulting, with which I had worked for nearly twenty years. This combination of business, family, and community felt to me like the Community of Inquiry, combining erotic work and friendship, that I had been edging towards all my adult life.

Oddly, from early on, my scholarly and consulting reputation grew more rapidly outside the US. I was invited to come every few years to play a leadership role in a four-day event, called Emerging Approaches to Inquiry held in the EU, and several of my books were published in the UK as well.

It was at one of these events around 1990 that I got to know Daniel and Kathleen, a bright, experimental, pixie-ish young couple who owned a growing consulting firm called Paynesdonne. Paynesdonne was ensconced in the French countryside just across the Channel. Soon we partnered in developing a professionally presented, commercially viable assessment and feedback process, based on the action-logic framework for adult development.

An endearing community of colleagues and friends and families gathered around our work at Paynesdonne, with ritual celebrations of inquiry at New Year's each year and in mid-summer, including weekend trips to music festivals and elaborate birthday celebrations at home, with skits and poetry to fit each occasion.

Kathleen and I were very definitely attracted to one another personally, as well as professionally, from the outset. Following my 'rule' for conversing with the senior partner, we raised the question with Daniel of how open he felt about Kathleen's and my potential sexual intimacy. He responded with definite emotional constriction that he did not want to open the marriage, nor to talk about it further. Although it was a sacrifice we never stopped feeling, she and I acceded to his preference. Our reward for prioritizing our trio'ing with Daniel over our coupling was a generation of joint work and friendship that I treasure, including moments widely spread apart when Kathleen and I might express some of our intimate feelings without breaking the agreed-upon boundary.

Paynesdonne had four directors including me. Although we generally made collaborative decisions on business matters, Daniel's voice in fact carried most weight.

By 2010, we moved to formalizing our collaborative decision-making process. For example, in cases where we did not reach consensus, a vote of all four directors was henceforward to be taken. Suddenly Juliette, a very bright and capable consultant/writer, arrived on the scene to help with our expanding enterprise. I was spending one of my two annual weeks with Paynesdonne, and it was obvious that Juliette was making an immediate positive contribution and working most intensively with Kathleen.

By the time of our first directors' meeting by Skype a few weeks later, it became clear that Kathleen had fallen in love with Juliette. It also became clear that she no longer had any intention of agreeing to a new voting procedure much less to any passive veto exercised by Daniel. For his part, Daniel was enraged and distraught, feeling a demon was haunting his family.

As the severity and the rancor of the split between the partner-couple began to emphasize themselves during that first autumn, I made a sudden trans-Atlantic flight to visit them, their children, and some of our close friends. Without knowing what I could do, it felt imperative to me to be present in the situation in whatever quiet way I could muster as the senior member of both the trio and the directors' quartet. It turned out that what I could mainly do was bear witness to the suffering, separately, of each member of the couple.

Daniel was unable to eat or to sleep (though still hard at work with clients) … and unable to feel support from any relationship with me or anyone else. I could empathize with him because of my experience forty years before with Linda … But it was shocking to realize what immediately became obvious – how fused the couple's two identities had been, and how disconnected his identity and mine suddenly seemed. This was a moment when I, were I he, would have appreciated masculine brotherhood. It was also a moment when I could feel why Kathleen needed to part to experience a fuller personhood.

I advised Daniel and Kathleen not to get separate lawyers, but rather a mediator to forge an agreement, which they could then seek further legal advice about … And this is how the process began. I also invited each of the three directors to come to Boston separately to visit me for a weekend in the early spring. Jill and Daniel did so, but Kathleen, amidst the juggling of business, family, new partner, and a divorce process, simply did not. At the time, the two weekends in Boston with Jill and Daniel felt like positive markers. But my communication with Kathleen was withering. Not only was no visit scheduled, for months we rarely spoke by phone. Even e-mails were scarce. At first, that seemed fine to me, because I assumed our relationship remained strong. But as events ran on I began to feel, to see evidence for, and finally to conclude that she was in fact actively avoiding contact with me.

Slowly, I realized that the business might not survive and that the future credibility of both our workshops on transformational leadership and the leadership measure were at stake. We, whose very business rested on integrating self with system and inquiry with action, were coming undone in apparently cliché'd ways.

When my e-mails went unanswered and directors' meetings went unheld, I realized my understanding of the company's interests were incompatible with the owners' behavior, and I resigned my role. I did not sue because I remain prudentially certain to this day that spending time and money on a court case is almost absolutely contrary to the primary goods of my life to date.

Finally Kathleen picked up communications with me, evidently guided by her intellectual property lawyer, to the effect that the copyright of the materials developed under the banner of Paynesdonne was vested in Paynesdonne as a legal entity (namely the partnership of Daniel and her). Stunned that Kathleen would allow a legal fact (that could be revised by our joint decision) to preempt our relationship and our joint decision-making capacity, I let the communication sit for a day. Next, I received yet another e-mail, this time from, of all people, Juliette. She professed despair that I was acting as a strategic game-player and not honoring Kathleen's choices, and asked that I join her in supporting Kathleen. Flummoxed by this interpretation of events, I wondered if Juliette, whom I did not know so well, might persuade Kathleen to talk to me in person. I attempted another outreach:

> Dear Juliette,
> Thank you for writing…
> I do want to honor and support Kathleen, and if she wishes to
> honor and support me as well, then maybe we can back away
> from a legalistic approach to the future (as I have asked in a
> letter sent yesterday to the Paynesdonne Directors), and talk
> on the phone this next week.
> With good wishes in this spiritually-grueling time for us,
> Bill

On the following day, Daniel wrote to oppose the legalistic approach of Kathleen. Almost before I could rekindle some hope, however, a next message arrived from Juliette, explaining to me at length that my own values of collaborative inquiry did not allow me to claim ownership of anything – not an argument in which I could find any sense. (One of the ironies of the struggle over ownership of the leadership measure and associated research is that the measure is not in itself a profit-making venture; I was trying to preserve my relationship to it, in order to continue the research necessary to maintain the ongoing validity of the measure.)

I remembered Kathleen as having had a strong voice in many ways during the twenty years of our friendship; now however, she seemed to have lost her voice with me, and Juliette and her lawyer were speaking in her stead. Nevertheless, Juliette's tone seems to throw reflected new light on Kathleen's state of mind as well. How would Kathleen – how would I? — now be seeing the world if Juliette's voice had been both the loudest, the softest, and the most frequent in my ear over the past year?

When Kathleen finally did talk with me by Skype, she dissolved into tears, saying she had to trust her new partner and her lawyer. I thereupon withdrew from the dispute, which continued for another year and a half.

The Dark Side of Camelot

In retrospect, as I worked through my grief over six months at the uprooting of this long, fruitful friendship and partnership, I realized that from an emotional perspective, I had too often indulged during the prior years in a sentimental illusion about Paynesdonne. We even talked about Paynesdonne as Camelot – half jokingly, but half in awe. And indeed, the rituals celebrated by the community of friendly families who converged on Paynesdonne itself or at a summer weekend's music festival were often mythic in their distinctiveness and memorableness. Who could ever forget the building and planting and burning of the 20-foot high wooden birds in their field for Kathleen's 50th? Or the poets' readings and the singer's arias at Daniel's 50th? Or the transformation of Paynesdonne's cobblestone courtyard into a Turkish seraglio for another of the communal celebrations that always included the children as full members? In some ways, one can criticize me for being falsely and sentimentally over-identified with our Paynesdonne trio and community... So much so that I remained blind to the real developmental patterns we were exhibiting... So much so that a significant proportion of my inquiring vigilance was missing in action.

In addition to gradually recognizing my emotional over-identification with Paynesdonne, I also developed a serious intellectual critique of my conduct in our trio relationship and our business relationship at Paynesdonne across the years. I had idealized our individual action-logics, treating my younger partners as operating at the Transforming action-logic with complex-system-leadership capabilities, when in fact both their actions and mine within Paynesdonne almost always reflected earlier action-logics instead. Moreover, none of us seriously applied my theory of how organizations develop to Paynesdonne, nor did Daniel and Kathleen apply that part of the theory to their client engagements. I can now also see with painful clarity that I did not encourage our trio to continue its development as a trio, nor in any of its three dyads. In the end, the trio and its dyads were spread-eagled across the Diplomat, Expert, Achiever, and Redefining action-logics, with the later Transforming and Alchemical action-logics manifesting themselves only on particular mythic occasions, in occasional participant breakthroughs in workshops, and in occasional organizational transformations through our consulting. Since I was the senior member of the team in terms of age, in terms of both scholarly and consulting experience, as well as in terms of my supposed action-logic, my culpability in the Lear-like outcome is therefore in some ways foremost among the four directors.

In sum, the Paynesdonne collapse became the worst personal, organizational, spiritual tragedy in which I've participated. I grieved deeply the loss of our Paynesdonne community, while trying to absorb what it teaches about impermanence, about the fragility of transformational inquiry, and about the partiality, rather than impartiality of my own attention in matters where love, power, and inquiry interweave. The fact that this collapse occurred after my retirement in my late sixties made me wonder whether my entire life project was, not the exploration of a new frontier for humankind, but rather nothing more than a quixotic dream. Eventually, however, I began to take note of the messages coming from colleagues and friends wishing to create a new, more power-symmetric, more truly inter-independent community of inquiry. The harsh lessons I took from my relative lack of active attentiveness to, and dearth of developmental analysis of, our organizing, our relational, and our individual patterns at Paynesdonne have been much more alive in me these past four years than ever before, in the midst of my most meaningful projects and relationships.

Hilary Comments:

> Bill, thank you for sharing this so honestly. It's a case for a Masters level class in the use of power and feedback. It's certainly not simple and for many it illustrates why unilateral power and seeking to master and control others may be the safer bet than seeking mutual power. Clearly that is not how you (or I) see it. And while you might have preferred a quite different outcome, the demise of Paynesdonne has been a positive catalyst for you to develop your work more actively (and with a little more consideration of intellectual property!). This is important to point out, because part of later adult development is really about trusting that breakdown will lead to breakthrough, even when it is at first entirely out of reach. Systems reconfigure. And I was delighted to hear that you managed to have dinner recently with Daniel, if only for old time's sake. You are good at keeping the chan-

nels of friendly communication open, waiting for the right moment for furthering the inquiry.

That said, I can't help but note, however, how uncomprehending you seem to me about Kathleen. Though strong, she may also have experienced herself as voiceless. My using the term "voiceless" here again throws me back to what I wrote earlier and from which I detoured into a reflection on a Nobel Prize winning novel by Coetzee about the effects of colonization. Kathleen was economically dependent on Daniel. It is indeed possible that she grew up used to being without her voice. Thinking of The Psychology of Women, a breakthrough book at the time (70's), Baker Miller points out that women's socialization as the one "who takes care of others" is so deep as to normalize loss of herself. This loss does not show up as psychosis or odd behavior; it is entirely normal! In fact retrieving that lost self – and often, as in this case, it may mean leaving the husband, may be seen – socially – as the problem of feminism. And it's quite a social "problem." Today over 70% of divorces are requested by women.

As hard as it is for you to hear it, which makes it hard for me to say it, it appears to be very hard indeed for men to understand their taken-for-granted-privilege. And this is especially the case for those who have inherited the trappings of social power, by virtue of their 'WASP heteronormativity,' as today's academic jargon would put it. And while it's not your personal fault, you're an enlightened man, it is your responsibility (as it is mine, as demonstrated by the spirit of this book) to take responsibility for the tortured male/female dance. But what is required of us? Is it that you take account, if you can, of the impersonal claim to power that just naturally accrues to you. But to do so you'd have to endeavor to become more aware of what is necessarily transparent to you? That's what makes it so tricky. Power works, as Foucault describes so well, by being invisible. We experience privilege differently. Perhaps that is where I can help, and we can help each other.

When I think of power that accrues to men who look like you, I see the power of social confidence, or to walk unimpeded by gnawing concerns for your safety if it's growing dark: the power to walk in a shopping mall and have customer service be ready to help you without assuming you want to steal, the power to have women and men listen to you first and foremost in a gathering, the power not to have to be so concerned with how you look, the power to have others want to unconsciously flatter and cajole you, the power to have women's ostensibly innate lack of confidence (or more positively, innate risk aversion) serve your freedoms in intimate relationship in that they will always be more careful with you/your relationship then you will be. The power to be paid well for your time, the power to see people like you in positions of power everywhere, to have the English language speak mostly of you. The power to not worry about being sexually harassed. The power to resist notions of structural power, insisting instead to look solely at power as primarily or solely concerned with individual acts. The power to think I am raving on a little too long here about white men's privileged power as if I have forgotten who I am talking to.

The power, the power…. OK, I won't go on. Not that there is even much to be done here, except to let it in. This impersonal privilege is not about you. It is not your fault. This privilege, however, is your responsibility. We are holding ourselves responsible for how power is manifest to and through us in first, second and third person guise. In truth it is most effective to address first person and then second person arenas. That's why we are writing this book. Yet clearly we also remain ever open to how third person forms of power outside ourselves operate and shape the first and second person personal and interpersonal expressions.

Bill comments:

Hilary, I mirror your language in thanking you for sharing this comment so honestly. You are right that it is difficult for me – in spite of my deep commitment to gender equality and relational mutuality my whole adult life, and in spite of my intellectual recognition that historic differences in gender and social class power privilege me and other men – to appreciate how deeply these power differences reach into life's every moment. I am therefore very glad you've spelled it out in (some) concrete detail above, both for me and for other white senior men to rub our faces in, to truly contemplate.

My way of taking on responsibility for my white, male privilege has been primarily to try to co-generate increasingly mutual relationships in all my work and leisure activities. This means engaging in vulnerable conversational inquiry, not buttoned-up, ideological monologue. It means sharing power, not wielding it unilaterally. It means exploring boundaries, not taking them for granted. But, since conventional wisdom has it that power comes from outside ourselves – from impersonal roles, institutions, and resources (guns and money) – such explorations toward mutuality by the 'high status' person are always at risk of being interpreted as illegitimate unilateral moves (especially since high status positions are usually enacted unilaterally)... and, the initiatives become unilateral by default, if the other does not overtly respond.

I think my difficulty is multiplied in regard to women like Celia when I was at Harvard, like Kathleen at Paynesdonne, and like you – women who have powerful voices in many regards. I would like to understand how I can do more to get beyond low-power responses that my reputed high status generates. Has Juliette done more to evoke Kathleen's voice? I think the evidence I present suggests that Juliette's voice may have amplified some aspects of Kathleen's voice, but seems also to have substituted itself for her voice once again. Bringing out our own and one another's full voices is clearly one of the ultimate 'tricks' (or liberating disciplines) of collaborative inquiry.

Invitation

Our aim with the book is to encourage deep inquiry into the trickster domains of eros and power with the hope that Eros/Power can flow more in all our lives.

How are your work-related relationships? Are some eros tinged? How have you been able to navigate the difficulties and opportunities? Are your work relationships creative? How might Eros/Power be enacted more powerfully for professional expression?

Chapter 12

Hilary's "Valentine Dharma":

Inquiry into the Eros of spiritual life

"Let the soft animal of your body love what it loves."
– Mary Oliver (Wild Geese)

My practice for decades, having felt no welcome in the Catholicism of my up-bringing, moved to the practice of Zen, which, like almost all patriarchal spiritual traditions today, has little place for eros. In the following I share reflections from a talk I offered to my community sangha on a recent St Valentine's Day in which I seek to consciously integrate eros, power and inquiry as spiritual practice.

It feels timely to share what's crystallized for me over my two years of almost full time spiritual 'work' here that ended with the start of the Year of the Snake which itself precipitated great transformation, too. For me this is the closing of a transformational time that began at the Solstice, and included the important festivals of Christmas and New Year.

I am wearing a version of St Brigid's cross around my neck, with its Celtic infinity and cycles, an integration of body with spirit. I grew up in Ireland and this time is part of the druidic/Pagan cycle of new year that starts on Feb 1 with St Brigid's day. Brigid is often overlooked in favor of that more famous Irish saint, St Patrick. He who chased the snakes away! Christianity and the patriarchal tra-dition generally don't like snakes. For the patriarchal tradition, the beginning was the word. For the snake types in the Chinese zodiac, however, the snake is the archetype of transformation (they shed their skin) and are considered quite erotic (check out the YouTube videos). There the beginning is love. Love in the body as we first know of love with the mother. Or with the sun that warms the Earth and brings all life, all mothers. It is for the sun that we honor the Solstice. As I like integrating things – indeed my journey these past two years has been a conscious journey of integration – I will put some words on this love I call eros.

I also love the further Greek synonym "Erota," with Erotes, plural. To remember that eros has plural forms is key.

Why all this mention of spiritual traditions? To hold this larger context, if lightly, is important. When you give up the centrality of the self – stop organizing life as only egocentric – context is more interesting. One finds oneself not by asking our mind but by finding ourselves in the environment we're in. And today it's Valentine's.

You may have heard of Eve Ensler's "The Vagina Monologues" – they are now often staged on Valentine's day. This is Eve Ensler whose work in the Congo has caught my admiration for years. The Congo has the world's most violent rape and at the highest levels. It's part of a war over natural resources that the West wants for our iPhones (and full disclosure, I own one). Eve, named for the mother of Creation, called the "Billion Rising" events into being. She has a very inspiring poem called "Over it" as in we are so sick and tired of the sexual violence everywhere. So I went on a dance-march on Thursday and I took my daughter. It's hard to explain the madness of rape to a little girl with an undefended heart. The undefended heart truly doesn't get that the hunger for love that we all feel could ever manifest as rape. It's so counter intuitive. Rape to love.

There is an interesting debate in the civilized societies of Northern Europe right now about legalizing prostitution. The state feminism of Scandinavia stands in contrast to France where prostitution is legal. One wonders if a Dominque Strauss Kahn could have been born Swedish? Alice Schwartzer (a German feminist of some renown) insists that prostitution is rape and that untransformed male sexuality is predatory, because it allows men to feel that they can have whatever they want as long as they pay for it, even if it is the use/abuse of another human being's body. There is pushback from men who say that normal male sexuality itself is being demonized by feminists. Confusing this civil discourse is that illegal human trafficking is very much a part of all prostitution nowadays and is something presumably few civilized people would defend. And there are those relatively few women who insist that sex work is their choice for capitalizing on their erotic capital. The debate is interesting because we are clearly transforming what is experienced as "natural" female and male sexuality as we fumble in updating ancient biological and cultural scripts about gender.

In San Francisco, always a little ahead of the curve, we see the work of Nicole Daedone's One Taste who calls her students, women and men, to hold the pleasuring of women within a rigorous spiritual practice. (The French must find us odd indeed!) Still it is an evolutionary leap that women's pleasure is put at the center of any movement much less a spiritual one. A common statistic is that 60% of American women do not experience orgasm. Presumably if the number for men were as high, funding of the Pentagon would be redirected with overwhelming congressional approval. But women, our comfort in our bodies, our joy and self-expression in life, somehow not quite so important.

And then there's good old St. Valentine's day itself – a lovely festival of love. In Europe St Valentine's is usually only a celebration between lovers. I was a little horrified at first when I came to the USA and saw little kinder-gardeners being encouraged to give Valentine cards to each other! How perverse I thought. Then I realized that love had lost some of its majesty because it had been infantilized, de-eroticized. But it certainly sells more Hallmark cards. This twisting of core life needs – what is greater than the need for love – makes for billion dollar industries after all. So starved are we all, it's an inexhaustible marketplace! Don't most spiritual traditions reinforce that very starvation? So my inquiry is in part about what has been lost in that disappearance of eros, that part of love, including spiritual love, that would be sexy.

My talk is also about the emergence of eros in my life over the past two years. But this emergence of eros through me was felt and acknowledged at first at a cellular, not an intellectual level. The body is the site of eros coming to awareness of herself, a body at home with herself.

My inquiry today which I have been hinting at is a little scary to me to be undertaking with you. My being scared is neither primary nor solely egocentric. It's a collective scared. Scared for how women all over the world are treated, and because of my own Irish and Catholic background scared especially for European women. There was a time when women were burned alive in the Middle Ages. Hundreds of thousands, some insist it was millions over centuries. Maybe that ended at the Salem witch trials, or maybe not, given that the report of pervasive rape (perhaps in its impact not so very different from burning at the stake in terms of its reinforcing fear) may still be the tip of the iceberg.

The crime of these witches (bitches?) was that they were bewitching, referred in old English as being "glamorous." Beautiful women, strong women, brainy women, priestess and healer types were burned for being glamorous. I like that this word has been retrieved even if most don't understand or reduce the importance of women's erotic glamor – which is an essence, a soul quality. Not a style of clothing – though it animates those kinds of choices too.

Let's imagine for a moment what it was like to be burned alive – in the town square no less. That's how it was for centuries in Europe. Your neighbors gawking. With the brief exception of Renaissance Venice, women's lives were awful before contemporary times. Today the lucky ones, those of us with a good enough life may live more fully in the public space once jealously defended by men. Imagine how glamorous women felt about themselves back then! Men who loved glamorous women must have been scared or guilty too. Gay men were their allies. They were thrown on the bonfires too, as kindling, hence the word "faggot." Women who had glamorous daughters were perhaps very scared. Think of how we parent our little girls. Repression works best when it is inculcated at the cellular level and defended as the right way to be.

The talk of women being burned alive induces an experience of body tension for me. One of my favorite Yiddish terms is verklemt – feeling of being tense, uptight, unexpressed, sexually repressed. Clearly this verklemt was not an accident. It's not me or mine. It's a cultural conditioning. Very deep. I have been intrigued to read Naomi Wolf's book. Stupendously, it's called Vagina. One of the important themes is that women's biochemistry is such that threat, especially of a sexual kind, not least those subtle ones we call "hostile work environment," impair the cognitive functioning of women. Sexual threat shuts women down. And women hold up half the sky as the Chinese say. Societies where women are repressed are repressive, femicidal and ecocidal. It all goes together – they kill off women, nature and political dissent – think of Pakistan or Saudi Arabia. The world of Taliban. The Tea Party! How we treat women, is how we treat nature and the world around us.

So if you want to repress women and men who love women (as well as men who love men and women who love women) – repress eros! This is, of course, exactly what the priests and rabbis and Taliban want. The conventional pornographers want it too, of course. That is one of the hugest industries of all. A repressed people is precisely an un-liberated people, an exploited people. Conventional pornography exploits its consumers as much, and certainly more profitably, than its actors and models.

The most foundational thing to share is precisely the hardest to share. Hard because to speak of the body and to speak personally is culturally taboo. It doesn't make sense – it's on a par with insisting that we not admit we breathe oxygen, except that it's been this way since Plato. He didn't hold the body or women – the two are linked – in high esteem. He didn't think much of practical matters – matter and mother have the same etymology. And the rest of Western civilization has been footnotes to Plato. It really matters what Plato thought and all the priests who followed him. All the way to today.

An erotic awakening happened for me some 18 months ago. It may, in retrospect, have been facilitated by a deep catharsis over the death of my brother. I had it during a meditation retreat. But whatever, I'll simply say that what we know as the second chakra, the sexual center, came alive in a most noteworthy way. The erotic awakening happened in the safety of my own home!

Little of human experience is unique. What I do know, however, is that almost no one speaks of such things. So I walk here between taboo and the tantalizing.

Frankly, at first I did not know what had hit me. I knew myself as an educated, intellectually centered woman. This "waking down" did not come through my head. It came through my body. I wondered OMG, what is this?!

I visited my doctor. It felt like an emergency so I met with a male doctor – nice guy but not ideal. He listened, puzzled. In the end he said there seems to be nothing actually wrong! He also asked if I were depressed in any way (perhaps he was considering if there were depressive episodes to match the apparent mania. Clearly, I was beaming!). I told him quite the contrary. After establishing that the primary symptom was the unusual but not life endangering experience of ongoing orgasm, he smiled and said "Well then Hilary – go enjoy yourself!"

So I followed the doctor's orders! Perhaps a little too much. The energetic quality was at first really un-integrated in me. I became, in a way, a little bundle of eros. Being a woman of the world I also had some delightful erotic dalliances with lovely people. After all I am a lay practitioner, I said to myself – which naturally led to the big insight on the difference between a monk and a lay practitioner: A lay practitioner gets laid. That'd be my path!

Finally I could slow down a little and I was able to look at all this. That is what a good meditator should do, right?! But had anyone said to me at the very start, "just be with the energy" I think I might have exploded with derisive laughter. But all changes. I began a daily practice of tai chi and then yoga – the practice of looking at how life wants to move (rather than me moving life), especially in these gentle traditions, was an important thing on seeking to integrate this new energy.

Tantra was an important practice during this time. Portland has a wonderful Tantra community. Tantra is often reduced to being "only" about sex. And if when something is about sex it must be diminished as part of our pervasive "either/or" dualism, it is yet another facet of the Cartesian catastrophe that warps the relationship between mind and body. Odd isn't it, that we get so alternatively derisive and diminishing over something that, let's face it, is literally about the possibility of the continuance of our species. What was important was that tantric yoga helped me reframe my experience of eros as a central part of my spiritual work? Practices are often as simple but unusual as "erotic meditation," which is the practice of giving and receiving touch with great attention to sensation, specifically our clinging to certain sensations and our aversions. The body speaks clearly. This body-mind feedback is therefore very ordinary but powerful to learn about with another.

At first I couldn't see the erotic as spiritual. Well why would that be easy? Our very conditioning relies on this separation. And for what? To be charitable we might say all the priests, knowing the power of eros, wanted to prevent predation of innocent bystanders by avoiding and exiling the Erotic. Hardly. Our society overstates the hurt of eros – when, ironically, it's the secrecy and repression of erotic development and full, sustainable mutuality that is probably doing way more damage. Certainly to the little children hurt by the priests.

I also began to read a little – the Internet is a great friend to the marginalized. Terms like "Kundalini awakening" and their descriptions of biochemical changes really resonated as true to my experience. I was also intrigued to learn of debates that still go on about women's (sexual) anatomy. Much of this confusion can be attributed to, I believe, a continuing mystification over women's bodies. Though, yes, it seems the biochemistry truly is more complex. Here is one little tidbit – women have, or at least can have, three different types of orgasm, in the sense that each type travels different neuro-circuitry. Men only have one type. And no doubt part of the mystification has resulted from too many male scientists assuming their own experience. I might even recommend some reading material – try Diana Richardson's Slow Sex. I see this work as decidedly revolutionary in how sexuality itself is practiced as a path to spiritual unfolding. It's also great fun to do the practice.

Something else came with the bodily/energetic awakening – a new experience of brain function. This intrigues me greatly. I would say that in effect I lost the capacity for neuroticism in most parts of my life. It used to be the case that I could spend forever noodling problems in a neurotic way. Now it is literally that my brain simply won't go there. At least for most issues. So when confronted with a problem I just relax and let life handle it. The right thing will happen. I trust that I will be moved to say the right thing. I will have time to do it when it's timely. Or so goes the relaxed thought. Seeing this separation my mind was making between sexual-erotic focus and spiritual focus created a lot of internal dissonance. But dissonance always seeks to reduce itself. So I finally got the connection – they are one thing. So obvious now, yet so hidden for too long.

The American Zen and Buddhist communities have not been spared our share of sordid, because covered up for too long, scandals. The Sasaki case comes to mind, famously notable perhaps because Sasaki was Leonard Cohen's teacher and was well over 100. Who needs viagra when you meditate daily?! When I hold all the sexual harassment he has created over decades in my heart, along with the too much sexual harassment I experienced when I was younger, I feel into the screaming silence of not enough listening to the truth about these intimate matters. An analogy we could learn from is the AIDS crisis in the West. In the mid 80's we began to learn that we will either die from embarrassment or we will learn to speak up. In speaking up we had to use embarrassing new words like 'condom,' which has almost become a household term today. Safe sex was the catch phrase then. Perhaps mindful sex may become the motto today. Let's speak up/clean up our erotic starvation and misery. Women and men. Together.

Speaking of this and the aspiration for women and men to partner in tackling the screaming silence, I also recall an occasion of sexual harassment that I experienced in a professional consulting context. What I recalled, apart from the demeaning and vulnerability inducing self-doubt, was what had happened with my consulting teammates. My mostly male teammates defended me with great energy. And that came as a surprise because there is the risk of pissing off a high paying client in any consulting context. But more than that, their empathy touched me. I realize I had expected they'd be oblivious and at best tell me to "get over it, move on." Perhaps and even likely, I was projecting my own lack of empathy with that more vulnerable part of me. Instead and happy-healingly, I felt loved and appreciated by these teammates, embraced in a protective bear hug. They were more punishing of the predatory client than I would have been at the time. This helped undo the extreme vulnerability that happens in a hostile work environment. One of the saddest things is that harassment can make women feel that all men will sell us out, because the vulnerability makes us so wary. And though we feel we can't ask for support, we also wonder why no one helps. But in fact so many men can and do bring support that liberates all women and men. Indeed that is the message of the new public health announcements to men and women on campuses, which we are learning are as plagued by sexual violence as is general society. We don't have to tolerate sexual harassment, predation by a few men, we can help one another already!

My erotic journey is a more collective women's erotic journey with its terror of being burned at the stake. And maybe in its modern form that's the fear of being a slut – or of not being taken seriously, of being abandoned. Can the feminine be intellectual and erotic and loved?! Of course there is also more joy and excitement when eros can show up.

During this erotic awakening unfolding, in my professional life I was promoted to Full Professor – which means going to the top of the academic hierarchy. Not to blow my own trumpet, ahem, but it's not an easy thing to achieve as it requires a round of anonymous evaluations from people around the world, adjudicated by a panel of professors from different disciplines, and so it is never a sure thing. I hadn't quite felt like I "needed" to become full professor... So when I was promoted I recall wondering how to use this gift to serve. What I felt was I had been given a gift of additional fortitude, of courage. The girl who had been sexually harassed could use a shot in the arm, so to speak. I wondered how I might be able to use this gift to support the courage I need to continue my journey wherever it takes me.

This feminine journey needs courage. Even with fortitude, it takes effort to speak. Women suffer too much from self-doubt, which may well be anchored in a biological difference between male and female brains that makes women more risk averse and hence less confident. But this compounds the subtle and gross repression of feminine eros. Time to speak up. In doing so I know how much this integration of eros on my path has allowed that I have come more alive – become more of myself. That my body gets to lead, with my mind following. That's still so surprising to me! It's about letting life come to me rather than shaping it to my will. So easy and so difficult for a mind so practiced in making things happen. My professional work, and life more generally have come more alive as a response.

Let Go, Let God.

For a long time, I used to think that Buddhism was a nice path, not really a religion in its Zen form, so rational, so amenable to scientific accounts of mindfulness. And in a way it is true. The Dalai Lama, America's teddy bear, hangs out with scientists. But if you take that we are relational quite seriously, (the Buddhist term is no self), what a fantastical metaphysical world we live in! There is sub atomic swirl in which these body-minds take form. Life itself lives through us, as opposed to we live our (individual) life. There were hints of this much bigger sense of self for me as an erstwhile student of Western philosophy For example Hegel's notion of Zeitgeist suggests that phenomena simply arise simultaneously, all over, rather than from the product of an individual mind. The term for this is "pan psychism." Asian thinking, of course, has always had more of a sense of the collective self.

I would say that one of those archetypes of the collective unconscious today arising is eros of the Feminine. Existence is calling something more joyful, more partnership oriented, more erotic and honest into existence. And Life/God/The Sacred Mystery/Shared Intelligence calls eros through these forms we call our bodies. So it's not really "my" business at all but to be a channel. Ideally to be a channel that releases from all that hinders all of us. So that is the impetus for sharing today. It is not really my story – it is our story – but I am the one speaking first.

I link eros with divinity. Inquiry into the intelligence of the body and sexual experience, is a way to allow more resilience of what is already healthy and whole (holy) in me and therefore in the world. Evolving humanity and devolving divine awareness in an erotic dance together, a kind of mutuality that gives life to a way of living that can serve all sentient beings. We can honor the hunger for love as honorable.

I know there is a global phenomenon of dark sexual – perverse sexual – grasping cruel sexual rapaciousness, the very opposite of eros. One thinks of that man in Cleveland not too long ago who kept malnourished women in chains in his basement, for over a decade. What intrigued me most in his trial was his insistence that he was not an abhorrent monster. Was this simply unrestrained male sexuality? Yet another sign that women must step forward and partner in leading us to a new society. I think women can do a good job (I can't think of a genocidal maniac who was a woman, can you?). It feels terribly important that we allow for the alchemical mix of eros with spirit, eros with intellect, eros with love. Rape of the body is not separate from rape of nature. Tremendous hunger, rapaciousness lingers in our DNA and can't simply be repressed the way patriarchy encourages – which of course makes sure that it lingers and grows. In Ireland we know sexual repression better than most and we have an avalanche of pedophilia to prove it. Repression will never help.

Eros can be embraced and danced with and honored for the joy it brings, acknowledged as the wellspring of creativity that eros is. We have been afraid far too long. I want a world in which eros speaks its name, with women playing a partnering role in that speaking together with men, regardless of sexual persuasion, giving space to all our hungers, all our energies, all our joys. We have had too much of the patriarchal take on eros. It's not been attractive. Though patriarchy's pornography sure sells well, much like cheap, fast food to an obese crowd. But I suspect we all yearn for slow food for the slim crowd. Slow sex, like slow food, for the erotically mindful. And you?

Invitation

Our aim with the book is to encourage depth of inquiry into the trickster domains of eros and power, of love under the sign of inquiry, with the hope that Eros/Power can flow more in all our lives.

How much more honesty about the eros of everyday life could there be for you? How much more permission could you give yourself to speak about what's true and real and emerging for you as eros comes to know herself in your life? What's to be liberated? What happens when you bring the light of inquiry to the energy of sexuality in your life? What can you share from that, be it as aspiration or as desperation?

Chapter 13

Eros/Power Fails Better?

Ever tried, ever failed, never mind, try again, fail better.

Samuel Beckett

Although this book is primarily about our, Hilary's and Bill's, attempts to exercise Eros/Power in our inter-gendered friendships earlier in our lives, we draw to the close by describing a little of the present...

Bill writes of his contemporary inter-gendered friendships:

As I have previously mentioned, a Community of Inquiry of about two dozen members, half men, half women, including both Hilary and myself, emerged after some years of inviting friends to Alchemists' Workparties. This far-flung community serves as a home base for the ongoing practice in everyday life of mutual power, love, and inquiry. Different subgroups of us meet twice annually for three days, to deepen our own capacity for practicing collaborative developmental action inquiry in a timely fashion with one another. We represent not only different genders and life stages, but also very different faith traditions, and very different human love commitments – from celibacy to monogamy to polyamory. In my case, for the past five years I have been exploring how erotic, emotional, intellectual, and spiritual intimacy can exist together in non-possessive intergendered relationships, even where we are rarely together in the same physical space and in which we collaborate to bound our expression short of sexual intercourse, but not short of the most tender and intimate of meditative touch and sensual dance. (This boundary-setting has admittedly become easier in my 70s, as I have experienced 'erectile relaxation,' a relaxation I find no urges nor reasons to try to undo with little blue pills.)

Influenced by my experience of writing and talking about my relationship with Hilary as we crafted this book, I have done so repeatedly with a number of the others in the Community of Inquiry as well, and our three-day meetings are characterized by honest and challenging feedback among all the men and women present, as we try to better understand the exercise of moment-by-moment mutuality among us. These exchanges and letter-writing exercises have helped me to untie long-time knots of fixed perceptions with several other members, bringing further understanding and relative ease to several of my ongoing relationships.

But speaking of these erotic same-gendered and inter-gendered relationships in the aggregate is somewhat unsatisfying, so, let me conclude by briefly characterizing one of my contemporary erotic friendships with a woman. This relationship is about a decade old, and, like virtually all my close friendships nowadays, involves our being in the same place no more than two or three times a year. E-mail and Skype has been our principal medium of contact during these years, and we have spoken once or twice a month. Thus, this is a story of how love can explore itself in the context of an outwardly narrowly-boundaried relationship and across vast distances. As Hilary does in sharing her contemporary story with Nathan next, I try here to offer fragments of an ongoing inquiry into intimacy. My friendship clearly includes an erotic quality and deep care for the other person, but is not a conventional couple-like or sexual-intercourse-like relationship. It is an intimacy in which we unsettle assumptions about love, we both carefully delineate boundaries, we both then maintain these boundaries in practice, each slow intimate touch or artistic performance generating a state of ecstasy in each of us. It is also an intimacy where both of us have primary, home-based commitments to another partner and family, which we mutually respect, prioritize and protect.

Do our self-ordained boundaries reduce the sense of active eroticism between us? If anything, my experience is that this condition of carefully-maintained limits has heightened our intimacy, with touch, when it infrequently occurs, losing its egoistic goal-orientation and becoming purely celebratory of presence to one another, to ourselves, and to the wider world– as Hilary says, an erotic meditation. I think it's important as well that humor is such a regular part of our rhythms in so many different ways… and weeping too.

What kind of love appears for us, with echoes in my other closest friendships with men and women? It is, as truly as I've been able to approximate, a love under the sign of inquiry. It is a love I trust deeply, and am always surprised again by. It is a love that at one and the same time puts me at ease and invites my best attention. It is a love that causes me deep, active suffering when some feeling separates us, but doesn't make me try to fix it. It is a love wherein I feel both deeply challenged and deeply supported. It is a love that permits us each to tell the other anything. It is a love that includes deep respect and admiration for one another's professional artistry, independence of perception, and capacity for economic self-sustainability. It is a love that makes me feel completely known and as if I know her as she does, but that leaves as a complete mystery what either of us will do next.

Or, in her words,

> By this point readers know that Bill has multiple beloveds, men and women, and multiple intimate relationships with women in particular. He has always been upfront about this with me, explicitly discussing his desire for post-conventional, mutually transforming love. I got to know him early on through pieces of his autobiographic writing in which his polyamorous attempts were described in detail. I was "warned" about him by other women and men in his life who spoke to me either directly or through the excerpts in his writing.
>
> I had lived a largely unexamined, relatively non-monogamous life up to that point myself. I felt untroubled by it, perhaps because of my generation's laissez-faire attitude toward such things, or because I come from a society where monogamy has not traditionally been the unquestionable norm (gendered double-standards notwith-standing). But this friendship has forced me to get serious about the inquiry into non-possessive and non-exclusive love, including facing the emotional implications of loving seriously under such terms.
>
> Can I be okay with sharing and being shared? Can I accept that he is not really mine at all? Can I be at peace with the reality that there have been lovers before me, some in parallel, and perhaps others to come after me? Can I enjoy the loving attention I am receiving, and continue to enjoy giving, even though it doesn't exactly make me feel special? Can I participate in love fully in the face of the possibility that it is a matter of time before he meets up with the next person with whom to have his next unprecedented experience?!
>
> The exploration in myself around these questions has been significant to me. It is not an exaggeration to say that it has transformed me and my relationship with eros. I wish I could say that these transformations are complete and stable, that I have figured these things out once and for all. In reality, I end up having to come to these insights over and over again, losing my clarity, then finding it again in a different light. A work in progress, as they say.
>
> First insight: Fairytale love is not the [only] kind of love worth pursuing. Knowing Bill's history (who else arrived in my life with a book about his love life?!) saved me a lot of trouble because it gave me a realistic (if unromantic) perspective on his relationship with me – I never expected it to be something it is not. This is not a fairy tale romance. It is not the kind of love that will get me a diamond

ring, or bear children or move me into his house. It is not the kind of love that can be there for me when I wake up in the morning, and take care of me, and never leave me. Nor is it a passionate love affair that I can run to when my primary home relationship falls short. I then have to ask myself: if this love isn't all of that, then what is it? The answer is not as important as the fact that the question is often there for me. With all the usual suspects turned away, new reasons to practice love come to mind on a regular basis, expanding my view, challenging me, not letting me get lazy.

Second Insight: The purpose of love is not to make me feel special. I used to continuously look for new love, partly, if I'm honest, because of how special the adoration of a new lover makes me feel. With Bill I can't feel special because of the possibility that I am simply one of many women going through the revolving doors of his adoration! This has somehow forced me to consider what it means to participate in love that doesn't feed my appetite for feeling special. There is some way in which I have come to feel special on my own terms, having dropped some of my attachment to external sources. Mostly, I have resolved the issue by coming to terms with a likely possibility: that I am not very special and I am special. And then a liberating realization: that I don't need to be so damn special. What a relief!

Third insight: Loving abundantly can serve the one I love most. I have come to see very clearly the possibility of loving multiple people, and of allowing one's lovers to love others without getting drowned in envy. Love is an abundant, infinite emergence. The fact that Bill loves others doesn't mean he doesn't love me. (This simple truth solidified with the birth of my second child and the delightful realization that I was crazy about him and that didn't take away anything from how much I loved my first.) If anything, he loves me so well because he has such a well-exercised love muscle! I feel that I am also getting better at loving the others in my life because I am growing my love muscle in new ways. I love my life partner more actively and more passionately (having at some point committed myself to spending twice as much time and effort on my home relationship as I do on all my other relationships combined – the math is tricky but the principle is good!) and I am more at ease with all of his relationships that exclude me. To get out of the grip of jealously, even if I can only do it sporadically, feels like a significant victory.

Fourth Insight: We love with all the joys and suffering of mortals. In relationship with Bill, I have come to appreciate love that is time-limited, not permanent, not happily-ever-after. With him, loss is pretty well guaranteed. Either he will leave me because he moves on to someone else, or he leaves me because he dies. (The possibility that I will die first is unthinkable!) Either way, I'm forced to find a way to remain open and vulnerable in love, with the myth of permanence having been properly shattered. I have dreams of him leaving, most of them still disturbing to me. Outside of my dreams he is also slowly leaving – having aged and deteriorated between each of our meetings in a visible way. It's not easy to love someone so old (!), someone you know you're going to lose. But of course I could lose any of my loved ones in the blink of an eye, no matter how hard I try and hold on to them. The awareness of their mortality – and my own – infuses our moments of joy with sweet heartbreak. When I feel most happy and connected with others, I also simultaneously feel the weight of loneliness. Sometimes I have to weep to relax into these potent moments, but I am so grateful for how fully human they make me feel. Perhaps I am also developing the muscle of loss.

Hilary Writes of Nathan

Bill introduced Nathan and me. At first we stumbled and failed painfully. Then, as Beckett puts it, in an Irish flourish of ambiguity, our failings, or perhaps our feelings about our failings, got better. Anyway, only a fool would claim success in the complex arena called romantic love in the middle years. Failing better will have to do.

Perhaps Cupid was at work through Bill. Or more prosaically because Nathan was the only other member of the new Community of Inquiry who lives in Oregon, with Bill's encouragement, Nathan got in touch when he had a business meeting in Portland. That it was just days after my second husband had asked for a divorce felt if not good, then at least interesting timing. I would really value the opportunity to talk with an intelligent friend, one who understands the complexity of the human heart and is slow to judge. I wasn't expecting him to be quite so handsome.

I'll share about our learning to work together toward the power of mutuality and its connection with the erotic part of our relationship, our practice with Eros/Power.

"I'm the mover and you are the follower!" I repeat to Nathan with unhidden exasperation. We find ourselves with less than 24 hours to go before we will stand in business attire in front of Nathan's loyal client. This client's 40 new employees have flown in from around the country and I have designed the two day process and organized the employees' GLP's intended to socialize them to their new company's culture of action inquiry. Nathan's client loves action inquiry.

She sees it as a prime reason for the profit gains under her leadership in the past five years as her leadership teams learn to speak and inquire, innovate and learn well together.

I had taken on most of the client management and design of his project over a month previously because Nathan had been consulting overseas. Feeling very capable in this particular context, I had emailed my detailed design to the client's manager of Organizational Development, after only the briefest conversation with Nathan. Nathan, in turn very busy, was simply relieved that this client could also be served. In fact by all measures the client was even very pleased. Thus, we all happily prepared to go into the employee orientation. Dangerously I had assumed Nathan would simply be eager to "get on board" with the workshop as designed, especially because the client had already signed off on it. The client had even made snazzy folders of the materials for the new employees. Time was now short.

Nathan finally took the time to talk. He started by thanking me for my work. Then he asked if we could "start our co-design." The word "start" came as a red rag to a bull. I was the bull. I blurted in response, "We have no time to start anything! What I have is exactly what they want and need." Nathan impatiently explained that this was his client after all and, less directly, that he was not about to act like my junior partner. Certainly not in front of his own client. I could see his rationale clearly. I could even accept it.

I knew Nathan as an excellent consultant, executive coach and group facilitator. I also loved him and our time together. We were partners "on all chakras," having ceremonially joined our lives some two years after meeting. But joining doesn't necessarily bring ease. Our disharmony now escalated. Nathan warned that this would be the last time we'd work together. His statement of abandonment acted like a meditation bell to me. A wake up call. I grew calm and replied, "Maybe so. But right now we are committed to working for this client and with each other. We'll make it as good as possible on all counts. After the workshop we can discuss the future. For now I request that we reschedule a time to talk." And then I hoped that a miracle would occur in the meantime.

When we spoke again, rather than holding back in the hopes of getting to sleep sooner, I simply leapt in, groping toward a bedrock of clarity from which I trusted we could manage most anything. I expressed straightforwardly how upset I felt to be asked to start over when I had already created a design that was near perfect. Nathan paused for a moment and said that under the circumstances it was best that he agree to "empower me to lead." That certainly sounded like a good idea. Deep breath and recognition that a partial miracle had occurred! But it didn't feel quite right. Not yet. I didn't want to be set up as the one who is solely accountable. We both acknowledged that my design was, at most, 50% of any work we'd do. The real work, as in any consulting engagement, is the timely response in the moment-to-moment. Such a response requires one to go "off road," away from any design, always guided by the client's needs. We'd need to do this work together. In the silence I became clear that I wanted to lead and be supported, which is different from being empowered. From the ensuing silence, Nathan affirmed, "You move; I'll follow you." The upset between us dissolved entirely. The miracle had come. We quickly rehearsed key moments for the following day.

In closing our call and practicing what has become a dear practice, I expressed why it had taken me so long to express that I needed to lead. In truth, as awake as we were, there remains a gender taboo by which I as a woman feel that I cannot enact my power over a man without somewhere fearing I will be punished for it. But the punishment is not burning at the stake, not anymore. In the domain of a romantic relationship, it can become emotional withdrawal or unconscious reduction of eros (or erotic polarity) between us. The trade off I feared is that by insisting that I lead, we could be excellent work partners, but we wouldn't be sexy lovers. Or vice versa. And this is not a sustainable choice. Nor is its danger easy to see. With the tables turned, when Nathan plays the role of lead it can actually enhance the polarity between us, making his leading a sexy thing. But vive la différence, as the French say. What is saucy for the gander is only saucy sometimes for the goose. Was will das Weib?!

The work here was merely to take on that we would dance together at this client engagement, and to start I would lead as my design had indeed been excellent. But AS important would be Nathan's moves throughout the following day to bring humor, deeper insight, relaxation and a spirit of collaborative inquiry to the new employees. Thus we would swap the lead position throughout the day in a new kind of relational tango. Thankfully, we received rave reviews from Nathan's client.

Relaxing as a couple over dinner that evening, we moved out of the work partner and into romantic partner mode. I felt the onus of taking charge naturally dissolve. Yes, I can take charge, but I very much like it when Nathan can. And vice versa. There is no rule to making this work, but we realized the need to tune into the purely erotic part of our Eros/Power as an important part to consider in the life/work balance we sought.

That we had gotten to this place of being able to acknowledge difficult things, address them practically, honestly, and decisively, and that we could overlook those patterns in the other that create difficulty for us and still end up with an erotic charge between us… well, all that is hardly a foregone conclusion. It is the fruits of awareness of the dynamics of Eros/Power. It takes pretty much all our effort! Truth be told, it was a lot of effort from the very start.

Alchemy of Relating: Turning Darkness into Light

That Nathan and I share a meditation practice feels very important along with our sense that relationship is itself a path to liberation. What comes up as difficult between us is now used as a gateway into letting go old patterns that don't serve. We also share an unusual degree of devotionality allowing me to laugh for joy at the ease with which we mix the sacred and profane. We do not look like a devotional couple (no flowing robes!). And as a woman who gives orgasms and Zen practice pride of place in her life, I knew early on that I would not find someone like Nathan, not easily. Not on match.com or even dharma match (which I secretly wanted to try even after we met!).

The push pull at the beginning was painful. But the whispering of my heart, now consulted far more regularly than clever calculations of my rational mind, had me see how much I wanted Nathan to be happy. I found I was happy making him happy, for he made me happy (and mad and maddened!). My early intuition was that we were good for one another. I might so easily have overlooked this previously, so lost in feeling myself sometimes to be the victim of his domineering ways (for the record not his chosen term). I realized that my nervous system had been jiggered with my sense of worth and lovability cast into doubt from earlier experiences. It's as though when love arrived the emotional circuit breakers snap. But we stuck at it and our deeper intuitions have proved true. While I had to learn to give up any romantic idea that he would get down on his knees and worship me, damn!, he did get down on his knee to propose marriage.

We laugh also in recognition of our different Enneagram types. Enneagram is a personality typing that Nathan had introduced me to. He is a classic "7," a Peter Pan type, always onto the next adventure. I am an "8," the Enneagram's "oral self reliant," sometimes called "the boss." Not an easy personality type for a woman in the US, as women in power never feel entirely welcome in our world (I am curious how the other Hillary, the one with two "L's," may well change that).

My power feels welcome to Nathan (we realized his Mom, a strong Jewish woman, was likely also an Enneagram 8 personality like me), so love and power in this combination also feels lovable and protective as well as guilt inducing. I feel my power welcomed enough, enough that I can allow myself not always be in charge. What a relief! And in response to learning of the Enneagram, I taught Nathan the finer details of the Myers Briggs (he ENFP, me INFJ) as well as the Kolb Learning Styles (we meet in concrete experience, but with him diverging and me converging, which translates into our being excellent complements, but only when we respect our differences. Easy to say!) We realize what good partners we can be to each other and seek to live up to that possibility. Each system allows us more insight and therefore more patience both with self and other, especially when the rub of the other's patterns seem difficult to take. Personality does not change that much over the years, but it smoothens. Learning his style gave me patience with his tendency to threaten abandonment, so he could move to the next adventure. His knowing mine gives him patience with my apparent invulnerability, so I don't have to feel the pain of neediness. Our personalities dance well together as long as we take time to do relational action inquiry.

When I look more closely at our years together, I also see that I have actually grown true confidence in this man, in this relationship. I feel I am allowed to be me, and I hope I offer that to him. I do not make him wrong for wanting to run away from my strong woman persona. He does not make me wrong for acting invulnerably. In turn I can relax as he and I can allow me to take the lead as in the consulting work described earlier and to hand it back when done.

In truth – and this is a difficult one to talk about – so I will be clear that it's my truth – I am not sexually attracted to men if they are not "stronger" than me in some important dimension. I simply don't want to be "in charge" any more than I have to be (which with my personality is probably much more than for the average woman, sigh). This is because I can't relax into my femininity when I am in charge and it is my femininity that responds to the dance of eros with Nathan's masculinity. This is the dance of the ages. And how does celebrating that dance land differently than regular reactionary patriarchal convention we might wonder? The difference is that life demands that I be in charge a lot of the time professionally. And I certainly want that, I am good at that! So herein lies the paradox of the professional and personal self. Eros/Power is different in the bedroom than in the boardroom (to use a useful if alliterative simplification). Indeed, the tremendous success of the book *50 Shades of Grey* at around the same time that CEO Sandberg's *Leaning In* was celebrated, may have something to do with contemporary woman trying to figure out when power is appropriate and in which hue it works best, as 'power over' or 'power with.' We have that choice now, if we are mindful.

Nathan's and my commitment is to a juicy relationship through our remaining years. Our polyamorous selves are granted free play, but we're both simply, at least for now, too careful. He fears betrayal, and I fear being ignored. We simply agree to not make things worse by bringing additional emotional entanglements. Anyway, we grow old and have little extra time what with all our relational action inquiry! What works between us feels possible, but only because accompanied by an uncommon commitment to loving candor. Sometimes I do feel ignored (when he is wrapped up in work), sometimes he does fear my betrayal (when I just "naturally" fall into what I consider a rather mild flirtation). So we remain attentive to regularly and frequently "clearing the space" between us; we share the truth of what is there. In this way – said spiritually – we can catch the old privations of our evolutionary, cultural and childhood habits. We can empower each other to transform this lead into gold. We can become relational alchemists. These leaden human stains are transformable into something worthy of our aspirations. That's alchemy. But only while doing the work it requires.

What madness brings the ego mind, especially in relationship – what a roller coaster even after all the years of self-inquiry, meditation, yoga and herbal tea! Vast is the field of benefaction and yet how ceaseless are our requests that the other be just a little different than how he is right now. To take on the practice of trusting and allowing is an ongoing practice everyday.

As I reflect on the damage of the early years, what in part stymied me so long has been an inability to see myself as the powerful woman I am. For too long I sought Eros/Power outside myself, as if I lacked it, as if what was there was too much or not enough. Oddly, but related, I could not allow vulnerability. My not really seeing this for so long may also point to the self-censorship in contemporary debates about women and power. First we have to own the power that is ours. Then we ask for what we want. The miracle is that men want that too.

I am reminded of Shantideva: we do not come to change the world, we come to let the world change us.

What remains unclear for us, even as we both see the 'almost if not quite perfect partner' in the other, is how we should navigate day-to-day life together having consciously joined our lives? Should Nathan and I live together in the same place (we currently maintain separate residences but spend a great deal of time together and talking when separated)? We are careful, however, not to require the fragile couple form to swim in the river of life all on its own, however common that is today. Because we want to support living in community in which sustainability, meditation and mutuality are integral to the community's agreements, we have become founding members of a cooperative housing community in Portland. So far we plan to live in one townhouse, with separate bedrooms! It will take a couple of years to build this community of private town houses around a shared community garden and commonspace with fireplace and room to dance. During the building phase Nathan and I practice living together. More importantly we practice relational action inquiry. For now it seems an auspicious and healthy way to dissolve the fragile couple in a larger community.

May We All Fail/Feel/Fare Better in Bringing Consciousness and Transforming the Ancient Dance between Women and Men

You will notice that only in the most recent years and only in this last chapter of our erotic autobiographies are either of us able to describe enduring intimate relationships, characterized by ongoing and mutual feedback to one another – relationships that in general demonstrate Transforming action-logic qualities, as well as occasional Alchemical qualities.

The Transforming action-logic qualities include: creative conflict resolution; awareness that paradox, not just unreconcilable contradiction; also, awareness that what one sees depends upon one's worldview. These qualities lead to the recognition of developing shared principles, contracts, and theories for making and maintaining good decisions – not just rules, customs, and exceptions. The Transforming partnership is process oriented as well as goal oriented; puts a high value on individuality, on unique market niches, and on particular historical moments. He or she enjoys playing a variety of roles, exercises witty, existential humor (as contrasted to prefabricated jokes). At the Transforming action-logic, one is beginning to become aware of the dark side, of the profundity of evil, and that it is inside oneself as well as outside, tempting in its promise of power.

Both Hilary and Bill (and maybe all of us?) seem to have found it easier to exercise the Transforming action-logic in other relationships at work and at home than in our eros-infused friendships.

Invitation

Our aim with the book is to encourage deep inquiry into the trickster domains of eros and power, of love with the hope that Eros/Power can flow more in all our lives.

This chapter describes more mature, conscious loving relationships in which eros-as-inquiry is given primacy of place, where Apollonian, structured love and Dionysian spontaneous love are care-fully balanced. While it is not always easy, the consciousness brought to this non-dual inquiry creates a container that can hold the misery.

Which relationships are best expressions of Eros/Power for you in your life today? How well do you tend them? Is that an inquiry you can engage in together? What have you learned in any relational action inquiry practices (see Interlude II) that you have tried?

Chapter 14

Reflecting Together: Extending our inquiry

Bill writes upon closing:

As we suggested briefly at the outset, the writing of this book has been a transformative experience for us. Now that we have completed two years of work on it, and are, in effect, turning it over to you, our readers, to discover whether our work can challenge and support you to engage in the mutually-transforming power of love in the spirit of inquiry… it seems important to make a final effort to name our own learning.

As we have received feedback on the manuscript from a few colleagues and close friends, a fair amount of the feedback to me (Bill) has had a decidedly negative edge. Some of this feedback follows the theme of Hilary's comments: that I have not enough recognized my power and privilege and its effect on women; that I am blind to my shadow side; that I choose by and large to relate to low-power, voiceless women, who don't call me to account; and that, just as Liz called my "living inquiry" "living Hell," so I seem in general overbalanced toward rational inquiry and lacking in emotional engagement. In Leonard Cohen's words, is it that "I couldn't feel, so I learned to touch"? Is my dedication to the possibility of multiple, non-possessive, erotic relationships, even in my postsexual old age, simply a rhetorical mask for the archetypal male unwillingness to commit to full partnership?

I am going to assume now that there is truth in this perspective, even though I have so rigorously dedicated my life to the minimal use of unilateral power, to encouraging usually-unheard voices to enter conversations… even though I have been called to account at many times by many – not least in the past two years by Hilary and other men and women in our community of inquiry… even though I count a rare number of decades-long close friendships with both men and women in my life… And even though I've made some changes in the text to try to convey my feelings a little better.

Assuming a truth to the critique has finally opened me to my most emotionally revealing insight about my friendships with women, as well as to my most promising analysis of the depth of the man-woman power conundrum. The emotionally revealing insight is how often I feel as though I am looking up to, and seeking the affirmation of, women (no matter how relatively powerful they or others may see me). I was introduced decades ago to the idea that in some ways I had won the Oedipal battle against my father for my mother (largely because she several times compared me favorably to my father), but I did not realize until Hilary's comments on my writing in this book that one impact of that so-called 'winning the Oedipal battle' has been to subordinate myself, as a general rule, to the power of women I love, just as I did (unawaredly) to the charm of my mother. I now see that this is one element that complexifies my early relationships with Louise, Sonia, Linda, and Celia. Sonia and Linda, in particular, seem low-power to Hilary, but inwardly I felt low-power in relation to them. I may very well have been experienced as high power by at least some of the women I have befriended at the very same time as I was feeling and enacting low power in relation to them... while consciously being aware only of my attempts at mutuality. Is it perhaps more generally a human tendency to identify more closely with ways we don't have power than the ways we do?

Thus, I belatedly come to see that the human power conundrum is even more deeply complex than can adequately be suggested by enumerating the types of power associated with developmental action-logics (even as I hope they provide a helpful framework for understanding and action). I am left to appreciate this by enumerating the following propositions:

1) Since, in patriarchal society, men in general come invested with more unilateral status and power than women, it is to men's advantage not to draw attention to power issues, nor even to be very articulately aware of them;

2) As women become aware of and disturbed by this inequity and gain enough protection of the laws to find some voice, their first focus may most often be on developing a strong critique of societal power and status inequities (this is also generally true of any developing social group [teenagers, racially-oppressed peoples, etc.]);

3) Thus, women's exercise of power may initially be concentrated in the mode of critique, and their more self-affirming and socially-constructing voices may largely be discovered somewhat later;

4) For some time (a time that most democratic societies, international corporations, and social enterprises are still experiencing), all power continues to be treated as unilateral (on the model of organizational, technological and military power), the notion of mutual power remains unarticulated, and the power question is simplified to surveillance of power

equity among role players (e.g., are there enough women executives, board members, and political office-holders in a given organization or nation?);

5) At the same time, the global complexity of feedback loops generated by individual and institutional actions is today making a mockery of claims that unilateral power can have intended outcomes (see the too many wars that are not improving situations [Iraq-Syria-Iran-Ukraine-Israel-Hamas], and closer in, family life in general, which is morphing well beyond the traditional hierarchy of generations);

6) As a result, new formulations of mutual power are beginning to appear;

7) However, few of us to date are sensitized enough to recognize, let alone successfully enact, mutual power with others on a consistent basis;

8) So, seen from a distance, mutual power initiatives exercised by members of the class societally-deemed more powerful may be mistaken for exercises of unilateral power by those societally-deemed less powerful (and vice-versa, mutual power initiatives by the one societally-deemed less powerful may be mistaken for submission by the one societally-deemed more powerful);

9) Moreover, those who are at the frontier of struggling to formulate their real wishes and real feelings with one another, whether they be men or women, begin to discover that the complexity of their own personal history gives them relatively easy access to some aspects of their 'voice of power' while rendering other aspects relatively inaccessible; and finally

10) The questions of power and love are so deeply entwined at the very core of our identities, that inquiry in the present about either is the most threatening and difficult kind of inquiry imaginable, and we allow ourselves to be constantly distracted from it.

Thus, the overall transformation for me in my understanding of Eros/Power in the spirit of inquiry has been to move me first from a shy, hesitant, and deeply woundable boy and young man, to a more confident knower and enactor of mutual inquiry and Eros/Power as a man in my thirties and forties. But this man also possessed a significant blind spot around just how mutual my intimate relationships felt to some of my women friends and just what kind of inquiry disciplines are necessary to create an ongoing container to hold such relationships. Now, in my elder years, I move toward appreciating the unfathomable complexities of power, as well as the stumbling and fumbling nature of my attempts to enact mutual power and true love.

Turning to the literal process of writing of this book, I have most often felt like the low-power member of Hilary's and my partnership. She has often been the pace-setter; she introduced the process of writing commentaries to one another; she introduced the end-of-chapter invitations; and she introduced the Interludes. I have usually felt quite happy about Hilary's power, because it seems overwhelmingly to be conducted under the sign of mutual inquiry, and because it brings our end product increasingly into alignment with our initial aspirations. For quite a while, I also accepted the critiques in her commentaries without reservation. Only late in the process did I begin to develop my own critical voice and quarrel (a little) with hers. Only late in the process have I taken a stronger role in the overall editing. Throughout, a pervasive feature of our writing, editing, and conversing about the book has been Hilary's extremely good-natured and kind support for my efforts.

What strikes me now is that – while there are faint echoes of our original relationship twenty-some years ago (she still seems to me more convinced of her point of view than I am of mine at any given time; she still feels how my power looms) – overall Hilary's power is today much more engaged with initiatives than with critique, much more inviting of my voice than before, much larger and more generous of spirit. I am, in turn, much older and more faltering, and have genuinely struggled with how to understand what is going on in the realm of erotic power, largely due to her gentle persistence. Most importantly, both of us have learned a difficult lesson we both needed to learn – namely, how to be emotionally vulnerable with one another. We have been helped to move in this direction not only by our two-day conversation in Portland at the outset of the writing project and by our exchange of letters thereafter, but also by Nathan's presence and deep listening with us on a later occasion, by several other friends' editorial comments in the final phases of the book, and by a renewed flurry of meaningful Skype meetings between us, and even more intense re-editings in the final weeks.

As you will be able to see – both from our longer story throughout the book and from the shorter story here of our writing of the book – the key to an increasing sense of Eros/Power in one's life appears to us to be an increasingly unremitting commitment to ongoing experiential inquiry that periodically undermines one's very assumptions about what power is, how one is exercising it, and what its impact on others actually is. Nietzsche claimed that the greatest power is the power of self-overcoming. Our stories give some indication of how this becomes true in relational action inquiry. And let us not forget that Nietzsche was extremely lonely, went insane, and died relatively early. I would say that the power and the inquiry of self-overcoming can only be sanely explored in loving relationships and communities of inquiry. We do not claim to have fully defined such relationships and communities in this book (nor fully created them in our lives). We have only pointed toward them with the aim of inspiring further adventures by you, our readers, and ourselves.

I owe my own gradually developing penchant for lifetime inquiry to many women and men close to me during my first age. This book I dedicate in particular to the powerful women of inquiry who influenced me during the first third of my life – my Christian-mystic-poet grandmother Alice Coyle Torbert, my charming-skeptical-independent mother Anne Holloway Torbert, and three of my teachers Mary Watt, Margaret Flinch, and Madame Jeanne de Salzmann.

Hilary closes:

The writing of this book has taken me by surprise. I have been more used to scholarly writing in which, from the start I have a clear idea of what I'm communicating. This book, however, unfolded in ways unimagined and likely unfinished. I am curious how it might help others start/deepen their journey of relational action inquiry, where we come to voice, to ourselves and then to others, in relational action inquiry.

The seeds of the inquiry emerged as this book sprouted from an exercise aimed at deeper understanding of personal development. As part of my own professional development, I had turned to Bill's action logic perspective of the many frameworks I know as an organizational psychologist. I believed that the theory and practices around developmental action inquiry could help me constructively confront a leadership challenge that I had encountered upon entering local politics at 40. I had experienced a head on collision between my fairly advanced systems thinking capacity and the toxic turf battles of local politics. After successfully navigating the larger hurdles, Bill suggested I continue to dig deeper by writing a developmental autobiography, which formed the early chapters. In turn this led him to suggest that I share this with the "only other person he'd seen write quite so much for this exercise." (What, 20 pages is unusual?!). The other colleague was male, ex-military and by all external markers, quite different from me. It was all the more interesting to see our similarity in terms of adult development stages and similarity above and beyond the different content of our life stories. Then there was the intense conversational connection occasioned by Bill's visit to my home in Portland, whereafter I shared a copy of what is now the chapter called "Dharma Valentine." Bill's feedback was so strongly supportive and his edits so helpful that I felt very touched. After all this was a very personal account that I was about to share publicly about eros and my spiritual life – hardly typical "public" content. His partnership was timely.

Bill's invitation to an Alchemist Workparty and then convening the Community of Inquiry with an invitation to me as a founding member allowed me a place in which to re-imagine my life. I needed people with whom I could more fully interweave personal and professional development as I was being re-created in the upheaval of my second divorce. This was also a time of meeting my partner to whom I dedicate the book, also a member of the Community of Inquiry, and who appears earlier in the guise of Nathan.

I feel that the key in my sense of transformation in relating to men has been in bringing the receptive feminine part of myself, the part most easily objectified by the masculine, to a more active self-sharing. Doing that means overcoming many years of silence that I myself had been deaf to. The inquiry that became this book started when Nathan facilitated Bill's and my deeper conversation about our early experience as professor and student. This dialogue was framed as supporting "women in coming to fuller voice about conscious relationship." I remember being touched by the framing, as I felt I didn't have to fight for acceptance of my undigested upset or ask permission to explore. Men and women have for so long bypassed each other so regularly on matters of eros. This bypassing is the source of umpteen scandals in which she tells and he balks. If we're lucky, we can learn to be in dialogue that seeks to unweave millennia of gendered socialization, anchored in the awkwardnesses we feel around this as if physically lodged as constrictions in our bodies. If writing this book has done anything, it has taught me that we can learn very quickly to relate in a new way; the feminine can come to voice when the masculine is in support. In this way I feel it is for women to invite men to bring a supportive role for us, allowing that none of us may know how to do this very well and so holding permission to make mistakes. To enter into this type of dialogue, which can feel so dangerous at first, is to shift the micro power dynamics that have been practiced unconsciously for millennia.

As we close I go to a yoga class with Nathan. We are both struck by a woman on her yoga mat across the beautiful studio floor. I think of the character called Hatsumomo in Memoirs of a Geisha because this woman is flawless in all ways from her porcelain skin to her Warrior pose. During class, the yoga instructor calls us to a moment of mindfulness after a particularly demanding set of poses. She advises that we place "hands on hearts" and "tell the truth of our experience right now." Over tea later Nathan, my partner, tells me that he'd realized at that moment that he'd been leering at Hatsumomo as a way to avoid the difficulty of the poses, as if to extract repose from her resplendent feminine aura. The call to mindfulness had broken the spell of oblivion. Upon "waking up" he sent her an energetic apology along with a blessing. I wondered if Hatsumomo had felt this inexplicable discomfort turn to blessing? How come we'd never spoken of this before I wondered? A lightbulb went off about this way in which a man externalizes his discomfort and, like a vampire, seeks comfort in the feminine, taking what is not given. This exploitative use of women's energy seemed all too familiar. What was new is that I had never heard it explained so straightforwardly. "We take, often unconsciously, to feel comfort, to overcome discomforts of all kinds," explained Nathan. He also explained that it's a little shameful to catch yourself doing it.

I wondered if I hadn't been feeling this male discomfort, externalized as the 'patriarchal gaze' for most of my life. I wondered how, when feeling this gaze, if I might also know it as it truly is, a bungled and exploitative call for help. But first I wondered if other men and women could corroborate this.

That evening Nathan and I had dinner with a male friend on the periphery of our Community of Inquiry. He is a single father of a sixteen year-old daughter. After enjoying his abundant hospitality and trading jokes with his daughter who left to play with her friends, I opened the inquiry into this parasitic energy exchange between men and women. I asked if he could corroborate, in his experience, what had happened with Hatsumomo. He listened nonplussed while I spoke and answered simply: "Hilary, that *is* the relational dynamic between men and women. This energy exchange is either malignant or munificent. For my daughter's sake I hope there can be more awareness about it." I was his daughter's age when I went as an au pair to the creepy Mr. Kelly. I too hope there can be more awareness. But for that men will have to move more often in what we've called the 4th territory of experience, that is being in touch with what they actually feel, where their awareness is fixated and why. And so too women, perhaps just like our yoga instructor of that morning, may feel externalized discomfort and start to call men to mindfulness and even apology. It seems much of this taking and healing can be done in silence also. But for now it is not the conventional mindset to even acknowledge, much less participate, in such an ethereal (quantum?) relational dance.

Remembering our first summer's work together some 20 years ago, I send my account of Hatsumomo to Bill.

Bill responds:

My response to the Hatsumomo story is to feel quite differently than Nathan did and to interpret it quite differently from your interpretation. Whereas Nathan speaks of 'leering' and 'taking' and 'apologizing,' if I were looking at her, I believe I would experience it more as 'appreciating,' 'being taken,' and 'recovering contact with the inner source of my attention,' and, possibly 'deepening my breathing and softening my body.' As your male friend said, the energy exchange can either be malignant or munificent. We don't know how the woman in this story received Nathan's gaze, nor how she would receive mine, nor whether she notices. Instead, wouldn't it be a good workshop exercise where men and women gaze at one another and try to articulate how their attention/energy dynamics are operating?

Hilary continues:

Indeed what about the women's experience. In truth I am wondering about me and how endless is this inquiry into how to draw energetic boundaries. It does require workshops and dedicated practice and I have been pleased to be designing some of those now that this book is finishing up. Coming to see and speak of this relational energy is very much informed by the psychoanalysis I entered into before starting this book. And hence I also dedicate this book to Dr. Larry Christensen because this book is also the product of our many conversations. In those sessions I found it helpful to frame my issues as a variation on "everywoman's" issues – for I keenly felt that most of the content of my life overlapped with many others. As if a chaperone of this larger spirit, it's curious to me how the heightened media concern with rape-murders in India and campus rapes of the USA have paralleled this book. My writing started the same day as the mass demonstrations in New Delhi in popular revulsion at the barbaric assault on Jyoti Singh on a New Delhi bus in the erstwhile cradle of civilization. My finishing is on the heels of a popular vote in Ireland, my country of origin, which makes Ireland the first nation in the world to legalize gay marriage. Transformation happens.

In sharing our relational action inquiry into what lies beyond domination based social systems, I hope to support others' work with their own inquiry. It is a precarious moment in human history in which a new relational (as opposed to dominance based) orientation among us may be possible at scale. This is the work sparked by the idea of democracy millennia ago, which began to catch a fire unquenched in the passionate work of the Mary Wollstonecrafts, Gandhis and Martin Luther Kings of the world. Now it is work for all of us to do, when we can. Truly it is time, perhaps already a little too late.

When we are quiet enough surely we all can feel that if we do not evolve in how we relate as a species we simply will not survive. Our domineering ways have already pushed myriad other (lesser, unappealing?) species to extinction. So when people ask if it's not too private to share the far from perfected articulations of this book, I say to the contrary! In this book the wounds of domination are addressed through the experiment of our relational inquiry. I hope others will perfect the effort started here. In actively giving up the privilege of not seeing and instead reaching to deeper honesty, Bill and I stumbled into a mutual inquiry that transformed us. This sharing is therefore an act of concern for public health – my own included. That sharing has softened me; it transformed me in unexpected ways that I needed but couldn't see for most of my life.

Most difficult to name, and have heard, is what nowadays is summarized as "privilege." To speak of privilege to Bill was difficult as it is precisely the arena to which Bill had explicitly and consciously dedicated so much of his of life to address and remediate. How to mention the unmentionable?! Yet there it was for me to see, this unacknowledged privilege in how Bill related to me and to women in general. We couldn't easily address or step around this elephant. First I had to see my own collusion in not addressing it squarely and then dig deeper and come to voice about areas I have been too passive with addressing. For how long we have been fooled, it always takes two to tango. This is not to assign blame, but to assign responsibility.

All domination efforts, be they the light touch of cruel jokes or the repressive hand of monstrous hate crimes, contain the same seeds of self privileging in a dance of cover up of that privilege. Writing this book has meant disciplined subjectivity and learning to talk about deeply vulnerable issues that walk a fine line between truth and love. It has allowed me to hold what would have been only misunderstood fury of my early years along with a new and surprising compassion for the appalling behavior of some men and the women who collude with them. For I too have come to know that women are forced to appeal to others for resources. In patriarchy this means women's appealing to empowered men. In all patriarchy's fraternal systems of domination, the many mini and minor totalitarian regimes all around us, it means subordinates' having to appeal (and be appealing) to those with entrenched 'superiority.' Moreover, those of us, like me, who are now afforded the privilege of liberation from many such oppressions, may clearly still find ourselves sidelined by our inherited and ongoingly unconscious dynamics. My hope is that as the ones coming to newfound privilege we can help further dismantle vestigial forms (as opposed to fighting each other over whose privilege has been worse). Imagine a world that works for all, all members of all species.

Perhaps because I grew up in a pretty homogeneous society I see inter-gender relations as an especially important domain in which to re-learn how to partner across the boundaries of our many labels and differences. Precisely because we meet gender differences early in life and in our own households, they are an especially potent vehicle of learning and potential re-learning. There in those relationships, where erotic possibility that evokes multiple expression (from flirtation to creating science or art together), life quickens in its evolutionary surge toward collaboration and integration.

The gender spectrum we will tolerate is more fluid than ever before in history, at least in the Enlightened West. We may choose more freely when expressing our feminine or our masculine in boardroom and bedroom. What will happen, I wonder, when our laws move to support the type of inquiry we discuss in this book. The "yes means yes" campaigns on campuses (which increasingly require explicit consent by both parties to sexual encounters) may likely translate into the law of the land. The diplomat practice of the feminine suffering but saying nothing must yield to a much more clearheaded articulation of what kind of relationship she wants. The age old question – was will das Weib – may yet be answered now that there is legally enforced attention. The masculine penchant for "taking" will no longer meet the feminine penchant for silence and looking the other way rather than risking break in relationship. It has taken a long time for the feminine to dare to speak in her own voice. We have no idea how this will play out, backlash is certain. So too deeper insights.

I release the book with the intention that women, with men, learn to partner in overcoming 'power over', so that human cruelty may be reduced. I end with gratitude for Nathan, Bill and Larry whose support allowed my feminine voice to emerge more clearly. Helping turn this support into something worthy of my aspirations came women friends, most notably Patricia Gaya and Marga Laube, along with other women and men friends in the Community of Inquiry and beyond, including those in my Zen community, whose alternating generosity and criticism was so valuable. Thank you.

Conclusion: Pursuing the Holy Grail of Inter-gendered Friendships

We see our time as the possible dawning of a Third Age of the Inter-Independence of Humankind. This age follows the First, Dependent Age of Humankind in which tribal logic was what counted most (an age we estimate as pre-eminent until about 1,500AD). This Third Age also follows the Second, Independent Age of Humankind in which modernism's scientific, political, commercial, and artistic logics have developed and are still pre-eminent today. In the Third Age we may now be learning how to contain our dependency and independency "issues" as we evolve toward increasing experience of the Inter-Independent action-logics (Transforming, Alchemical, and Ironic). It is the place in which many of us consciously seek sexual equality, but oriented by a feminine voice that, as Helene Cixous says, writes in mothers' milk, that is to say, using a script that is difficult to discern given the patriarchal privileging of expert, codified knowledge.

Brilliant minds of different eras twigged the preciousness of friendship for transformation of self and setting. Aristotle associated friendships of preference with youth, and friendships of interest with adults. But he also wrote about a rare kind of friendship that he thought the best, and that he called friendships of virtue.

A friendship of virtue is Inter-Independent in that it is concerned with developing one another's virtues – integrity, mutuality, humor, and just/enuf/ness – over the course of a lifetime. Whereas Dependent relationships are based on unilateral patriarchal power, and Independent relationships are based on contract law or formalized agreements such as organization charts, Inter-Independent relationships are fundamentally mutual and thus transformable (or even dissolvable) at will. Thus, friendship and communities of inquiry, fully understood and enacted, constitute the archetypal Inter-Independent relationship.

There may be rare examples of such friendship constellations across history… Socrates, his female teacher and his friends? The Buddha and his male and female sangha? Hildegaard of Bingen, her confessor, and her sister nuns? Ficino whose network of 100 friends was the catalyst for the Renaissance in Italy – imagine all it took were one hundred men (and a few women!) to bring the Western world out of the witch-burning dark ages, let us have hope yet! Then there is the friendship circle of Margaret Fuller, Emerson, and Thoreau near Boston in the 19th century, all the way up to Warren and Susie Buffett and their friends in the late 20th and early 21st century. Buffett suggests that women are the necessary ingredients for the economic-social leap forward needed in the 21st Century. We would suggest they are equally necessary for the political step of more generally and more consistently giving mutual power primacy over unilateral power in relations within families, organizations, religions, and countries.

Broadly speaking, this Inter-Independent, Third Age Friendship among non-possessive beloveds, a futuristic tribalism if you will, invites us all to a journey well beyond the ethnocentric boundaries of previous tribalism in attempting to cultivate an extended family beyond blood relatives. How remains a mystery. We intuit only that persons – perhaps especially women in their Third Age, can begin to lead their friendship constellations generating quite distinct versions of such non-possessive, mutually-beloved friendships toward this promised land… between now and 2035. We can begin, if YOU wish to learn to interact mutually.

Annotated References

On the Web

Invitation to learn more about practicing relational action inquiry: http://www.integratingcatalysts.com/erospower/

Invitation to learn more about Action-logics:

You can take the Global Leadership Profile and see what the analysis of that psychometric instrument suggests about your centre-of-gravity action-logic. You can find the GLP at actioninquiryleadership.com.

The Authors' Recent Publications

Hilary Bradbury's other most recent book, Bradbury, H. Ed. (2015). Handbook of Action Research. Sage: London, Thousand Oaks and New Delhi, offers a wealth of action research with multiple forms of relational inquiry and practice.

Bill Torbert's other most recent book – Action Inquiry: The Secret of Timely and Transforming Leadership [Berrett-Koehler, 2004] – provides fuller chapters on the developmental action-logics.

Other Helpful Books

Bourgeault, C. (2010). The Meaning of Mary Magdalene: Discovering the woman at the heart of christianity. Boston : Shambhala Publications.

Benjamin, J. (1988). The Bonds of Love: Psychoanalysis, feminism, and the problem of domination. New York: Pantheon Books:.

Daedone, N. (2011). Slow Sex: The art and craft of the female orgasm. New York: Grand Central Life & Style.

Daly, M. (1978). Gynecology: The metaEthics of radical feminism. Boston: Beacon Press.

Easton, D. and Hardy, J. (2009). The Ethical Slut (2nd ed.). New York: Crown Publishing Group.

Eisler, R. (1996). Sacred Pleasure: Sex, myth, and the politics of the body: New paths to power and love. New York: Harper One.

Fisher, D. and Torbert, W. (1995) Personal and Organizational Transformations. London : McGraw-Hill.

Garvey-Berger, J. & Johnston (2015). Simple Habits for Complex Times. Palo Alto: Stanford Business Books.

Irigaray, L. 1985. This Sex Which Is Not One. Cornell Press: Ithaca NY.

Nicholson, S. (2013). The Evolutionary Journey of Woman. Tucson: Integral Publishers.

Richardson, D. (2003). Slow Sex: The path to fulfilling and sustainable sexuality. Randoph, VT; Destiny Books.

Ryan, C. and Jethá, C. (2010). Sex at Dawn. New York: HarperCollins.

Scharmer, O. & Kaufer, K. (2013). Leading from the Emerging Future. Berrett-Koehler, San Francisco: Berrett-Koehler.

Savage, D. (1998). Savage Love. New York: Plume.

Torbert, W. (1972). Being for the Most Part Puppets: The interplay among men's labor, leisure, and politics. Cambridge MA: Schenkman Publishing.

Torbert, W. (1973). Learning from Experience: Toward consciousness. New York: Columbia University Press,.

Torbert, W. (1976). Creating a Community of Inquiry: Conflict, collaboration, transformation. London : Wiley Interscience.

Torbert,W. (1987). Managing the Corporate Dream. Homewood IL: Dow Jones-Irwin, .

Torbert, W. (1991). The Power of Balance: Transforming Self, Society and Scientific Inquiry. Thousand Oaks CA: Sage.

Torbert, W. (1993). Sources of Excellence. Boston : Edge\Work Press.

Torbert, W. (2013). Listening into the Dark: An essay testing the validity and efficacy of Collaborative Developmental Action Inquiry for describing and encouraging the transformation of self, society, and scientific inquiry. Integral Review. 2013, 9(2), 264-299.

Wolf, N. (2012). Vagina: A new biography. London: Virago Press.

Zimmerman, J. and McCandless, J. (1998). Flesh and Spirit: The mystery of intimate relationship. Bramble Books.

Hilary Bradbury

Hilary Bradbury, PhD, is a scholar-practitioner whose work focuses on the human and organizational dimensions of creating collaborative learning communities. Hilary's own research is on personal integration as a key for advancing human capacity for collaborative organizing. She obtained her undergraduate degree in German/Theology at Trinity College Dublin, Ireland and continued at graduate level at Harvard and University of Chicago's Divinity Schools. Starting her professional academic career at Case Western Reserve University's department of Organization Behavior, she became Professor of Management in Oregon's Health Sciences University (OHSU) in 2012. Hilary is also Visiting Professor of Action Research for the Business School of Lausanne in Switzerland. Hilary's work with action research originally took off in collaboration with Peter Reason. She has since edited three volumes of the Handbook of Action Research and serves the peer reviewed journal Action Research as Editor-in-Chief. Today in support of practitioners and educators, Hilary convenes AR+, a virtual community for participatory action researchers to nurture global interactivity and working partnerships between scholars and practitioners: actionresearchplus.com. Hilary's journal articles on the action research response to systemic collaborative challenges of our time, such as collaboration for sustainability, healthcare and education have appeared in *Organization Science, Leadership Quarterly, Journal of Applied Behavioral Science, Academy of Management Learning and Education, Sloan Management Review,* among others. In 2014 Hilary founded an executive coaching and action research consultancy, Integrating Catalysts. She practices collaborative living with her family and various cooperative communities in her adopted home of Portland, Oregon. Hilary is a senior practitioner in the Soto Zen tradition and happily offers mindfulness instruction. e: hilary@hilarybradbury.net.

Bill Torbert

Having received both his BA in Politics and Economics and his PhD in Individual and Organizational Behavior from Yale, Bill served as Founder and Director of both the War on Poverty Yale Upward Bound Program and the Theatre of Inquiry. He also taught leadership at Southern Methodist University, the Harvard Graduate School of Education, and then, from 1978-2008 at the Carroll Graduate School of Management in Boston College, winning local and national teaching awards. He first served as Graduate Dean (the BC MBA program's rank rising from below the top 100 to #25 during his tenure) and later as Director of the Organizational Transformation Doctoral Program. Bill has consulted to dozens of companies, not-for-profits, and governmental agencies and has served on numerous Boards, notably at Harvard Pilgrim Health Care when it was rated the #1 HMO nationally in the US, and, for twenty years, at Trillium Asset Management, the original and largest independent Socially Responsible Investing firm. He has also published eleven books and over 60 articles, based in part on the Global Leadership Profile psychometric measure of leadership development, articulating and illustrating the Collaborative Developmental Action Inquiry meta-paradigm of social science. Since 2012, Bill has served as a Principal of Action Inquiry Associates. Along with numerous teaching and book awards, Bill's co-authored HBR article has been repeatedly reprinted as one of the ten all-time best HBR reads on leadership, the Center for Creative Leadership has given him the Ulmer Career Award for Applied Research on Leadership in 2013, and the Academy of Management has offered him the Chris Argyris Career Achievement Award in 2014.

Lightning Source UK Ltd.
Milton Keynes UK
UKOW03f0109280217
295449UK00001B/48/P